# Mastering COBOL Programming

## From Basics to Expert Proficiency

# Contents


**1 Introduction to COBOL** **9**

1.1 History of COBOL . . . . . . . . . . . . . . . . . . . . . . 9
1.2 Importance and Use Cases . . . . . . . . . . . . . . . . . 12
1.3 COBOL Language Overview . . . . . . . . . . . . . . . . 16
1.4 Structure of a COBOL Program . . . . . . . . . . . . . . 19
1.5 Understanding COBOL Divisions . . . . . . . . . . . . . . 21
1.6 The Role of Different Divisions . . . . . . . . . . . . . . 24
1.7 Basic COBOL Program Example . . . . . . . . . . . . . . 26
1.8 Summary and Future of COBOL . . . . . . . . . . . . . . 28

**2 COBOL Environment Setup** **31**

2.1 Introduction to COBOL Development Environments . . 31
2.2 Setting Up a Local COBOL Environment . . . . . . . . . 34
2.3 Installing and Configuring GnuCOBOL . . . . . . . . . . 37
2.4 COBOL Integrated Development Environments (IDEs) . 40
2.5 Setting Up Online COBOL Environments . . . . . . . . 43
2.6 Writing Your First COBOL Program . . . . . . . . . . . . 46
2.7 Compiling and Running a COBOL Program . . . . . . . 47
2.8 Troubleshooting Common Setup Issues . . . . . . . . . 50

**3 Basic COBOL Syntax** **55**

3.1 COBOL Program Structure . . . . . . . . . . . . . . . . . 55

3.2 COBOL Keywords and Reserved Words . . . . . . . . . . 58
3.3 Understanding COBOL Statements . . . . . . . . . . . . 60
3.4 COBOL Identifiers and Naming Conventions . . . . . . 63
3.5 Comments in COBOL . . . . . . . . . . . . . . . . . . . . 65
3.6 Paragraphs and Sections . . . . . . . . . . . . . . . . . 67
3.7 Importance of Columns and Formatting . . . . . . . . . 69
3.8 Using Literals and Constants . . . . . . . . . . . . . . . 71
3.9 Writing a Simple Hello World Program . . . . . . . . . . 74

**4 Data Types and Variables** **77**
4.1 Introduction to Data Types in COBOL . . . . . . . . . . 77
4.2 Defining Variables in COBOL . . . . . . . . . . . . . . . 79
4.3 Numeric Data Types . . . . . . . . . . . . . . . . . . . . 82
4.4 Alphanumeric Data Types . . . . . . . . . . . . . . . . . 84
4.5 Picture (PIC) Clauses and Their Usage . . . . . . . . . 86
4.6 Understanding Level Numbers . . . . . . . . . . . . . . 89
4.7 Working with Redefines and Renames . . . . . . . . . . 91
4.8 Data Initialization and Value Assignment . . . . . . . . . 93
4.9 Using Figurative Constants . . . . . . . . . . . . . . . . 95

**5 Conditional Statements** **99**
5.1 Introduction to Conditional Statements . . . . . . . . . . 99
5.2 IF...ELSE Statements . . . . . . . . . . . . . . . . . . . 102
5.3 Nested IF Statements . . . . . . . . . . . . . . . . . . . 105
5.4 EVALUATE Statements (Case Statements) . . . . . . . 107
5.5 Conditions and Relational Operators . . . . . . . . . . . 110
5.6 Logical Operators in COBOL . . . . . . . . . . . . . . . 114
5.7 Combining Conditions . . . . . . . . . . . . . . . . . . . 116
5.8 Using Sign and Class Conditions . . . . . . . . . . . . . 119
5.9 Conditional Abbreviations . . . . . . . . . . . . . . . . . 121

**6 Looping and Iteration** **125**
6.1 Introduction to Looping in COBOL . . . . . . . . . . . . . 125
6.2 Performing Iterative Processes . . . . . . . . . . . . . . . 128
6.3 Simple Perform Loop . . . . . . . . . . . . . . . . . . . . 131
6.4 Perform Varying Loop . . . . . . . . . . . . . . . . . . . . 133
6.5 Perform Until Loop . . . . . . . . . . . . . . . . . . . . . 135
6.6 Nested Loops in COBOL . . . . . . . . . . . . . . . . . . 138
6.7 Using the EXIT Statement . . . . . . . . . . . . . . . . . 141
6.8 Working with Inline Perform . . . . . . . . . . . . . . . . 144
6.9 Best Practices for Looping . . . . . . . . . . . . . . . . . 146

**7 Arrays and Tables** **151**
7.1 Introduction to Arrays and Tables . . . . . . . . . . . . . 151
7.2 Defining Single-Dimensional Arrays . . . . . . . . . . . . 153
7.3 Accessing and Modifying Array Elements . . . . . . . . . 156
7.4 Working with Multi-Dimensional Arrays . . . . . . . . . . . 159
7.5 Table Handling and Indexing . . . . . . . . . . . . . . . . 161
7.6 Using the OCCURS Clause . . . . . . . . . . . . . . . . . 164
7.7 Dynamic Arrays in COBOL . . . . . . . . . . . . . . . . . 166
7.8 SEARCH and SEARCH ALL Statements . . . . . . . . . . 169
7.9 Common Use Cases for Tables . . . . . . . . . . . . . . . 171

**8 File Handling in COBOL** **177**
8.1 Introduction to File Handling . . . . . . . . . . . . . . . . 177
8.2 Types of Files in COBOL . . . . . . . . . . . . . . . . . . 180
8.3 Defining Files in COBOL Programs . . . . . . . . . . . . . 182
8.4 File-Control and File Section . . . . . . . . . . . . . . . . 185
8.5 File Operations: OPEN, CLOSE . . . . . . . . . . . . . . 188
8.6 Reading Data from Files . . . . . . . . . . . . . . . . . . 191
8.7 Writing Data to Files . . . . . . . . . . . . . . . . . . . . 195

8.8 Rewriting and Deleting Records . . . . . . . . . . . . . . 198
8.9 Handling Sequential Files . . . . . . . . . . . . . . . . . 204
8.10 Handling Indexed Files . . . . . . . . . . . . . . . . . . 208
8.11 Handling Relative Files . . . . . . . . . . . . . . . . . . 210
8.12 Error Handling in File Operations . . . . . . . . . . . . . 213

**9 Subroutines and Functions** **219**
9.1 Introduction to Subroutines and Functions . . . . . . . . 219
9.2 Creating Subroutines . . . . . . . . . . . . . . . . . . . 222
9.3 CALL Statement and Its Variants . . . . . . . . . . . . . 224
9.4 Passing Parameters to Subroutines . . . . . . . . . . . 227
9.5 Using COPY and INCLUDE Statements . . . . . . . . . 230
9.6 Writing Functions in COBOL . . . . . . . . . . . . . . . 232
9.7 Intrinsic Functions in COBOL . . . . . . . . . . . . . . 236
9.8 Calling Subroutines from Other Programs . . . . . . . . 240
9.9 Error Handling in Subroutines . . . . . . . . . . . . . . 243
9.10 Best Practices for Modular Programming . . . . . . . . 246

**10 Debugging and Error Handling** **249**
10.1 Introduction to Debugging . . . . . . . . . . . . . . . . 249
10.2 Identifying Common COBOL Errors . . . . . . . . . . . 252
10.3 Using Debugging Tools . . . . . . . . . . . . . . . . . . 255
10.4 Setting Up Breakpoints . . . . . . . . . . . . . . . . . . 257
10.5 Step-by-Step Execution . . . . . . . . . . . . . . . . . . 260
10.6 Viewing and Modifying Variable Values . . . . . . . . . . 263
10.7 Understanding COBOL Error Codes . . . . . . . . . . . 266
10.8 Handling SYNCHRONIZED and ALIGNMENT . . . . . . 269
10.9 Using DISPLAY for Debugging . . . . . . . . . . . . . . 271
10.10Writing Fault-Tolerant Code . . . . . . . . . . . . . . . 274
10.11Logging and Tracing Techniques . . . . . . . . . . . . . 278

10.12 Best Practices for Error Handling . . . . . . . . . . . . . . 282

# Introduction

COBOL (Common Business-Oriented Language), conceived in 1959, marks one of the earliest high-level programming languages. Its creation was driven by the need for a language that could be used across various hardware and software platforms, making it a linchpin in the realms of business, finance, and administrative systems.

With an enduring presence in the software landscape, COBOL remains critical to today's enterprise ecosystems. The language underpins mission-critical systems in government agencies, financial institutions, and myriad large-scale industries. A testament to its robustness and reliability, COBOL applications handle everything from payroll processing to credit card transactions, tasks which require unfailing accuracy and performance.

COBOL's syntax is designed to be readable and self-documenting. The language's verbosity might seem anachronistic in the context of modern programming paradigms, but it provides unparalleled clarity. This explicit nature is a boon for maintenance and troubleshooting, allowing developers to understand and modify code with greater ease.

This book, "Mastering COBOL Programming: From Basics to Expert Proficiency," aims to furnish readers with a thorough understanding of COBOL from fundamental principles to advanced techniques. We will embark on a structured educational path that introduces you to COBOL's core components, guiding you through the setup of your development environment, and acquainting you with essential syntax and programming constructs.

Beginning with the history and significance of COBOL, we will dive into its distinctive divisions—the Identification Division, Environment Division, Data Division, and Procedure Division—each serving a specific purpose within a COBOL program. An exploration of data types and variable handling will illuminate how COBOL manages data, an essential aspect given the language's primary application in data processing tasks.

Conditional statements and looping constructs form the backbone of any programming language's control flow. In COBOL, these constructs are straightforward yet powerful. We will examine their syntax and practical applications, providing a solid foundation for writing efficient and logical COBOL programs.

Arrays and tables in COBOL are critical for handling collections of data and facilitating operations on these collections. Our comprehensive coverage will include defining, accessing, and manipulating single- and multi-dimensional arrays, with a focus on efficient data handling techniques.

File handling, another cornerstone of COBOL programming, will receive extensive treatment. From defining files within a COBOL program to performing read, write, rewrite, and delete operations, you will gain the expertise needed to manage various file types—sequential, indexed, and relative files—essential for real-world applications.

Procedural abstraction through subroutines and functions will be discussed in detail, emphasizing best practices for modular programming and code reuse. We will explore intrinsic functions and the CALL statement, equipping you with the tools to write maintainable and scalable COBOL applications.

Debugging and error handling are crucial skills for any programmer. You will learn to utilize debugging tools, set breakpoints, and step through code. Techniques for handling runtime errors, understanding error codes, and logging will also be covered to ensure your programs are robust and reliable.

This book strives to balance theoretical knowledge with practical application. Each chapter is designed to build on the previous ones, creating a coherent and comprehensive guide to mastering COBOL programming. By the end of this journey, you will possess both the foundational and advanced skills necessary to excel in the field of COBOL programming.

As you proceed through the chapters, it is our hope that you will not only gain proficiency in COBOL but also appreciate its enduring importance in the modern world. Whether you are re-skilling, up-skilling, or simply broadening your technical horizons, "Mastering COBOL Programming: From Basics to Expert Proficiency" will serve as a valuable resource in your learning journey.

# Chapter 1

# Introduction to COBOL

**COBOL, an acronym for Common Business-Oriented Language, was developed in 1959 to address the need for a universal programming language across disparate computer systems. It remains a cornerstone of enterprise-level and governmental data processing. This chapter covers the history, significance, and structure of COBOL programs, providing a foundational understanding of its divisions and their respective roles, complemented by a basic example to illustrate core concepts. The enduring relevance of COBOL in modern computing is also discussed.**

## 1.1 History of COBOL

COBOL, short for Common Business-Oriented Language, was initiated in response to the 1959 Conference on Data Systems Languages (CODASYL). The objective was to create a universal programming language capable of running on multiple machines, thereby facilitating business and administrative computing tasks across different hardware platforms. The development of COBOL is attributed to the collaborative efforts of multiple stakeholders, including computer manufacturers, guided by the principles of achieving both machine independence and readability akin to English.

The genesis of COBOL can be traced back to the recommendations of a committee formed by the United States Department of Defense. The primary challenge was the lack of compatibility between different programming languages used in business applications, which hindered efficient data processing. As a result, the committee aimed to create a language that possessed excellent compatibility, making inter-system portability achievable and simplifying user training.

Early development of COBOL was spearheaded by several key individuals, with Grace Hopper often heralded as a pioneer due to her significant contributions in designing early compilers. A notable moment in COBOL's history was the delivery of the first COBOL specifications on January 3, 1960, known as COBOL-60. The language's syntax and semantics were developed over an extensive period of meetings and refinements, leading to COBOL's first successful compilation and execution on both an RCA 501 and a Remington-Rand UNIVAC computer.

To facilitate the understanding of COBOL's historical progression, consider the timeline of significant milestones:

- **1959:** Development initiated by CODASYL, with the foundational goal of creating a universal business-oriented language.
- **1960:** Delivery of the first COBOL specifications (COBOL-60). The language was designed to be easily readable, with a verbose English-like syntax to minimize the learning curve.
- **1961:** COBOL demonstrated the practical feasibility of its design by running successfully on different computer brands, proving its machine-independent capabilities.
- **1968:** The American National Standards Institute (ANSI) adopted COBOL as a standard, designated as ANS COBOL. This standardization provided substantial momentum, propelling widespread adoption.
- **1974:** Introduction of the revised standard, COBOL-74, which included numerous enhancements to improve reliability and performance across various systems.
- **1985:** Further standardization efforts result in COBOL-85, which introduced important features such as structured programming constructs, improved debugging capabilities, and enhanced data processing functions.
- **2002:** ANSI and the International Organization for Standardization (ISO) released COBOL 2002, enhancing object-oriented capabilities, adding support for user-defined functions, and extending the language's internationalization features.

- **2014:** The most recent standard, COBOL 2014, includes modern features such as dynamic memory allocation, improved interoperability with other languages, and better integration with contemporary software environments.

COBOL's development has been pragmatic, focusing on meeting the evolving needs of business data processing. Initially, it was predicted that COBOL would fade as newer programming languages emerged. However, its adaptability and enduring efficiency in handling large-scale transaction processing have ensured its continued relevance, particularly in legacy systems of financial, governmental, and administrative domains.

The sustainability of COBOL is partially attributed to its backward compatibility. Programs written in older versions of COBOL can generally run on newer systems without substantial modifications. This characteristic reduces the risk and cost associated with migrating to new systems and technologies.

As the migration from old systems proves costly and risky, many organizations prefer to upgrade their existing COBOL-based systems. Additionally, COBOL's performance in processing extensive datasets and complex transactions remains unmatched by many modern languages. Hence, extensive investment in training and maintaining a proficient workforce skilled in COBOL persists.

```
IDENTIFICATION DIVISION.
PROGRAM-ID. HELLO-WORLD.
PROCEDURE DIVISION.
    DISPLAY 'HELLO, WORLD'.
    STOP RUN.
```

HELLO, WORLD

The above COBOL code represents an archetypical starting point, illustrating the language's straightforward syntax. The IDENTIFICATION DIVISION and PROCEDURE DIVISION exemplify COBOL's emphasis on readability and structure, reflecting its historical design principles. Over the years, COBOL has maintained its core philosophy while incorporating necessary modernizations to stay relevant.

COBOL's historical evolution is emblematic of sustained adaptation and specialization, rooted in practical requirements of business data processing. Considering the massive codebases and critical systems dependent on COBOL, its history provides vital insights into foundational computing principles that continue to inform modern practices, ensuring its prominence in enterprise computing environments.

## 1.2 Importance and Use Cases

COBOL's significance in the field of information technology is deeply rooted in its capabilities as a robust and versatile programming language designed specifically for business applications. Since its inception, COBOL has played a crucial role in various industries due to its readability, maintainability, and ability to handle large volumes of data. The importance of COBOL can be classified into several key areas:

- **Business and Financial Applications:** COBOL is extensively used in the financial sector including banking, insurance, and governmental agencies. These applications require precise calculations and the capability to handle extensive records, which COBOL's data processing abilities cater to effectively.
- **Maintainability and Readability:** COBOL's syntax resembles the English language, which makes it more accessible for business professionals. This readability ensures that even non-programmers can understand and contribute to the development and maintenance of COBOL programs.
- **Legacy Systems:** Many legacy systems, which are still operational, have been written in COBOL. These systems continue to function efficiently in critical applications, making it essential to maintain and occasionally enhance COBOL code.
- **Interoperability with Modern Systems:** Despite its age, COBOL has been adapted to work with modern technologies, including web services and cloud environments. This ensures that COBOL-based systems can be integrated seamlessly with contemporary IT infrastructures.

**Use Cases:**

*1. Banking and Financial Services:* COBOL is deeply embedded in the banking industry. A significant portion of core banking systems, such as transaction processing systems, customer information management, and credit card processing systems, is written in COBOL.

The language's ability to process heavy transaction loads with precision makes it indispensable in these environments.

Consider a simple COBOL program designed to process a batch of financial transactions:

```
IDENTIFICATION DIVISION.
PROGRAM-ID. TRANSACTION-PROCESSOR.

DATA DIVISION.
FILE SECTION.
FD TRANSACTION-FILE.
    01 TRANSACTION-RECORD.
        05 ACCOUNT-NUMBER PIC 9(10).
        05 TRANSACTION-AMOUNT PIC S9(9)V99.
        05 TRANSACTION-TYPE PIC X(3).

WORKING-STORAGE SECTION.
01 WS-TOTAL-DEPOSIT PIC S9(11)V99 VALUE ZEROS.
01 WS-TOTAL-WITHDRAWAL PIC S9(11)V99 VALUE
    ZEROS.

PROCEDURE DIVISION.
OPEN INPUT TRANSACTION-FILE.
PERFORM UNTIL EOF = TRUE
    READ TRANSACTION-FILE INTO
        TRANSACTION-RECORD
        AT END MOVE 'YES' TO EOF
        NOT AT END
            EVALUATE TRANSACTION-TYPE
                WHEN 'DEP'
                    ADD TRANSACTION-AMOUNT TO
                        WS-TOTAL-DEPOSIT
                WHEN 'WDR'
                    ADD TRANSACTION-AMOUNT TO
                        WS-TOTAL-WITHDRAWAL
            END-EVALUATE
END-PERFORM
CLOSE TRANSACTION-FILE.
DISPLAY 'TOTAL DEPOSIT: ' WS-TOTAL-DEPOSIT.
DISPLAY 'TOTAL WITHDRAWAL: '
    WS-TOTAL-WITHDRAWAL.
STOP RUN.
```

The combination of simplicity and precision in COBOL's syntax allows for efficient batch processing of financial transactions. This particular program reads a file of transactions and calculates the total amounts for deposits and withdrawals.

2. *Government and Public Sector:* Governments utilize COBOL for managing public records, payroll systems, and welfare programs. This is attributed to the reliability and scalability of COBOL programs, which can effectively handle and process large datasets inherent in public sector applications.

A typical COBOL application in this domain might involve the computation of social security benefits based on various parameters such as income, age, and contribution history.

```
IDENTIFICATION DIVISION.
PROGRAM-ID. BENEFIT-CALCULATOR.

DATA DIVISION.
WORKING-STORAGE SECTION.
01 WS-INCOME PIC 9(7)V99.
01 WS-AGE PIC 99.
01 WS-CONTRIBUTIONS PIC 9(7)V99.
01 WS-BENEFIT-AMOUNT PIC 9(7)V99.
01 WS-MULTIPLIER PIC V99 VALUE 1.05.

PROCEDURE DIVISION.
DISPLAY 'ENTER INCOME: '.
ACCEPT WS-INCOME.
DISPLAY 'ENTER AGE: '.
ACCEPT WS-AGE.
DISPLAY 'ENTER CONTRIBUTIONS: '.
ACCEPT WS-CONTRIBUTIONS.

COMPUTE WS-BENEFIT-AMOUNT = (WS-INCOME +
    WS-CONTRIBUTIONS) * WS-MULTIPLIER.
DISPLAY 'BENEFIT AMOUNT: ' WS-BENEFIT-AMOUNT.

STOP RUN.
```

In this example, the program calculates benefits by accepting user inputs for income, age, and contributions, and then applying a multiplier to determine the benefit amount.

*3. Insurance:* The insurance industry also relies heavily on COBOL for policy management systems, claims processing, and actuarial computations. The language's ability to perform accurate and reliable data processing is critical in managing the vast amounts of data associated with policies and claims.

A COBOL-based insurance claim processing system might process claims as follows:

```
IDENTIFICATION DIVISION.
PROGRAM-ID. CLAIM-PROCESSOR.

DATA DIVISION.
FILE SECTION.
FD CLAIM-FILE.
    01 CLAIM-RECORD.
        05 POLICY-NUMBER PIC 9(10).
        05 CLAIM-AMOUNT PIC S9(9)V99.
        05 CLAIM-DATE PIC X(10).

WORKING-STORAGE SECTION.
01 WS-TOTAL-CLAIMS PIC S9(11)V99 VALUE ZEROS.
01 WS-CLAIM-COUNT PIC 9(5) VALUE ZEROS.
01 WS-AVG-CLAIM PIC S9(9)V99 VALUE ZEROS.

PROCEDURE DIVISION.
OPEN INPUT CLAIM-FILE.
PERFORM UNTIL EOF = TRUE
     READ CLAIM-FILE INTO CLAIM-RECORD
         AT END MOVE 'YES' TO EOF
         NOT AT END
             ADD CLAIM-AMOUNT TO
                 WS-TOTAL-CLAIMS
             ADD 1 TO WS-CLAIM-COUNT
END-PERFORM
CLOSE CLAIM-FILE.
IF WS-CLAIM-COUNT > 0
    COMPUTE WS-AVG-CLAIM = WS-TOTAL-CLAIMS /
        WS-CLAIM-COUNT
END-IF
DISPLAY 'TOTAL CLAIMS: ' WS-TOTAL-CLAIMS.
DISPLAY 'NUMBER OF CLAIMS: ' WS-CLAIM-COUNT.
DISPLAY 'AVERAGE CLAIM AMOUNT: ' WS-AVG-CLAIM
```

```
.
STOP RUN.
```

This program reads a file containing claim records, calculates the total claims, the claim count, and the average claim amount. The simplicity and readability of COBOL ensure that these calculations are performed accurately and efficiently.

The importance and use cases of COBOL extend beyond these examples, reinforcing the language's continued relevance in modern computing environments. Its ability to evolve and adapt to new technological paradigms ensures its enduring presence in the IT landscape.

## 1.3 COBOL Language Overview

COBOL, or Common Business-Oriented Language, is a high-level programming language primarily designed for business, finance, and administrative systems. Its syntax and structure are purposefully crafted to be accessible for those with a business background, emphasizing readability and straightforward data manipulation. COBOL excels in processing bulk data, and its verbosity ensures that programs are self-documenting to a considerable extent.

A COBOL program is typically composed of four main divisions: Identification Division, Environment Division, Data Division, and Procedure Division. Each of these divisions serves a distinct role and contributes to the overall structure and functionality of the program.

The Identification Division is mandatory and provides metadata about the program, including the program's name and any relevant author information. It establishes a unique identifier for the program and is crucial for documentation and maintenance.

The Environment Division specifies the computer environment in which the program will run. It includes details about the configuration, such as file system organization and device allocations. This division ensures that the program can interact correctly with its surrounding hardware and operating system.

The Data Division is where all data items the program manipulates are defined. The division is subdivided into several sections:

- File Section: Describes the files utilized by the program, their structure, and record layouts.

- Working-Storage Section: Declares variables that retain their values throughout the program's execution.
- Local-Storage Section: Similar to Working-Storage, but variables in this section are freshly allocated and de-allocated with each program invocation.
- Linkage Section: Specifies data items passed to the program from other programs or systems.

The Procedure Division contains the actual code that manipulates the data declared in the Data Division. This division is composed of a series of paragraphs, each containing COBOL statements that define the program's logic and operations. The statements in the Procedure Division are notably English-like, which enhances the readability and maintainability of the program.

Here's an illustrative COBOL program structure:

```
IDENTIFICATION DIVISION.
PROGRAM-ID. HELLO-WORLD.

ENVIRONMENT DIVISION.

DATA DIVISION.
WORKING-STORAGE SECTION.
01 WS-MESSAGE PIC X(12) VALUE 'HELLO WORLD!'.

PROCEDURE DIVISION.
DISPLAY-MESSAGE.
    DISPLAY WS-MESSAGE.
    STOP RUN.
```

In the example above, the Identification Division includes the PROGRAM-ID attribute, uniquely identifying the program as HELLO-WORLD. The Environment Division is present but empty, as no environmental specifications are required. The Data Division includes a Working-Storage Section defining a data item WS-MESSAGE as a 12-character string containing the value 'HELLO WORLD!'. The Procedure Division contains a single paragraph, DISPLAY-MESSAGE, which executes a display command to output the message and then halts the program with STOP RUN.

COBOL's syntax is designed to mirror natural language, making it relatively easy for business professionals to understand. Each statement in COBOL consists of a verb, such as DISPLAY, followed by a subject, such as WS-MESSAGE, which contributes to the intuitive nature of the language.

To manage complexity, COBOL allows the use of sections and paragraphs to structure the Procedure Division. Sections consist of one or more paragraphs, and each paragraph is a block of one or more sentences containing COBOL statements. Grouping related statements into paragraphs and sections helps organize code logically and facilitates readability and maintenance.

The key features of COBOL include extensive file handling capabilities, comprehensive data manipulation functions, and powerful debugging and error-handling mechanisms. COBOL supports both sequential and random file processing, which is vital for enterprise-level applications that rely on large databases and transaction processing systems. Its data manipulation capabilities handle fixed-format records, making it ideal for traditional business applications that require precise control over data structure and format.

Error handling in COBOL is managed through status codes and exceptions. Programs can check the status of I/O operations and take appropriate action if an error occurs. This feature is particularly useful in critical business environments where reliability and accuracy are paramount.

One of COBOL's strengths is its ability to handle legacy data and integrate with modern systems, making it an effective language for maintaining and upgrading long-standing enterprise applications. Its compatibility with various data formats and communication protocols allows seamless interaction with contemporary software and technologies.

As COBOL programmers continue to be in demand, understanding the fundamental structure and capabilities of the language is essential for contributing to and maintaining the vast array of existing COBOL-based systems. The progression from basic concepts to advanced features enables programmers to develop robust, efficient, and reliable applications tailored to the specific needs of business and administrative operations.

## 1.4 Structure of a COBOL Program

COBOL programs are generally characterized by their high degree of structure and readability. The structure of a COBOL program is divided into four main parts or divisions: Identification Division, Environment Division, Data Division, and Procedure Division. Each of these divisions serves a specific purpose and contains precise sections that further organize the code. Understanding the function and organization of these divisions is crucial for mastering COBOL programming. Let us delve into each division in detail.

**1. Identification Division**

The Identification Division is the first division of a COBOL program and it is mandatory. It provides essential information about the program, such as the program name, which is used for program identification.

```
IDENTIFICATION DIVISION.
PROGRAM-ID. ExampleProgram.
AUTHOR. John Doe.
```

In the example above, PROGRAM-ID. specifies the name of the program, which is 'ExampleProgram'. The AUTHOR. clause specifies the name of the program's author. Other optional clauses that can be included here are INSTALLATION., DATE-WRITTEN., and DATE-COMPILED.

**2. Environment Division**

The Environment Division describes the environment in which the program will run. This division is subdivided into two sections: Configuration Section and Input-Output Section.

```
ENVIRONMENT DIVISION.
CONFIGURATION SECTION.
SOURCE-COMPUTER. IBM-370.
OBJECT-COMPUTER. IBM-370.

INPUT-OUTPUT SECTION.
FILE-CONTROL.
    SELECT IN-FILE ASSIGN TO 'INPUT.DAT'.
    SELECT OUT-FILE ASSIGN TO 'OUTPUT.DAT'.
```

In the Configuration Section, SOURCE-COMPUTER. and OBJECT-

COMPUTER. clauses specify the types of computers that are used for compiling and running the program, respectively. The Input-Output Section defines how files are handled during program execution. The FILE-CONTROL. paragraph maps logical file names to physical file names using the SELECT statements.

### 3. Data Division

The Data Division is where all the variables and data structures used in the program are defined. This division can have several sections, but the most commonly used are the File Section, Working-Storage Section, and the Local-Storage Section.

```
DATA DIVISION.
FILE SECTION.
FD IN-FILE.
01 IN-RECORD PIC X(100).

FD OUT-FILE.
01 OUT-RECORD PIC X(100).

WORKING-STORAGE SECTION.
01 WS-COUNTER PIC 9(4) VALUE ZERO.
01 WS-SWITCH PIC X(1) VALUE 'N'.
```

In the File Section, File Descriptors (FD) are defined for each file, specifying the structure of the records within those files. In the Working-Storage Section, variables such as WS-COUNTER and WS-SWITCH are declared. The PIC clause specifies the data types and sizes of these variables, with VALUE clauses providing initial values.

### 4. Procedure Division

The Procedure Division contains the program's logic, or instructions that the computer will execute. This division is organized into paragraphs and sections, allowing for structured programming and modularization.

```
PROCEDURE DIVISION.
MAIN-PARAGRAPH.
    OPEN INPUT IN-FILE.
    OPEN OUTPUT OUT-FILE.
    PERFORM READ-PROCESS-FILE.
    CLOSE IN-FILE.
    CLOSE OUT-FILE.
```

```
    STOP RUN.

READ-PROCESS-FILE.
    READ IN-FILE INTO IN-RECORD
        AT END MOVE 'Y' TO WS-SWITCH.
    IF WS-SWITCH = 'N'
        MOVE IN-RECORD TO OUT-RECORD
        WRITE OUT-RECORD
        PERFORM READ-PROCESS-FILE.
```

The Procedure Division starts with MAIN-PARAGRAPH. Here, the program opens the defined files, performs a sequence of operations using the PERFORM statement to control the flow, and finally closes the files. The READ-PROCESS-FILE paragraph demonstrates reading a record and using conditional logic (IF) to continue processing multiple records in a recursive manner.

These four divisions collectively form the structure of a COBOL program, ensuring that the code is organized, maintainable, and readable. Understanding the purpose and role of each division is imperative for effective COBOL programming, easing the task of both writing new programs and debugging existing ones.

## 1.5 Understanding COBOL Divisions

COBOL is structured in a hierarchical manner, comprising four primary divisions that form the skeleton of any program. Each division has a unique purpose and set of statements that define the structure and behavior of the program. Understanding these divisions is crucial for mastering COBOL programming.

The four main divisions in a COBOL program are:

- Identification Division
- Environment Division
- Data Division
- Procedure Division

**Identification Division:** This division is the program's header and contains metadata about the program itself. It typically includes the program's name and can contain other details such as author, date written, and other comments. The syntax is straightforward:

```
IDENTIFICATION DIVISION.
PROGRAM-ID. SampleProgram.
AUTHOR. Jane Doe.
```

The PROGRAM-ID paragraph is mandatory and must be specified. It uniquely identifies the program.

**Environment Division:** This division specifies the environment in which the program will run. It can be further divided into the CONFIGURATION SECTION and the INPUT-OUTPUT SECTION, though not all sections are mandatory for every program.

```
ENVIRONMENT DIVISION.
CONFIGURATION SECTION.
SOURCE-COMPUTER. IBM-370.
OBJECT-COMPUTER. IBM-370.
```

In the CONFIGURATION SECTION, the SOURCE-COMPUTER and OBJECT-COMPUTER paragraphs define the type of computer where the program is compiled and run, respectively.

INPUT-OUTPUT SECTION handles file-related configurations:

```
INPUT-OUTPUT SECTION.
FILE-CONTROL.
    SELECT input-file ASSIGN TO 'input.dat'.
    SELECT output-file ASSIGN TO 'output.dat'.
```

The FILE-CONTROL paragraph within this section maps logical file names used within the program to physical files.

**Data Division:** This division declares the data items that the program will use. It is divided into multiple sections, such as the FILE SECTION, WORKING-STORAGE SECTION, and optional sections like LINKAGE SECTION. The FILE SECTION is used to define the structure of the files referenced in the ENVIRONMENT DIVISION.

```
DATA DIVISION.
FILE SECTION.
FD input-file.
01 input-record.
    05 employee-id PIC 9(5).
```

```
    05 employee-name PIC A(30).

WORKING-STORAGE SECTION.
01 temp-variable PIC 9(5) VALUE ZEROS.
```

In the FILE SECTION, the FD entry defines a file descriptor followed by its record structure. The WORKING-STORAGE SECTION is used to declare variables needed for processing.

**Procedure Division:** This is where the executable instructions are written. It contains the complete procedural logic of the program. The procedural code is divided into paragraphs, which can be further subdivided into sections.

```
PROCEDURE DIVISION.
MAIN-PARA.
    OPEN INPUT input-file.
    OPEN OUTPUT output-file.
    PERFORM UNTIL end-of-file
        READ input-file
            AT END
                MOVE "YES" TO end-of-file
            NOT AT END
                WRITE output-record FROM input-record
        END-READ
    END-PERFORM.
    CLOSE input-file.
    CLOSE output-file.
    STOP RUN.
```

The PROCEDURE DIVISION begins with a paragraph name such as MAIN-PARA. Here, file operations like OPEN, READ, WRITE, and CLOSE are performed. Control structures such as PERFORM are used for iteration and conditional mechanisms.

Understanding these divisions is fundamental to structuring and organizing COBOL programs effectively. Each division serves to modularize the program, clearly demarcating sections for metadata, environment configuration, data definitions, and executable instructions. This modular structure aids in both the development and maintenance of complex COBOL applications.

## 1.6 The Role of Different Divisions

COBOL programs are organized into four main divisions: Identification Division, Environment Division, Data Division, and Procedure Division. Each division has a specific role and set of functionalities that collectively facilitate the program's overall operation. Understanding the function and structure of these divisions is crucial for writing effective COBOL programs.

**Identification Division:**

The Identification Division serves as the header section of a COBOL program. This division contains metadata about the program itself, such as the program's name and other optional descriptive details like the author, installation, date written, and security information. The Identification Division helps to document the program and ensures that anyone reading the code later can easily understand its purpose and authoring context.

```
IDENTIFICATION DIVISION.
PROGRAM-ID. SAMPLE1.
AUTHOR. JOHN DOE.
INSTALLATION. XYZ COMPANY.
DATE-WRITTEN. 2023-01-01.
SECURITY. CLASSIFIED.
```

**Environment Division:**

The Environment Division is responsible for defining the program's operating environment. This division specifies the physical and logical configuration under which the program operates. Comprising two sections, the Configuration Section and the Input-Output Section, it describes the system's hardware setup and the files the program will use.

Configuration Section declares specifics about the computer and its installations, while the Input-Output Section defines the files the program accesses, including their physical devices and file organization used.

```
ENVIRONMENT DIVISION.
CONFIGURATION SECTION.
SOURCE-COMPUTER. IBM-370.
OBJECT-COMPUTER. IBM-370.
INPUT-OUTPUT SECTION.
FILE-CONTROL.
```

```
SELECT IN-FILE ASSIGN TO DISK-IN.
SELECT OUT-FILE ASSIGN TO DISK-OUT.
```

**Data Division:**

The Data Division is crucial as it describes all the data items the program manipulates. It is divided into several sections, including the File Section, Working-Storage Section, Local-Storage Section, and Linkage Section.

- The File Section defines the structure of data files. - The Working-Storage Section is used for declaring temporary variables retained during the program's execution. - The Local-Storage Section is similar to Working-Storage, but variables here do not retain values between invocations. - The Linkage Section describes data from outside the program, such as parameters passed by a calling program.

```
DATA DIVISION.
FILE SECTION.
FD IN-FILE.
01 IN-RECORD PIC X(100).

FD OUT-FILE.
01 OUT-RECORD PIC X(100).

WORKING-STORAGE SECTION.
01 WS-VAR1 PIC 9(3) VALUE 0.
01 WS-NAME PIC X(20).
```

**Procedure Division:**

The Procedure Division contains the executable code and logic of the COBOL program. This division specifies what operations are to be performed and in what sequence. User-defined sections, called paragraphs, structure the code within this division. Each paragraph typically contains a coherent set of COBOL statements designed to perform a specific functionality.

```
PROCEDURE DIVISION.

BEGIN.
    PERFORM FILE-INPUT
    PERFORM PROCESS-DATA
    PERFORM FILE-OUTPUT
```

```
    STOP RUN.

FILE-INPUT.
    OPEN INPUT IN-FILE
    READ IN-FILE INTO IN-RECORD
    CLOSE IN-FILE.

PROCESS-DATA.
    MOVE IN-RECORD TO OUT-RECORD.

FILE-OUTPUT.
    OPEN OUTPUT OUT-FILE
    WRITE OUT-RECORD
    CLOSE OUT-FILE.
```

Ensuring correct division usage enhances program clarity, maintainability, and structure. Identification Division aids in program documentation, Environment Division specifies system interactions, Data Division manages data definitions, and Procedure Division lays down the executable logic. Collectively, these divisions form the backbone of any COBOL program, facilitating organized and systematic coding.

## 1.7 Basic COBOL Program Example

To provide a practical illustration of COBOL's structure and functionality, we will dissect a basic COBOL program. This example will guide you through each part of the program, explaining its purpose and exemplifying its use. The core components covered in the program include the Identification Division, Environment Division, Data Division, and Procedure Division.

A typical COBOL program can be divided into four main divisions. Below is an example of a simple COBOL program followed by an explanation of each section:

```
IDENTIFICATION DIVISION.
PROGRAM-ID. Hello-World.

ENVIRONMENT DIVISION.

DATA DIVISION.
```

```
WORKING-STORAGE SECTION.
01 WS-MESSAGE PIC X(12) VALUE 'Hello World!'.

PROCEDURE DIVISION.
BEGIN.
    DISPLAY WS-MESSAGE.
    STOP RUN.
```

The IDENTIFICATION DIVISION is the first and simplest part of a COBOL program. It provides basic metadata about the program, identifying it to the compiler and maintenance personnel. The PROGRAM-ID is a mandatory entry defining the program's name.

The ENVIRONMENT DIVISION, although necessary for most COBOL programs, is omitted in our basic example because it generally specifies the system-specific details such as file handling and hardware dependencies, which are not utilized here.

In the DATA DIVISION, essential variables and their types are declared. In our case, we have declared a single variable WS-MESSAGE in the WORKING-STORAGE SECTION. The WS-MESSAGE variable is declared as a string (PIC X(12)) with a length of 12 characters and initialized with the value 'Hello World!'. The picture clause (PIC) is used to define the data type and size of WS-MESSAGE:

- 01 level number indicates the data item is at the highest level.
- WS-MESSAGE is the name of the variable.
- PIC X(12) signifies an alphanumeric string of 12 characters.
- VALUE 'Hello World!' sets the initial value to 'Hello World!'.

The PROCEDURE DIVISION contains the code that manipulates the data declared in the DATA DIVISION. It consists of a sequence of instructions to be executed by the computer. The BEGIN section here starts the execution:

- DISPLAY WS-MESSAGE displays the value of WS-MESSAGE on the standard output.
- STOP RUN ends the program.

This minimalistic example demonstrates the fundamental structure and functionality of a COBOL program. More complex programs will generally involve additional sections and a more intricate PROCEDURE DIVISION, but the basic principles remain consistent. Understanding this example should equip you with the foundational knowledge necessary to explore more advanced COBOL programming concepts.

## 1.8 Summary and Future of COBOL

Since its inception in 1959, COBOL has maintained a pivotal role in business and financial systems. Its development was driven by a need for an accessible and universal programming language that could operate across various hardware platforms. As one of the oldest high-level programming languages, COBOL's structure and syntax were significantly influenced by English, making it more readable and easier to understand.

**Summary of COBOL's Importance and Applications**

COBOL has been engineered specifically for business data processing, which encompasses a broad spectrum of applications, including customer relationship management (CRM), banking systems, and government operations. It was designed to be:

- **Readable:** COBOL syntax is detailed and verbose, aligning closely with straightforward English phrases, mitigating the potential for ambiguity and errors.
- **Portable:** The language's design allows programs to run on different machines with minimal modifications, ensuring consistency across various hardware environments.
- **Durable:** COBOL systems have exhibited remarkable longevity, with many applications developed decades ago still in active use today. This has contributed to its continued relevance in contemporary IT environments.

Despite advancements in newer programming languages, COBOL remains integral to the functioning of a substantial number of legacy systems. It is estimated that millions of lines of COBOL code are still in operation, particularly within critical systems like banking infrastructure, insurance companies, and government agencies. COBOL applications are known for their reliability and efficiency in processing large volumes of data.

**The Future of COBOL**

The future trajectory of COBOL is an intriguing area of speculation and development. Several factors highlight COBOL's continued significance:

- **Legacy Systems:** The vast number of crucial legacy systems written in COBOL necessitate ongoing maintenance and updates. Companies and governments often prefer to update existing COBOL applications rather than undertake expensive and risky migrations to entirely new systems.
- **Modernization Efforts:** Efforts are ongoing to modernize COBOL, integrating it with contemporary software development practices. These attempts include updating development environments, integrating COBOL systems with web services, and utilizing cloud computing platforms.
- **Skill Demand:** There is a sustained demand for COBOL programmers to maintain and enhance existing systems. Educational initiatives and training programs have been set up to address this need, ensuring a new generation of developers can work with COBOL.

An example of modernization can be seen in the integration of COBOL with Java technology. Below is a basic illustration of how COBOL can interface with a Java component using the Java Native Interface (JNI):

```
public class COBOLInterface {
    public native void performCOBOLTask();

    static {
        System.loadLibrary("coboltask");
    }

    public static void main(String[] args) {
        new COBOLInterface().performCOBOLTask();
    }
}
```

The corresponding COBOL program might look like this:

```
IDENTIFICATION DIVISION.
PROGRAM-ID. COBOLTASK.

DATA DIVISION.
WORKING-STORAGE SECTION.
77 WS-MESSAGE PIC X(50) VALUE 'Hello from COBOL using JNI'.


PROCEDURE DIVISION.
DISPLAY WS-MESSAGE.
STOP RUN.
```

When executed, this integration allows COBOL to operate alongside modern technologies, thus extending its usefulness and bridging the gap between historical and contemporary programming paradigms.

### Challenges and Considerations

Implementing any significant changes or modernizations to COBOL systems involves several challenges:

- **Resource Availability:** The pool of experienced COBOL programmers is shrinking as many approach retirement, posing a challenge for sustaining legacy systems.
- **System Complexity:** Legacy COBOL systems can be highly complex, with bespoke customizations that have evolved over decades. This complexity makes system updates and migrations inherently risky.
- **Technology Integration:** Blending older COBOL systems with modern technologies requires careful planning and thorough understanding to avoid disruptions and ensure seamless interoperability.

However, the intrinsic value and stability of COBOL cannot be overstated. Continuous innovation within the realm of COBOL, alongside new technological integrations and educational outreach, ensures that it will remain a steadfast component of the global computing landscape.

# Chapter 2

# COBOL Environment Setup

**Setting up a COBOL development environment is essential for writing, compiling, and running COBOL programs. This chapter details the steps to configure both local and online COBOL environments, including the installation of GnuCOBOL and the use of Integrated Development Environments (IDEs). Additionally, it covers writing your first COBOL program and troubleshooting common setup issues, ensuring a smooth initiation into COBOL development.**

## 2.1 Introduction to COBOL Development Environments

COBOL (Common Business Oriented Language) is a high-level programming language that has been integral to business, finance, and administrative systems for decades. Setting up a COBOL development environment involves configuring the necessary tools and software that allow for writing, compiling, and executing COBOL programs efficiently.

A comprehensive COBOL development environment includes several components:

- A COBOL compiler: This translates the COBOL source code into machine language that can be executed by the computer.

- An Integrated Development Environment (IDE): This provides a user-friendly interface that includes features such as syntax highlighting, debugging tools, and code management utilities.

- Supporting libraries and dependencies: These ensure that the COBOL programs can interact with the underlying operating system and hardware.

- Version control systems: These are essential for managing changes to the source code, especially in team environments.

To understand the setup process better, let's delve into each component briefly before diving into hands-on setup instructions.

**COBOL Compiler** The COBOL compiler is integral to transforming your high-level instructions into an executable format. Several compilers are available, but GnuCOBOL is one of the most popular due to its open-source nature and extensive support for various COBOL standards. A typical compilation process can be summarized as follows:

```
$ cobc -x -o program_name program_name.cob
```

Here, cobc is the GnuCOBOL compiler command, -x indicates that an executable should be created, -o specifies the output file name, and program_name.cob is the source file.

**Integrated Development Environment (IDE)** An IDE is software that provides comprehensive facilities to programmers for software development. There are several IDEs tailored for COBOL:

- Eclipse with the COBOL plugin

- Visual Studio Code with COBOL extensions

- NetBeans with COBOL support

These IDEs enhance productivity by offering features such as syntax highlighting, code completion, debugging tools, and project management capabilities.

**Supporting Libraries and Dependencies** COBOL programs often require specific libraries and dependencies to execute properly. For example, database connectivity libraries, transaction processing systems, and specific operating system libraries. Ensuring all necessary dependencies are installed is crucial for the smooth execution of COBOL applications. Installation and configuration of these will be detailed in subsequent sections.

**Version Control Systems** Version control systems like Git play an essential role in modern software development. They help in tracking changes, maintaining code integrity, and facilitating collaboration among developers. Basic Git commands for initializing a repository and committing changes are as follows:

```
$ git init
$ git add program_name.cob
$ git commit -m "Initial commit"
```

Implementing a robust version control practice is recommended for effective COBOL development, especially in large projects or team settings.

**Integration in a Development Workflow** Setting up a COBOL development environment is not just about installing software; it's also about integrating these tools into a seamless workflow that enhances productivity and code quality. Consider the following integration tips:

- Configure the IDE to use the GnuCOBOL compiler directly.
- Setup build scripts to automate the compilation and linking processes.
- Use the IDE's debugging capabilities to step through the code and inspect variables.
- Leverage the version control system to manage source code effectively.

**Example** To illustrate, let's walk through a simple example of setting up a basic COBOL project in an IDE, compiling it with GnuCOBOL, and running it.

First, create a new source file named hello.cob with the following content:

```
IDENTIFICATION DIVISION.
PROGRAM-ID. HELLO-WORLD.
PROCEDURE DIVISION.
DISPLAY "Hello, World!".
STOP RUN.
```

Next, compile the file using GnuCOBOL:

```
$ cobc -x -o hello hello.cob
```

Finally, execute the compiled program:

```
$ ./hello
Hello, World!
```

This example demonstrates the basic workflow of writing, compiling, and running a COBOL program in a development environment. Subsequent sections will expand on these concepts, covering more advanced configuration and troubleshooting techniques.

The COBOL development environment's setup might seem daunting initially, but with the right tools and understanding, the process becomes intuitive and significantly enhances your programming efficiency.

## 2.2 Setting Up a Local COBOL Environment

To successfully set up a local COBOL environment, one must follow a series of precise steps to install the necessary software, configure the environment to ensure compatibility, and validate the setup through a series of basic operations. This section covers each of these steps in detail, providing a comprehensive guide that caters to diverse operating systems, with particular attention to the installation of GnuCOBOL.

**Prerequisites:**

- A computer with administrative access.
- Internet connection for downloading necessary files.

- Basic knowledge of operating system-specific commands (Terminal for Linux and macOS, Command Prompt or PowerShell for Windows).

### Step 1: Downloading the GnuCOBOL Compiler

GnuCOBOL is a robust and widely-used COBOL compiler that is open-source and supports a range of operating systems. The first step involves downloading the correct version of GnuCOBOL for your operating system.

```
# On Linux using apt package manager:
sudo apt-get update
sudo apt-get install open-cobol

# On macOS using Homebrew:
brew install gnu-cobol

# On Windows, download the installer from:
# https://sourceforge.net/projects/open-cobol/files/
# Follow the instructions on the download page to complete the
    installation.
```

### Step 2: Verifying the Installation

After installation, it is important to verify that GnuCOBOL has been correctly installed and that the PATH environment variable includes the location of the GnuCOBOL binaries.

```
# On Linux/macOS:
cobc -v

# On Windows:
COBC -v
```

The output should display the version of GnuCOBOL installed, indicating that the installation was successful.

```
cobc (GnuCOBOL) 3.1.2
built Aug 30 2021 17:45:09
```

### Step 3: Configuring the Development Environment

To streamline the development process, configure the environment to recognize COBOL source files and compile them efficiently. This typically involves setting environment variables and paths.

For Linux/macOS:

```
# Open or create .bashrc or .zshrc file in your home directory
nano ~/.bashrc # or ~/.zshrc for Zsh users

# Add the following lines
export PATH=\$PATH:/usr/local/gnu-cobol/bin
export COB_CONFIG_DIR=/usr/local/gnu-cobol/etc

# Apply the changes
source ~/.bashrc # or source ~/.zshrc
```

For Windows:

```
# Open the System Properties -> Advanced -> Environment
    Variables
# In the System variables section, find and select the 'Path' variable.
    Click 'Edit'

# Add a new entry with the path to the GnuCOBOL bin directory, e.
    g., C:\\gnucobol\\bin

# Click OK to apply the changes and close the dialogs
```

### Step 4: Writing a Simple COBOL Program

Create a basic COBOL program to ensure that the compiler and environment are configured correctly.

```
// Create a file named hello.cob
IDENTIFICATION DIVISION.
PROGRAM-ID. HELLO-WORLD.
PROCEDURE DIVISION.
DISPLAY 'Hello, World!'.
STOP RUN.
```

### Step 5: Compiling and Running the COBOL Program

Compile the COBOL program using the GnuCOBOL compiler, and then run the resulting executable file to verify the setup.

```
# On Linux/macOS:
cobc -x -o hello hello.cob # Compiles the COBOL program to an
    executable named hello
./hello # Runs the compiled executable
```

```
# On Windows:
COBC -x -o hello.exe hello.cob # Compiles the COBOL program to
    an executable named hello.exe
hello.exe # Runs the compiled executable
```

```
Hello, World!
```

The output should display "Hello, World!", indicating that the COBOL environment has been successfully set up and that the program can be compiled and executed correctly.

**Additional Considerations:**

- Ensure all dependencies for GnuCOBOL are installed (e.g., GCC for Linux users).
- Regularly update the GnuCOBOL package to leverage performance improvements and bug fixes.
- Utilize Integrated Development Environments (IDEs) or text editors like VS Code, which offer extensions for COBOL, to enhance your development experience.

## 2.3 Installing and Configuring GnuCOBOL

GnuCOBOL is a modern COBOL compiler that allows you to convert COBOL code into executable files that can run on various operating systems. This section provides a step-by-step guide on how to install and configure GnuCOBOL. Let's walk through the process for both Linux and Windows environments to ensure comprehensive coverage.

**Linux Installation**

For most Linux distributions, you can install GnuCOBOL using the package manager. Below are the steps for two common distributions: Ubuntu and Fedora.

On Ubuntu or Debian-based systems, open a terminal and execute the following commands:

```
sudo apt update
sudo apt install gnu-cobol
```

On Fedora or Red Hat-based systems, use:

```
sudo dnf install gnu-cobol
```

After the installation completes, you can verify that GnuCOBOL is installed correctly by checking its version:

```
cobc -v
```

The expected output should display the version of GnuCOBOL installed:

```
cobc (GnuCOBOL) 3.1.2
Copyright (C) 2018-2020 Free Software Foundation, Inc.
This is free software; see the source for copying conditions.
There is NO warranty; not even for MERCHANTABILITY or FITNESS FOR A PARTICULAR PURPOSE.
```

### Windows Installation

Installing GnuCOBOL on Windows requires slightly more steps. One popular method involves using MSYS2, a software distribution and building platform for Windows. Follow these steps:

1. Download and install MSYS2 from the official website: https://www.msys2.org/.

2. After installing, run the MSYS2 MSYS terminal from the Start menu.

3. Update the package database and core system packages:

```
pacman -Syu
```

4. Restart the MSYS2 terminal and update the remaining packages:

```
pacman -Su
```

5. Install GnuCOBOL:

```
pacman -S mingw-w64-x86_64-gnucobol
```

6. To add GnuCOBOL to your path, append the following line to your .bashrc file:

```
export PATH="/mingw64/bin:$PATH"
```

7. Reload the .bashrc file:

```
source ~/.bashrc
```

Verify the installation by checking the GnuCOBOL version:

```
cobc -v
```

The output should confirm the correct installation, similar to the Linux example.

**Configuring GnuCOBOL**

After installation, configuring GnuCOBOL to fit your development environment and workflow is essential. The configuration involves setting environment variables and understanding the basic usage of the GnuCOBOL compiler.

1. Setting Environment Variables

On Linux, you can add the GnuCOBOL binaries to your PATH in your shell configuration file (e.g., .bashrc or .bash_profile). Add the following line:

```
export PATH="/path/to/gnucobol/bin:$PATH"
```

For example, if GnuCOBOL is installed in /usr/local/bin, the command would be:

```
export PATH="/usr/local/bin:$PATH"
```

On Windows, as previously mentioned, ensure MSYS2 and its binaries are in your PATH. This can be verified by opening a new terminal and typing:

```
echo $PATH
```

You should see the directory where GnuCOBOL is installed listed in the output.

2. Basic Usage of GnuCOBOL Compiler

Understanding the primary commands of the GnuCOBOL compiler can simplify your development workflow.

- cobc: The compiler command.

- cobc -x source.cob: Compile the COBOL program and create an executable.

```
cobc -x hello.cob
```

- ./hello: Run the compiled executable (applicable for Linux).

```
./hello
```

In a Windows environment, simply run the executable by typing its name in the terminal:

```
hello
```

Lastly, always check the manual for detailed options and configurations available in GnuCOBOL using:

```
man cobc
```

By following these steps, you ensure a proper setup and configuration of GnuCOBOL, paving the way for efficient COBOL program development.

## 2.4 COBOL Integrated Development Environments (IDEs)

Integrated Development Environments (IDEs) provide a comprehensive environment to facilitate the development, debugging, and testing of COBOL programs. IDEs compile numerous functionalities into a single interface, enhancing productivity and reducing the complexity involved in managing multiple tools. This section delves into various popular COBOL IDEs and explains how to leverage their features for efficient COBOL development.

**Visual Studio Code**

Visual Studio Code (VS Code) is a highly customizable and versatile text editor that can be leveraged for COBOL development with the aid of extensions. To set up VS Code as a COBOL IDE, follow these steps:

1. Install Visual Studio Code from the official website.
2. Launch Visual Studio Code and open the Extensions view by clicking on the Extensions icon in the Activity Bar.
3. Search for the COBOL extension and install it. A popular choice is the bitlang.cobol extension by BitLang.
4. Configure the GnuCOBOL compiler path in VS Code settings to enable inline compilation and error checking.

An exemplary configuration for GnuCOBOL in VS Code settings might look like this:

```
{
    "bitlang.cobol.linter": "path/to/gnucobol/compiler",
    "bitlang.cobol.linterArgs": ["-m"]
}
```

BITLANG.COBOL provides syntax highlighting, code snippets, and linting support for COBOL.

**Eclipse**

Eclipse with the Enterprise COBOL plugin is another popular choice for COBOL development. Eclipse offers comprehensive support for project management, code editing, and debugging. To set up Eclipse for COBOL development:

1. Download and install Eclipse IDE for Java Developers from the official Eclipse website.
2. Install the Enterprise COBOL plugin:
    - Open Eclipse and navigate to Help -> Eclipse Marketplace.
    - Search for Enterprise COBOL and install the plugin.
3. Create a new COBOL project by selecting File -> New -> Project -> COBOL -> COBOL Project.
4. Configure the COBOL compiler settings within the project properties to use GnuCOBOL or another preferred COBOL compiler.

The plugin provides features such as syntax highlighting, code completion, and debugging tools tailored for COBOL programming.

**NetBeans**

NetBeans is another powerful IDE suited for COBOL development through the use of the COBOL NetBeans Plugin. Setting up NetBeans involves:

1. Download and install NetBeans IDE from the official website.
2. Install the COBOL NetBeans Plugin:
    - Open NetBeans and navigate to Tools -> Plugins.

   - In the Plugins window, switch to the Available Plugins tab and search for COBOL.
   - Install the COBOL NetBeans Plugin from the list.

3. Create a new COBOL project by navigating to File -> New Project -> Others -> COBOL Project.
4. Configure the compiler settings in the project properties to point to your COBOL compiler.

NetBeans provides syntax highlighting, code folding, and debugging capabilities tailored for COBOL.

**Online COBOL IDEs**

Online COBOL IDEs offer a browser-based environment for developing and running COBOL programs without the need for a local setup. Some noteworthy online COBOL IDEs include:

- JDoodle: An online compiler that supports COBOL programming.
- Rextester: Another online IDE with support for COBOL. Users can write, compile, and run COBOL code directly from a web browser.
- OnlineGDB: Featuring a COBOL compiler and debugger, this online tool supports code sharing and collaboration.

To use these online IDEs, simply navigate to their respective websites and select the COBOL language option. The interface typically includes an editor and a console for running and debugging your code.

**Debugging and Testing Tools**

Regardless of the chosen IDE, debugging and testing are critical components of the COBOL development process. IDEs enhance these activities through features such as breakpoints, variable inspection, and stack trace analysis. Typical debugging steps in an IDE might include:

1. Setting breakpoints at crucial lines of code to pause execution and inspect program state.
2. Running the program in debug mode to step through the code line by line.
3. Inspecting variable values and expressions during execution to identify logical errors.

4. Analyzing the call stack to trace back the origin of errors.

Example of setting breakpoints and inspecting variables in VS Code:

```
WORKING-STORAGE SECTION.
01 NUM-A PIC 9(2) VALUE 10.
01 NUM-B PIC 9(2) VALUE 0.
01 RESULT PIC 9(3).

PROCEDURE DIVISION.
    MOVE NUM-A TO RESULT.
    DISPLAY "Initial Result: " RESULT.

    SET BREAK-POINT AT LINE 12.
    PERFORM UNTIL NUM-B = NUM-A
        ADD 1 TO NUM-B
        ADD NUM-B TO RESULT
        DISPLAY "NUM-B: " NUM-B " RESULT: " RESULT
    END-PERFORM.

    DISPLAY "Final Result: " RESULT.
```

Outputs will be visible in the debug console, and breakpoints will halt execution to allow variable inspection.

The detailed execution, highlighting, and error-tracing capabilities provided by IDEs significantly enhance the COBOL learning and development experience. For complex COBOL applications, utilizing an IDE can streamline the development process and improve code quality through integrated tooling and automation.

## 2.5 Setting Up Online COBOL Environments

Online environments provide a convenient platform for programming without the need to set up local infrastructure. For those new to COBOL or seeking to quickly prototype and test code, online COBOL environments offer an accessible alternative.

A variety of online COBOL compilers and Integrated Development Environments (IDEs) are available. These platforms remove the burden of local installation and configuration, providing a ready-to-use environment that typically includes an editor, compiler, and runtime for executing COBOL programs.

To set up and use an online COBOL environment, follow these steps:

1. **Choose an Online COBOL Compiler or IDE**
    - Several options are available, such as JDoodle, PaizaCloud IDE, CompileOnline, and Rextester. Each platform provides COBOL support, often embedded within a broader suite of programming languages.
2. **Register or Log in to the Platform**
    - Some platforms require user registration, while others allow guest access.
    - Registering can provide additional features such as saving your code, accessing advanced functionalities, and sharing code snippets.
3. **Creating a New COBOL Project**
    - Upon accessing the platform, create a new project or file and select COBOL as the programming language.
    - This will often present a text editor where you can write your COBOL code.
4. **Writing Your COBOL Program**
    - Enter your COBOL code in the provided text editor. For example, input the following simple COBOL program to print "Hello, World!".

```
IDENTIFICATION DIVISION.
PROGRAM-ID. HelloWorld.
PROCEDURE DIVISION.
    DISPLAY 'Hello, World!'.
    STOP RUN.
```

5. **Compiling the COBOL Program**
    - Most online COBOL environments provide a compile button or command for compiling your code. Click this button or enter the respective command to compile the program.

```
Compiling...
Compilation finished successfully.
```

6. **Running the COBOL Program**
    - After compilation, run the program using the run button or command provided by the platform.
    - Observe the output in the designated area, typically located below or next to the editor.

```
Hello, World!
```

7. **Debugging and Troubleshooting**
    - Use the platform's debugging tools to assist with any issues. Errors will usually be highlighted, and messages are displayed in an output console.
    - Modify your code as necessary, recompile, and rerun it to verify fixes.

These steps ensure a straightforward initiation into COBOL programming without local setup complications. Online environments are particularly useful for educational purposes, rapid prototyping, or when working on systems where installation privileges are restricted.

**Example of JDoodle Usage**

JDoodle is an accessible online compiler that supports numerous programming languages, including COBOL. To use JDoodle:

1. Navigate to https://www.jdoodle.com/.
2. Select COBOL from the list of available languages.
3. Follow the steps outlined previously to write, compile, and run your COBOL code.
4. JDoodle provides options to save your code and obtain a link for sharing or future reference.

JDoodle and similar platforms aid in bridging the gap for beginners and professionals alike, ensuring that the capabilities of COBOL can be explored efficiently.

Another notable platform, PaizaCloud IDE, offers additional features such as file management and a broader development environment that can be useful for larger or multi-file COBOL projects. This level of flexibility makes online COBOL environments a vital tool in contemporary software development practices.

## 2.6 Writing Your First COBOL Program

To create your first COBOL program, we will go through the process from opening your text editor to executing the compiled program. This section introduces the structure of a COBOL program, which includes the identification, environment, data, and procedure divisions. We will write a simple program that prints "Hello, World!" to the terminal.

Begin by opening your preferred text editor. Save the new file with a .cob or .cbl extension, for example, hello.cob.

A COBOL program is distinctively divided into four divisions:

- **Identification Division**
- **Environment Division**
- **Data Division**
- **Procedure Division**

Below is an example of a basic COBOL program that outputs "Hello, World!".

```
IDENTIFICATION DIVISION.
PROGRAM-ID. HelloWorld.
AUTHOR. ComputerScienceProfessor.

ENVIRONMENT DIVISION.

DATA DIVISION.

PROCEDURE DIVISION.
DISPLAY 'Hello, World!'.
STOP RUN.
```

Now let's dissect each part of this program:

1. IDENTIFICATION DIVISION: This is mandatory and comes first in every COBOL program. It typically contains metadata about the program. Here, PROGRAM-ID specifies the program name, which is HelloWorld, and AUTHOR identifies the author of the code.

2. ENVIRONMENT DIVISION: This section is generally used to specify machine-dependent parameters and configurations. For this simple program, there are no parameters to set, so the section remains empty.

3. DATA DIVISION: This segment is where we define and describe the data used by the program. In our example, we do not use any data items, thus this section is also empty.

4. PROCEDURE DIVISION: The core of the COBOL program, where the logic and operations are defined. Here, we use the DISPLAY statement to output the string 'Hello, World!' to the terminal. The STOP RUN statement terminates the program.

Having written the program, the next step is to compile and run it. Assuming you have already installed and configured GnuCOBOL (as detailed in the previous sections of this chapter), you can compile hello.cob using the cobc compiler.

Open your terminal and navigate to the directory where your source file is located. Use the following command to compile the program:

```
cobc -x -o hello hello.cob
```

Here, -x tells cobc to create an executable, -o hello specifies the output file name as hello, and hello.cob is the source file to be compiled.

If there are no errors, running the command will produce an executable file named hello. Execute this file with:

```
./hello
```

You should see the following output in your terminal:

```
Hello, World!
```

This completes the process of writing, compiling, and running a simple COBOL program.

## 2.7 Compiling and Running a COBOL Program

Once you have successfully set up your COBOL development environment, the next step is to compile and run a COBOL program. Understanding this process is fundamental to COBOL programming as it allows you to transform your written code into an executable form that the machine can understand and perform.

To illustrate, we will use GnuCOBOL, a popular and freely available COBOL compiler. The steps outlined here can be seamlessly integrated into your workflow, whether you are using a terminal on a Unix-like system or a command prompt on Windows.

- **Writing the COBOL Program:**

Start with a simple COBOL program. Create a file named hello.cob with the following content:

```
000100 IDENTIFICATION DIVISION.
000200 PROGRAM-ID. HELLO.
000300*
000400 PROCEDURE DIVISION.
000500 DISPLAY 'Hello, COBOL World!'.
000600 STOP RUN.
```

In this program, the IDENTIFICATION DIVISION and PROCEDURE DIVISION are used to define the program name and the main logic respectively. The DISPLAY statement outputs the text "Hello, COBOL World!" to the screen, and the program ends with the STOP RUN statement.

- **Compiling the COBOL Program:**

To compile the COBOL program into an executable form, use the GnuCOBOL cobc command:

```
cobc -x -o hello hello.cob
```

Explanation of the flags used: - -x: This flag tells the compiler to create an executable file. - -o hello: This specifies the output filename for the executable (hello in this case). - hello.cob: The COBOL source file to compile.

If the compilation is successful, an executable file named hello (or hello.exe on Windows) will be created in the current directory.

- **Running the COBOL Program:**

After compilation, the next step is to run the executable. This can be done using the following command:

```
./hello
```

On Windows, execute the program with:

```
hello.exe
```

The expected output will be:

Hello, COBOL World!

This confirms that the compilation and execution have been carried out successfully.

- **Handling Compilation Errors:**

It is common to encounter errors during compilation. Here are typical error messages and their meanings:

- Identifier not declared: This indicates a variable or name used in the program is undefined. - Syntax error: This suggests there is a syntactic issue in your code, often due to a typo or incorrect COBOL syntax. - Cannot open input file: This error occurs if the COBOL source file path is incorrect or the file does not exist.

To resolve these, review the line numbers indicated in the error messages, check your syntax, and ensure all identifiers are properly declared. Re-compiling the code after corrections should ideally eliminate the errors.

- **Optimizations and Options:**

GnuCOBOL provides various options to optimize and control the compilation process:

- -W: Enables warning messages to alert you to potential issues in your code. - -debug: Generates additional debugging information, useful for troubleshooting logic errors. - -static: Compiles the program as a static binary, useful for distributions where dynamic libraries might not be compatible.

For instance, to compile with debugging information enabled:

```
cobc -x -debug -o hello hello.cob
```

Utilizing these options can aid in refining your program and understanding potential issues more clearly.

Mastering the steps of compiling and running your COBOL programs is essential. It ensures that errors are correctly identified and addressed before execution, contributing to more efficient development cycles. Transition smoothly from writing to executing COBOL code by adopting these practices diligently.

## 2.8 Troubleshooting Common Setup Issues

When setting up a COBOL development environment, it's not uncommon to encounter various issues that can hinder progress. This section aims to address some of the most prevalent problems and provide detailed solutions to ensure a smooth setup process. These issues can arise during the installation of GnuCOBOL, configuring Integrated Development Environments (IDEs), or running COBOL programs.

**Common Installation Issues and Solutions**

When installing GnuCOBOL, users might face several types of errors. Ensuring that these steps are followed correctly can prevent many of these common issues.

- **Incorrect Dependencies**
  - **Issue:** Missing or incorrect versions of dependencies.
  - **Solution:** Before installing GnuCOBOL, ensure you have all the necessary dependencies. Typically, these can be installed using package managers. For example, on a Debian-based system:

```
sudo apt-get update
sudo apt-get install gcc libcob4 libcob-dev
```

  gcc and libcob4 are essential for compiling COBOL programs and running the GnuCOBOL runtime.

- **Environment Variables Not Set**
  - **Issue:** The system environment variables are not properly set, leading to issues in locating GnuCOBOL binaries and libraries.
  - **Solution:** Verify and set the necessary environment variables. Adding the following lines to your shell configuration file (e.g., ~/.bashrc or ~/.zshrc) may resolve these issues:

```
export PATH=/usr/local/bin:$PATH
export LD_LIBRARY_PATH=/usr/local/lib:
    $LD_LIBRARY_PATH
```

After making these changes, make sure to source the configuration file or restart your terminal:

```
source ~/.bashrc
```

### Configuration Problems in IDEs

When using Integrated Development Environments (IDEs) for COBOL development, configuration issues might arise, disrupting the development workflow. Here are some solutions to common problems encountered with popular IDEs like Eclipse and NetBeans.

- **Eclipse IDE Configuration Issues**
  - **Issue:** Eclipse fails to recognize the COBOL compiler.
  - **Solution:** Ensure the COBOL compiler is correctly configured in Eclipse. Navigate to Window >Preferences >COBOL >Installed Compliers, and add the correct path to the GnuCOBOL compiler.
- **NetBeans IDE Configuration Issues**
  - **Issue:** NetBeans does not compile COBOL programs.
  - **Solution:** NetBeans requires proper configuration of the build tools. Go to Tools >Options >C/C++ and set the compiler and make command paths to the locations where GnuCOBOL is installed.

### Common Compilation and Execution Issues

- **Compilation Errors**
  - **Syntax Errors**
    - **Issue:** The compiler throws syntax errors.
    - **Solution:** Double-check the syntax of your COBOL program. A common pitfall is not adhering to COBOL's column-specific formatting requirements. Ensure that division names, section names, and statements start in the correct columns.

- **Missing Libraries**
  - **Issue:** Compilation fails due to missing libraries.
  - **Solution:** Verify that all required libraries are correctly installed and available in LD_LIBRARY_PATH. Use ldd your-program-name to identify missing libraries.

- **Execution Issues**
  - **Runtime Errors**
    - **Issue:** The program encounters runtime errors.
    - **Solution:** Inspect error messages carefully. Common runtime errors include file handling issues. Ensure that input and output files exist and have the correct permissions.
  - **Program Does Not Produce Output**
    - **Issue:** The program runs but does not produce any output.
    - **Solution:** Verify that output statements are included in the correct places in the program. Check logical flow with debugging options such as using the DISPLAY statements for tracing the execution.

### Debugging Tools

Utilizing debugging tools can assist in pinpointing the issues during both compilation and execution phases.

- **GDB COBOL Debugging**
  - **Issue:** Difficulty in tracing and understanding program behavior.
  - **Solution:** The GNU Debugger (GDB) can be used to debug COBOL programs, provided they are compiled with debugging information. Compile using:

```
cobc -g -x your-program.cob
```

and then start GDB:

```
gdb ./your-program
```

GDB allows setting breakpoints, stepping through code, and inspecting variables.

Attention to detail and careful configuration play crucial roles in successfully setting up and running a COBOL development environment. By addressing these troubleshooting steps thoroughly, many common setup issues can be effectively mitigated, enabling productive COBOL development.

# Chapter 3

# Basic COBOL Syntax

**Understanding basic COBOL syntax is fundamental for writing effective programs. This chapter provides an overview of COBOL's program structure, including keywords, reserved words, and essential statements. It covers the use of identifiers, naming conventions, comments, paragraphs, sections, and the significance of formatting. Additionally, the chapter introduces literals, constants, and concludes with a simple "Hello World" program to demonstrate these concepts in practice.**

## 3.1 COBOL Program Structure

A fundamental aspect of mastering COBOL programming involves a clear understanding of its program structure. The structure defines how a COBOL program is organized and dictates the sequence and hierarchy of the various components that constitute a complete program. The typical structure of a COBOL program is divided into four main divisions: Identification Division, Environment Division, Data Division, and Procedure Division. Each division has a specific role and purpose, as outlined in this section.

**Identification Division**
The Identification Division is the first division in any COBOL program. It provides basic information about the program and is a mandatory division. It typically includes the program's name and other documentary information that provides a brief description of the program. The

primary entry in this division is the PROGRAM-ID statement.

```
IDENTIFICATION DIVISION.
PROGRAM-ID. ProgramName.
AUTHOR. YourName.
DATE-WRITTEN. January 1, 2023.
```

ProgramName is a user-defined identifier that uniquely identifies the program. The AUTHOR and DATE-WRITTEN clauses are optional but highly recommended for documentation purposes.

**Environment Division**

The Environment Division specifies the computer environment in which the program will run. It describes the configuration of the hardware and software on which the program depends. This division is divided into two sections: Configuration Section and Input-Output Section.

```
ENVIRONMENT DIVISION.
CONFIGURATION SECTION.
SOURCE-COMPUTER. IBM-PC.
OBJECT-COMPUTER. IBM-PC.

INPUT-OUTPUT SECTION.
FILE-CONTROL.
    SELECT FileName ASSIGN TO 'file-path'.
```

The SOURCE-COMPUTER and OBJECT-COMPUTER entries specify the source and object systems for the program. The FILE-CONTROL paragraph within the Input-Output Section describes the files the program will use. FileName is a user-defined name assigned to the file, while 'file-path' specifies the physical location of the file on the system.

**Data Division**

The Data Division is crucial as it defines the variables used in the program. It contains sections and paragraphs that declare various types of data, including files and working storage. The primary sections within the Data Division are File Section, Working-Storage Section, and Local-Storage Section.

```
DATA DIVISION.
FILE SECTION.
FD FileName.
01 FileRecord.
```

```
    05 DataField1 PIC X(10).
    05 DataField2 PIC 9(4).

WORKING-STORAGE SECTION.
01 WS-Variable1 PIC X(10) VALUE 'Hello'.
01 WS-Variable2 PIC 9(4) VALUE 2023.
```

In the File Section, FileRecord defines the structure of each record in the file FileName. The Working-Storage Section declares in-memory variables such as WS-Variable1 and WS-Variable2, with specified storage formats (PIC X(10) for alphanumeric and PIC 9(4) for numeric).

**Procedure Division**

The Procedure Division contains the program's logic. It comprises a series of statements and instructions that the computer will execute. This division is where the actual computation and processing occur. It consists of paragraphs, which are groups of related statements, and sections, which are groups of related paragraphs.

```
PROCEDURE DIVISION.
Main-Section.
    DISPLAY 'Starting the program'.
    PERFORM Initialize.
    PERFORM Process-Data.
    PERFORM Terminate.

Initialize SECTION.
    DISPLAY 'Initialization complete'.

Process-Data SECTION.
    DISPLAY 'Processing data'.

Terminate SECTION.
    DISPLAY 'Ending the program'.
    STOP RUN.
```

The Main-Section paragraph defines the main flow of the program, with each PERFORM statement invoking a different section. The statements within each section, such as DISPLAY and STOP RUN, determine the specific actions taken during program execution.

Understanding and adhering to this structure is essential for writing efficient and readable COBOL programs. Each division serves a distinct purpose and contributes to the overall functionality and maintainability of the code. Proper organization and clear definition of each component ensure that the program performs its intended tasks effectively and is easier to debug and update.

## 3.2 COBOL Keywords and Reserved Words

In COBOL, certain words are designated as keywords or reserved words. These words have predefined meanings and serve specific purposes within the language, forming the backbone of the COBOL syntax. It's crucial to understand these terms to effectively interact with the compiler and ensure that the programs execute correctly.

Keywords in COBOL are used to identify elements such as data, variables, and operations. They are integral to the COBOL syntax, dictating how instructions and commands are interpreted. Reserved words, on the other hand, are words that are reserved by the language for specific use and cannot be used as identifiers such as variable names or paragraph names.

**Examples of Keywords**:

- IDENTIFICATION DIVISION
- DATA DIVISION
- PROCEDURE DIVISION
- IF
- ELSE
- MOVE
- PERFORM
- STOP RUN

**Examples of Reserved Words**:

- ACCEPT
- ADD
- CALL

- CLOSE
- COMPUTE
- CONTINUE
- COPY
- DELETE

These keywords and reserved words are case-insensitive, meaning that IF, if, and If are considered the same by the COBOL compiler. Here's a detailed exploration of some frequently used keywords and reserved words:

IDENTIFICATION DIVISION: This is the first division of a COBOL program. It contains metadata about the program, such as the program name and author.

```
IDENTIFICATION DIVISION.
PROGRAM-ID. HelloWorld.
AUTHOR. Jane Doe.
```

DATA DIVISION: This division is used for defining data items. It specifies the variables that will be used in the program.

```
DATA DIVISION.
WORKING-STORAGE SECTION.
01 WS-NAME PIC A(10) VALUE 'COBOL'.
```

PROCEDURE DIVISION: This division contains the executable code of the program. Here, the operations and logic are defined through procedures and paragraphs.

```
PROCEDURE DIVISION.
DISPLAY 'Hello, ' WS-NAME.
STOP RUN.
```

The IF and ELSE keywords are used to introduce conditional statements to control the flow of execution based on specific conditions.

```
IF WS-NAME = 'COBOL'
    DISPLAY 'Welcome to COBOL Programming.'
ELSE
    DISPLAY 'Unknown Program.'
END-IF.
```

The MOVE keyword assigns a value to a variable. This is one of the fundamental operations in COBOL for data manipulation.

```
MOVE 'COBOL Programming' TO WS-NAME.
```

PERFORM is used to execute a sequence of instructions multiple times or to call paragraphs/sections.

```
PERFORM UNTIL WS-NAME = 'END'
    DISPLAY WS-NAME
    MOVE 'END' TO WS-NAME
END-PERFORM.
```

The STOP RUN keyword signifies the end of the program. It tells the COBOL runtime environment that the program has finished executing.

```
STOP RUN.
```

Reserved words like ACCEPT, ADD, CALL, CLOSE, COMPUTE, CONTINUE, COPY, and DELETE perform specific functions and operations that are integral to program execution and cannot be repurposed as identifiers.

ACCEPT can be used to take input from the user or system.

```
ACCEPT WS-NAME.
```

ADD is utilized for arithmetic addition operations.

```
ADD 1 TO WS-COUNTER.
```

Learning to utilize these keywords and reserved words accurately is essential for mastering COBOL programming. As you continue to develop and debug programs, acknowledging the function and limitation of each keyword and reserved word will enhance the clarity and efficiency of your code.

## 3.3 Understanding COBOL Statements

Understanding how to effectively write and utilize COBOL statements is essential for developing proficient programs. COBOL statements offer a structured way to perform computational tasks, and they follow a syntactic form unique to the language. These statements are the building blocks of any COBOL program and must be written correctly to ensure accurate functionality.

COBOL statements typically fall into several categories, including DATA DIVISION statements, PROCEDURE DIVISION statements, and control statements. Each class of statements serves a distinct purpose and adheres to specific formatting rules.

**Data Division Statements**: These statements are used for defining the structure and format of data used within the program. They declare variables and constants and set up the data environment for the program.

```
DATA DIVISION.
WORKING-STORAGE SECTION.
01 EMPLOYEE-NAME PIC X(30).
01 EMPLOYEE-ID PIC 9(5).
```

In the example above, two data items, EMPLOYEE-NAME and EMPLOYEE-ID, are declared in the WORKING-STORAGE SECTION. The PIC clause specifies the data type and format, where X denotes alphanumeric characters, and 9 indicates numeric value placeholders.

**Procedure Division Statements**: The PROCEDURE DIVISION contains the logic and operational instructions for the program. Statements in this division include arithmetic operations, conditional statements, iteration constructs, and input/output control.

```
PROCEDURE DIVISION.
DISPLAY "Enter Employee ID: ".
ACCEPT EMPLOYEE-ID.
IF EMPLOYEE-ID > 10000 THEN
    DISPLAY "Employee is a senior staff member."
ELSE
    DISPLAY "Employee is a junior staff member."
END-IF.
```

In the PROCEDURE DIVISION, the above sequence of statements illustrates basic input and output controls. The DISPLAY statement outputs text to the standard display, while ACCEPT reads input. The IF...ELSE...END-IF construct provides conditional branching based on the value of EMPLOYEE-ID.

**Control Statements**: COBOL uses control statements to manage the flow of the program. These include conditional statements such as IF and EVALUATE, loop constructs like PERFORM, and sequence control using GO TO.

```
...
IF EMPLOYEE-ID IS NUMERIC THEN
    DISPLAY "Processing Employee ID ".
    PERFORM PROCESS-EMPLOYEE-ID
ELSE
    DISPLAY "Invalid Employee ID. Please enter a numeric value."
END-IF.

PROCESS-EMPLOYEE-ID.
    MOVE EMPLOYEE-ID TO WS-ID.
    DISPLAY "Employee ID is: " WS-ID.
    GO TO END-PROCESS.

END-PROCESS.
...
```

The PERFORM statement in the IF block illustrates how to execute a sequence of statements grouped under a paragraph name, in this case, PROCESS-EMPLOYEE-ID. The GO TO statement allows for immediate transfer of control to another part of the program, which can be suitable for certain algorithmic implementations.

**Loop Constructs**: Setting up loops can be performed using the PERFORM statement. The PERFORM statement can iterate through procedural logic based on conditions or a specified range.

```
...
PERFORM VARYING I FROM 1 BY 1 UNTIL I > 10
    DISPLAY "Current iteration: " I
END-PERFORM.
...
```

In this example, PERFORM VARYING establishes a loop that iterates from 1 to 10, incrementing I by 1 in each cycle. The DISPLAY statement within the loop outputs the current iteration count.

Each of these statements needs to be formatted within the specific column rules intrinsic to COBOL. For instance, the Area A starts from column 8, and Area B starts from column 12. Comprehending these formatting constraints is necessary to ensure the program compiles and runs correctly.

While understanding the syntax and structure of COBOL statements may seem complex initially, mastering them is vital for writing effective programs. Recognizing the distinction between data declarations in the DATA DIVISION and operational instructions in the PROCEDURE DIVISION is foundational to COBOL programming.

## 3.4 COBOL Identifiers and Naming Conventions

COBOL identifiers are crucial components used to name various elements within a program, such as variables, data items, and sections. An identifier is a sequence of characters used to uniquely identify a given element in the program. Understanding the rules and conventions for creating valid identifiers is essential for writing readable and maintainable COBOL programs.

**Rules for COBOL Identifiers**

1. **Composition**: An identifier must be composed of alphabetic characters (A-Z) and digits (0-9). 2. **Length**: The length of an identifier can range from 1 to 30 characters. 3. **First Character**: The first character of an identifier must be an alphabetic letter. 4. **Special Characters**: Hyphens (-) are allowed but should not appear at the beginning or end of the identifier. Underscores (_), dollar signs ($), hash signs (#), and percent signs (%) are not allowed. 5. **Case Sensitivity**: COBOL is not case-sensitive, meaning that EmployeeID and employeeid are considered different representations of the same identifier.

**Examples of Valid Identifiers**

- CUSTOMER-NAME
- EMPLOYEE-ID
- SALES-FIGURE
- ACCOUNT1
- TOTAL-SUM

**Examples of Invalid Identifiers**

- -CUSTOMER-NAME (Cannot begin with a hyphen)
- EMPLOYEE-ID- (Cannot end with a hyphen)
- SALES_FIGURE (Underscores are not allowed)
- TOTAL$SUM (Dollar signs are not allowed)
- 123ACCOUNT (Cannot begin with a digit)

### Importance of Meaningful Identifiers

Using meaningful identifiers enhances the readability and maintainability of the program. Identifiers should be descriptive enough to convey the purpose or content of the element they represent. For example, an identifier like DESCRIPTION is much clearer than a vague identifier like DESC.

### Using Naming Conventions

Adhering to standardized naming conventions helps maintain consistency throughout the codebase, making it easier to understand and maintain. Common naming conventions in COBOL include:

- **Uppercase Letters**: Identifiers are often written in uppercase letters.
- **Hyphen Separation**: Words in identifiers are separated by hyphens to improve readability.
- **Prefixes and Suffixes**: Specific prefixes or suffixes may be added to standardize certain types of identifiers. For instance, data items might use a common prefix like DATA-, while flags might use the suffix -FLAG.

### Example of a Well-Named COBOL Program Segment

```
IDENTIFICATION DIVISION.
PROGRAM-ID. SAMPLEPROGRAM.

DATA DIVISION.
WORKING-STORAGE SECTION.
01 CUSTOMER-RECORD.
   05 CUSTOMER-ID PIC X(10).
   05 CUSTOMER-NAME PIC X(30).
   05 CUSTOMER-BALANCE PIC 9(5)V99.
```

```
PROCEDURE DIVISION.
DISPLAY-CUSTOMER.
    DISPLAY 'CUSTOMER ID: ' CUSTOMER-ID.
    DISPLAY 'CUSTOMER NAME: ' CUSTOMER-NAME.
    DISPLAY 'CUSTOMER BALANCE: ' CUSTOMER-BALANCE.
STOP RUN.
```

In this example, the identifiers CUSTOMER-RECORD, CUSTOMER-ID, CUSTOMER-NAME, and CUSTOMER-BALANCE are clear and descriptive, adhering to the convention of using uppercase letters and hyphens to separate words.

**Avoiding Common Pitfalls**

To ensure identifiers are effective, avoid common pitfalls such as using overly abbreviated names or combining different naming conventions. For instance, an identifier like CSTMRID lacks clarity, whereas CUSTOMER-ID is more explicit. Mixing naming conventions can lead to inconsistent and confusing code, so it's important to adopt a standard approach and apply it consistently across the entire program.

Utilizing meaningful identifiers and consistent naming conventions not only improves readability but also significantly enhances the maintainability of COBOL programs, facilitating easier collaboration and reducing the potential for errors.

## 3.5 Comments in COBOL

Comments play a significant role in COBOL, aiding in code readability, maintainability, and documentation. They provide useful context and explanations for the code, which can assist anyone reading or modifying the program in the future. COBOL supports several ways to include comments within the code.

COBOL comments begin with an asterisk (*) in column 7 of a line. Any text following this asterisk on the same line is treated as a comment and is not executed by the compiler. For example:

```
      * This is a comment line in COBOL.
      * The below line is an executable statement
       MOVE 'HELLO, WORLD' TO GREETING.
```

Another method to include comments within a COBOL program is by using the *> symbol. This method is especially useful for in-line comments, which can be placed alongside COBOL statements to explain their purpose or logic:

```
MOVE 'HELLO, WORLD' TO GREETING *> Assign '
    HELLO, WORLD' string to GREETING variable
```

Using comments effectively in COBOL involves a few best practices:

- **Clarity and Brevity**: Comments should be clear, concise, and directly related to the code they describe. Avoid verbose or redundant explanations.
- **Consistency**: Maintain a consistent style and format for comments throughout the program. This includes the placement of comment symbols and the capitalization of comment text.
- **Relevance**: Ensure comments add value by explaining non-obvious portions of the code, describing important decisions, and outlining complex algorithms. Avoid stating the obvious.
- **Maintenance**: Regularly update comments to reflect changes in the code. Outdated comments can lead to confusion and misinterpretation.

Here is an illustrative example of a small COBOL program with comments adhering to these best practices:

```
IDENTIFICATION DIVISION.
PROGRAM-ID. HELLO-WORLD.
AUTHOR. JOHN DOE.

* This program displays "HELLO, WORLD" on the screen

ENVIRONMENT DIVISION.
CONFIGURATION SECTION.

DATA DIVISION.
WORKING-STORAGE SECTION.
01 GREETING PIC X(12) VALUE SPACES.

* Assign the greeting message
PROCEDURE DIVISION.
```

```
    MOVE 'HELLO, WORLD' TO GREETING
    *> Output the greeting message
    DISPLAY GREETING
    STOP RUN.
```

In this example, comments are used to describe the program's purpose, data division components, and specific COBOL statements. Notice the use of * for whole line comments and *> for inline comments.

Understanding the role of comments in COBOL is crucial for developing clear and maintainable code. Properly utilized, comments serve as valuable documentation that can significantly ease the process of code review and modification.

Comments also play an integral role during the collaborative development of COBOL applications. When multiple developers work on the same codebase, well-placed comments ensure that everyone can understand the code's logic without extensive verbal explanations, thus enhancing team productivity.

To summarize, comments are an essential feature in COBOL for improving code readability and maintainability. They assist developers in understanding the code and facilitate effective collaboration in large programming projects. Adhering to best practices when writing comments will make your COBOL programs easier to read and maintain over time.

## 3.6 Paragraphs and Sections

Understanding the logical structure of a COBOL program is essential for effective coding and maintenance. In COBOL, the primary structural units are paragraphs and sections. Each unit serves a distinct purpose, promoting clarity and organization in the program's flow.

A paragraph in COBOL is a block of code that performs a specific function. Paragraphs are defined within a section and are typically used to encapsulate a particular task. They are identified by a paragraph name, followed by a period. Paragraph names must be unique within a section and provide a means of directing the flow of control within the program using various control statements such as PERFORM.

Here is a synthesis of a COBOL paragraph:

```
PARA-NAME.
```

```
        COBOL statements...
```

Each paragraph can include multiple COBOL statements that collectively perform a single, cohesive task. The choice of meaningful paragraph names improves the readability and maintainability of the program.

Sections in COBOL aggregate multiple paragraphs and serve as broader units of code organization. A section in COBOL consists of a section header, followed by one or more paragraphs. Like paragraph names, section names must be unique throughout the program. Sections can contain data definitions or procedural code segments, often representing a major functional component of the program.

Here is a conceptual illustration of a COBOL section:

```
SECTION-NAME SECTION.
    PARA1.
        COBOL statements...

    PARA2.
        COBOL statements...
```

Sections often help delineate the phases of program execution, dividing the program into initialization, processing, and termination sequences. Sections can be invoked by PERFORM statements, which allow the program's execution flow to jump to the respective section and execute its paragraphs.

To highlight how paragraphs and sections interact in a typical COBOL program, consider the following example wherein a section processes customer records:

```
PROCESS-RECORDS SECTION.
    READ-NEXT-RECORD.
        READ CUSTOMER-FILE
            INTO CUSTOMER-RECORD
            AT END
            MOVE 'Y' TO END-OF-FILE-FLAG
    .

    PROCESS-RECORD.
        IF END-OF-FILE-FLAG NOT = 'Y'
            PERFORM DISPLAY-RECORD
```

```
        PERFORM UPDATE-RECORD
        PERFORM READ-NEXT-RECORD
    END-IF
    .

DISPLAY-RECORD.
    DISPLAY CUSTOMER-RECORD
    .

UPDATE-RECORD.
    MOVE CUSTOMER-DATA TO CUSTOMER-RECORD
    REWRITE CUSTOMER-RECORD
    .
```

In this example, the SECTION "PROCESS-RECORDS" encompasses four paragraphs: "READ-NEXT-RECORD", "PROCESS-RECORD", "DISPLAY-RECORD", and "UPDATE-RECORD". Each paragraph performs logically distinct operations, such as reading, processing, displaying, and updating customer records. The PERFORM statement within "PROCESS-RECORD" directs the flow to other paragraphs, ensuring an organized and modular program structure.

The distinction between paragraphs and sections allows for modularization. This modular approach is pivotal for breaking down complex tasks into manageable sub-tasks, enhancing both clarity and error isolation. It permits finer granularity of control, especially when combined with PERFORM statements that facilitate iterative and conditional execution of these modular units.

In summary, paragraphs and sections form the backbone of COBOL's structural organization. They play an indispensable role in delineating and modularizing functional components of the program, fostering improved readability, maintainability, and logical coherence. By mastering the use of these structural units, programmers can write more efficient, comprehensible, and maintainable COBOL programs.

## 3.7 Importance of Columns and Formatting

In COBOL programming, adherence to proper formatting practices is crucial not only for readability and maintainability but also because the COBOL compiler relies heavily on the structure and placement of code.

The significance of columns and formatting in COBOL cannot be understated, as it aligns the program with the language's syntax rules and conventions.

A COBOL program is divided into various areas based on columns, which serve distinct purposes:

- **Columns 1-6: Sequence Number Area**
- **Column 7: Indicator Area**
- **Columns 8-11: Area A**
- **Columns 12-72: Area B**
- **Columns 73-80: Identification Area**

**Sequence Number Area (Columns 1-6)**: This area is optional in modern usage but was historically used to hold line numbers. Sequence numbers allowed for easier management and reordering of punched cards. Contemporary compilers may ignore this field, but understanding its place helps grasp the legacy structure of COBOL programs.

**Indicator Area (Column 7)**: This column serves multiple purposes:

- *: Denotes a comment line.
- -: Continuation of a nonnumeric literal from the previous line.
- /: Indicates a page eject (form feed).
- D: Marks lines as debug lines, executed only when debugging is enabled.

Example of a comment:

```
      * This is a comment line
```

**Area A (Columns 8-11)**: Area A is used for the division, section, and paragraph names, and for major headings. These entities must start in Area A:

```
       IDENTIFICATION DIVISION.
       ENVIRONMENT DIVISION.
```

**Area B (Columns 12-72)**: Used for actual COBOL statements and to specify detailed data descriptions. This is the primary area for writing executable code, and everything in this area should be aligned to enhance readability:

```
MOVE 'HELLO, WORLD' TO WS-MESSAGE.
```

**Identification Area (Columns 73-80)**: Originally designed to hold a programmer-defined identification or sequence number. Modern practice generally disregards this area, and it serves no function in the code execution.

The visual structure of COBOL code matters because it affects the syntactical correctness and interpretation by the compiler. Misaligned or improperly placed code can lead to syntax errors, resulting in failed compilations. The following example illustrates a properly formatted COBOL statement:

```
IDENTIFICATION DIVISION.
PROGRAM-ID. HELLO-WORLD.
DATA DIVISION.
WORKING-STORAGE SECTION.
01 WS-MESSAGE PIC X(20).
PROCEDURE DIVISION.
    MOVE 'HELLO, WORLD' TO WS-MESSAGE
    DISPLAY WS-MESSAGE
    STOP RUN.
```

Attention to each column's purpose facilitates not just correctness but also code reviews and maintenance. It is easier to detect and debug issues when the code is neatly organized and adheres to convention.

Understanding and applying proper indentation and alignment practices are pivotal. This ensures that the structure of a COBOL program is clear and conforms to expected standards, reducing the likelihood of errors and making it manageable for other programmers to read and comprehend.

## 3.8 Using Literals and Constants

In COBOL, literals and constants are crucial for representing fixed values throughout a program. They can be classified into different types based on their usage and type of data they represent: numeric literals, non-numeric literals, and figurative constants.

**Numeric literals** are used to represent integer and decimal values. Numeric literals are composed solely of digits and may include a decimal point to indicate a non-integer value. The following are examples of numeric literals:

- 123
- 45.67

When specifying numeric literals, it is important to be aware of the range and precision that the COBOL implementation supports. Integer literals (or integers) must not include commas or spaces.

**Non-numeric literals** represent string values and are enclosed within quotation marks (either single or double). The following are examples of non-numeric literals:

- 'Hello, World!'
- "COBOL Programming"

Non-numeric literals should be enclosed consistently using the same type of quotation mark at both the beginning and end. They support special symbols and alphabets, depending on the character set supported by the COBOL compiler.

Literals are used in COBOL in various contexts, such as initializing variables, defining text to be printed, and controlling program flow with conditional statements. For example:

```
MOVE 123 TO NUM-VAR.
DISPLAY 'Hello, World!'.
```

**Constants** in COBOL are defined in the Data Division using the VALUE clause within **level-78** variables. Constants are named entities that retain a fixed value throughout the execution of a program. They are defined as follows:

```
78 MAX-STUDENTS VALUE 50.
78 COURSE-NAME VALUE 'COBOL Programming'.
```

The **figurative constants** in COBOL are predefined values that can be used directly in the program. These include ZERO, SPACE, ALL

SPACES, HIGH-VALUE, and others. Each figurative constant has a specific purpose:

- ZERO, ZEROS, ZEROES represent the numeric value 0.
- SPACE, SPACES are used to denote one or more spaces.
- HIGH-VALUE, HIGH-VALUES represent the highest value in the collating sequence.
- LOW-VALUE, LOW-VALUES represent the lowest value in the collating sequence.
- QUOTE, QUOTES represent the quotation mark (").

These figurative constants offer greater readability and maintainability. For example, instead of writing ' ' (seven spaces), it is clearer to write:

```
MOVE SPACES TO MY-VAR.
```

A practical example of using numeric and non-numeric literals, as well as figurative constants in a COBOL program, can be seen below:

```
IDENTIFICATION DIVISION.
PROGRAM-ID. LiteralExample.

DATA DIVISION.
WORKING-STORAGE SECTION.
01 NUM-EXAMPLES.
   05 COUNT-A PIC 9(3) VALUE 10.
   05 COUNT-B PIC 9(3) VALUE 20.

01 STR-EXAMPLES.
   05 WELCOME-MSG PIC X(25) VALUE 'Welcome to
       COBOL!'.
   05 EMPTY-MSG PIC X(25) VALUE SPACES.

PROCEDURE DIVISION.
DISPLAY COUNT-A.
DISPLAY COUNT-B.
DISPLAY WELCOME-MSG.
DISPLAY EMPTY-MSG.
STOP RUN.
```

When executed, the output of the above program will be:

```
010
020
Welcome to COBOL!
```

The VALUE clause initializes COUNT-A and COUNT-B with numeric literals 10 and 20, respectively. Similarly, WELCOME-MSG is initialized with a non-numeric literal, and EMPTY-MSG is assigned SPACES. The DISPLAY statements output these initialized values.

Understanding and effectively using literals and constants in COBOL is essential for defining immutable values, initializing variables, and improving program readability. By leveraging fixed values through the VALUE clause, programmers can avoid hardcoding literals directly in the procedure logic. This practice enhances both the maintainability and clarity of COBOL programs.

## 3.9 Writing a Simple Hello World Program

To illustrate the fundamental aspects of COBOL syntax and demonstrate the practical application of concepts discussed in this chapter, we will write a simple "Hello World" program. This program will embody the typical structure of a COBOL program and use various elements such as divisions, sections, and statements.

We begin by analyzing the standard structure of a COBOL program, which is typically divided into four main divisions:

- Identification Division
- Environment Division
- Data Division
- Procedure Division

Each division serves a specific purpose and is mandatory in a COBOL program.

**Identification Division:**

The Identification Division is the first part of any COBOL program. It includes metadata about the program, such as the program name and the author information.

```
IDENTIFICATION DIVISION.
PROGRAM-ID. HelloWorld.
AUTHOR. YourName.
```

PROGRAM-ID is a mandatory entry that specifies the name of the program. AUTHOR is optional but provides valuable information about the program's creator.

**Environment Division:**

In more complex programs, the Environment Division is used to specify machine-dependent parameters. However, it is not necessary for our simple Hello World program.

```
ENVIRONMENT DIVISION.
```

**Data Division:**

The Data Division is where all variables and constants used in the program are defined. Since our Hello World program does not utilize any data items, this section will remain minimal.

```
DATA DIVISION.
```

**Procedure Division:**

The Procedure Division contains the executable instructions of the program. This is where the actual logic is implemented. For our Hello World program, we will define the main section and include a single instruction to display the message.

```
PROCEDURE DIVISION.
    DISPLAY 'Hello, World!'.
    STOP RUN.
```

The DISPLAY statement outputs the literal 'Hello, World!' to the standard display device. The STOP RUN statement terminates the program.

Combining all these divisions, our complete program looks as follows:

```
IDENTIFICATION DIVISION.
PROGRAM-ID. HelloWorld.
AUTHOR. YourName.

ENVIRONMENT DIVISION.
```

```
DATA DIVISION.

PROCEDURE DIVISION.
    DISPLAY 'Hello, World!'.
    STOP RUN.
```

This simple program showcases the structured nature of COBOL and how each division plays a role in organizing the program. When executed, the output of the program will be:

```
Hello, World!
```

Understanding this basic "Hello World" program lays a foundation for more complex COBOL program development. The clear, hierarchical structure of COBOL ensures that even as programs grow in complexity, they remain readable and maintainable..readlines

# Chapter 4

# Data Types and Variables

**Understanding data types and variables is crucial for effective COBOL programming. This chapter explores the various data types available in COBOL, including numeric and alphanumeric types, and how to define variables using the Picture (PIC) clause. It delves into level numbers, the use of redefines and renames clauses, data initialization, value assignment, and the application of figurative constants to facilitate efficient data management.**

## 4.1 Introduction to Data Types in COBOL

In COBOL (Common Business Oriented Language), data types are fundamental constructs that allow programmers to define the nature and scope of data they wish to process. Unlike many modern programming languages, COBOL does not use explicit data type declarations such as int or string. Instead, COBOL utilizes the Picture (PIC) clause to describe the type and size of the data.

**Data Types Overview**

Three primary data types are prevalent in COBOL:

- **Numeric Data Types**: These are used to represent numbers, both integer and decimal. They are crucial for calculations and arithmetic operations.
- **Alphabetic Data Types**: These represent alphabetic characters

(A-Z). They are often used for names or other text-based data that does not involve numbers or special characters.

- **Alphanumeric Data Types**: These account for all character types including numbers, letters, and special characters. They are used for data that can include any combination of these characters.

### Numeric Data Types

Numeric data types in COBOL are used to represent whole numbers or decimal numbers. They are denoted in the PIC clause with the symbols 9 (which stands for a digit) and V (which stands for an implied decimal point). For example:

```
01 INTEGER-VAR PIC 9(5).
01 DECIMAL-VAR PIC 9(4)V9(2).
```

In the above definitions:

- INTEGER-VAR can hold a value up to 99999.
- DECIMAL-VAR can hold values like 9999.99.

The S symbol in the PIC clause can be used to denote that a number includes a sign (either positive or negative). For instance:

```
01 SIGNED-NUMBER PIC S9(6)V9(2).
```

### Alphabetic Data Types

Alphabetic data types are used for fields that contain only letters. They are represented in the PIC clause using the symbol A. For example:

```
01 ALPHA-VAR PIC A(10).
```

This indicates that the variable ALPHA-VAR can contain up to 10 alphabetic characters.

### Alphanumeric Data Types

These types are highly versatile as they can store a mix of letters, numbers, and special characters. The X symbol in the PIC clause is used to define alphanumeric data types. For example:

```
01 ALPHANUM-VAR PIC X(15).
```

This definition allows ALPHANUM-VAR to hold a string of up to 15 characters, which can be any combination of alphabetic and numeric characters as well as other symbols.

**Specialized Data Types**

Beyond the basic types, COBOL also supports specialized data formats, including:

- **Computational (COMP) Types**: These are used for efficient arithmetic processing, and their internal representation may depend on the hardware's architecture. For instance, COMP-1 and COMP-2 are used for floating-point numbers, while COMP-3 (Packed Decimal) is utilized for decimal numbers stored in a packed format.

Here's an example of how a computational type might be defined:

```
01 PACKED-VAR PIC S9(7)V99 COMP-3.
```

This specifies a signed packed decimal number with 7 digits before the decimal and 2 digits after.

Understanding the variety and functionality of data types in COBOL is critical to building robust and efficient programs. Whether dealing with large volumes of numeric data in financial applications or managing textual data, the correct utilization of these data types will enhance both performance and accuracy.

## 4.2 Defining Variables in COBOL

Defining variables in COBOL is a fundamental aspect that forms the backbone of efficient data management within a program. In COBOL, variables are defined using the Data Division, which is one of the four divisions in a COBOL program. The Data Division is crucial as it specifies the data types and structures that the program will utilize. Within the Data Division, we find several sections, each dedicated to different aspects of data handling. For defining variables, the Working-Storage Section or the Local-Storage Section is commonly used.

The general structure for defining a variable in COBOL includes specifying a level number, a data name, and a Picture (PIC) clause. The level number determines the hierarchy of data items, the data name identifies the variable, and the PIC clause defines the type and size of the variable.

```
01 CUSTOMER-NAME PIC A(30).
01 CUSTOMER-AGE PIC 99.
01 CUSTOMER-ID PIC X(10).
```

In the example above, CUSTOMER-NAME, CUSTOMER-AGE, and CUSTOMER-ID are variables defined with level number 01. The level number 01 indicates that these variables are top-level data items. The PIC clause specifies the type and size of each variable:

- CUSTOMER-NAME is defined as a 30-character alphanumeric field.
- CUSTOMER-AGE is established as a 2-digit numeric field.
- CUSTOMER-ID is outlined as a 10-character alphanumeric field.

Variables in COBOL can be grouped under a common name using higher-level group items. Group items allow for the definition of a hierarchical data structure, where multiple related elements are nested within a parent element.

```
01 CUSTOMER-DETAILS.
    05 CUSTOMER-NAME PIC A(30).
    05 CUSTOMER-AGE PIC 99.
    05 CUSTOMER-ID PIC X(10).
```

In this hierarchical structure, CUSTOMER-DETAILS is a group item with three subordinate elementary items: CUSTOMER-NAME, CUSTOMER-AGE, and CUSTOMER-ID. The group item does not have a PIC clause of its own; instead, it aggregates the PIC clauses of its constituent elements. Group items are useful for managing collections of related data elements efficiently.

Another essential feature for defining variables is the usage of initializing clauses such as VALUE. The VALUE clause can be employed to assign initial values to variables upon their definition.

```
01 TOTAL-CUSTOMERS PIC 9(4) VALUE 0.
01 STATUS-INDICATOR PIC X(1) VALUE 'A'.
```

In the examples above, TOTAL-CUSTOMERS is initialized to 0, and STATUS-INDICATOR is set to 'A'. Using the VALUE clause helps in setting default values that ensure variables have defined data at the start of the program's execution.

A particular consideration in COBOL variable definition is the usage of redefines. The REDEFINES clause allows a variable to occupy the same memory location as another variable, effectively providing a way to interpret a data item in multiple ways.

```
01 CUSTOMER-INFO.
   05 CUSTOMER-ID PIC X(10).
   05 CUSTOMER-DATA REDEFINES CUSTOMER-ID.
      10 CUSTOMER-NAME PIC A(30).
      10 CUSTOMER-AGE PIC 99.
```

Here, CUSTOMER-DATA redefines CUSTOMER-ID. This means the same 10-character space allocated for CUSTOMER-ID can alternatively be interpreted as a group consisting of CUSTOMER-NAME and CUSTOMER-AGE. This technique is beneficial for memory optimization and for interpreting data in different contexts.

COBOL also utilizes the RENAMES clause, allowing the renaming of a contiguous sequence of elementary data items under a new name. This clause is mainly used to provide an alternative view of the data structure.

```
01 EMPLOYEE-RECORD.
   05 EMP-NAME PIC A(30).
   05 EMP-AGE PIC 99.
   05 EMP-DEPT PIC X(10).
66 EMP-DETAILS RENAMES EMP-NAME THRU EMP-DEPT.
```

In this instance, EMP-DETAILS renames the sequence from EMP-NAME to EMP-DEPT. With the RENAMES clause, grouped data items can be referenced collectively under a new name, thus enhancing readability and manageability.

Defining variables in COBOL meticulously ensures accurate data representation and effective memory utilization. The thoughtful combination of level numbers, hierarchical structures, initializing clauses, and redefinition techniques aids in creating clear, maintainable, and efficient COBOL programs.

## 4.3 Numeric Data Types

Numeric data types in COBOL enable the storage and manipulation of numerical values, which are fundamental for calculations, processing transactions, and general data handling. These data types are primarily divided into two categories: COMP (computational) and DISPLAY. Understanding these distinctions, along with their application through the Picture (PIC) clause, is vital for leveraging the full potential of COBOL in numerical data management.

Numeric data types in COBOL are defined using the PIC clause, which specifies the type and size of the data. A numeric PIC clause contains the symbols 9, S (for the sign), and V (for the implied decimal point). A typical definition for a numeric data item might look like:

```
01 NUM-VAR PIC S9(5)V99.
```

Here, NUM-VAR is a signed numeric variable with five digits before the decimal point and two digits after it. The PIC clause's role is crucial in defining the structure and constraints of numeric variables.

**Computational (COMP) Usage:**

The COMP and its variants (COMP-1, COMP-2, COMP-3) provide ways to store and handle numeric data in binary format, optimizing performance on arithmetic operations. Each COMP variant has a specific utility:

- COMP-1: Used for single-precision floating-point arithmetic. It corresponds to a four-byte floating-point number.
- COMP-2: Used for double-precision floating-point arithmetic. This is an eight-byte floating-point number, allowing more significant precision and range.
- COMP-3: Known as packed decimal or Binary-Coded Decimal (BCD), it allows for efficient storage of decimal numbers. Each nibble stores one decimal digit, making it space-efficient while enabling accurate decimal arithmetic.

For instance, a packed decimal declaration might look like this:

```
01 PACKED-NUM PIC S9(5)V99 COMP-3.
```

PACKED-NUM will be stored in a compact binary format, with each digit taking up half a byte. The sign is typically stored in the last four bits of the last byte.

**Display Usage:**

Numeric data with the DISPLAY type is stored as character data, where each digit is represented in its ASCII or EBCDIC equivalent. This format is straightforward but less efficient for arithmetic operations compared to COMP. However, it is beneficial for applications involving substantial input/output operations.

Consider the following definition for a display numeric variable:

```
01 DISPLAY-NUM PIC 9(6).
```

DISPLAY-NUM is a six-digit unsigned integer, stored in standard character format. This makes interaction with human-readable displays, such as reports and screens, more intuitive.

**Handling Signed Numbers:**

The PIC clause allows the inclusion of an optional S to denote signed numeric data. COBOL enables the signing of both leading and trailing positions, depending on system and implementation specifics.

An example of a signed numeric field is:

```
01 SIGNED-NUM PIC S9(4).
```

This example shows a four-digit signed integer. The representation of the sign can either be in a leading or trailing position with a sign character (typically '+' or '-').

**Implied Decimal Point:**

The V (virtual decimal point) within the PIC clause signifies an implied decimal position without occupying a storage position. It is pivotal for fixed-point arithmetic, ensuring precision without additional complexity in managing decimal points physically.

For example:

```
01 DECIMAL-NUM PIC 9(3)V99.
```

In DECIMAL-NUM, we define a total of five digits, three before and two after the implied decimal point. This simplifies the storage and monetary calculations, ensuring data accuracy and readability.

**Examples and Practical Usage:**

To illustrate the practical applications, consider converting currency data for a payroll system:

```
01 EMPLOYEE-SALARY PIC 9(6)V99.
01 BONUS-AMOUNT PIC S9(4)V99 COMP-3.
01 TOTAL-PAY PIC 9(6)V99.
```

```
MOVE 50000.75 TO EMPLOYEE-SALARY
MOVE 1500.50 TO BONUS-AMOUNT
ADD BONUS-AMOUNT TO EMPLOYEE-SALARY GIVING TOTAL-PAY
```

In this example, the numeric data types designated for salaries and bonuses enable precise arithmetic operations essential for accurate payroll processing.

A firm understanding of numeric data types is indispensable for COBOL programmers, as it ensures accurate data representation, efficient processing, and precise arithmetic operations essential for business-critical applications.

## 4.4 Alphanumeric Data Types

Alphanumeric data types play an integral role in COBOL, providing the ability to manage and manipulate data consisting of both letters and numbers. These data types are versatile and widely used for handling a variety of data inputs such as names, addresses, and other textual information. In COBOL, alphanumeric data types are specified using the keyword PIC X, where X stands for any character and the number following X specifies the length of the string. Additionally, the PIC A clause can be used to denote alphabetic data, where A represents an alphabetic character only and the length specified afterwards dictates the total number of alphabetic characters.

**Defining Alphanumeric Data Types:** To define an alphanumeric variable in COBOL, the PIC X clause is used. Here is an example of its usage:

```
01 CUSTOMER-NAME PIC X(30).
```

The above code declares a data item CUSTOMER-NAME which can hold up to 30 characters. Each character can be a letter, digit, or any other valid symbol.

Another example using the PIC A clause, which restricts the data to alphabetic characters only, is shown below:

```
01 ALPHA-ONLY PIC A(10).
```

In this instance, ALPHA-ONLY is defined to contain exactly 10 alphabetic characters. If a non-alphabetic character is assigned to ALPHA-ONLY, an error will be raised.

**Working with Alphanumeric Data:** Alphanumeric data can be manipulated using different operations provided by COBOL. Common tasks include concatenation, comparison, and substring operations.

```
* Example of concatenation:
MOVE "John" TO FIRST-NAME.
MOVE "Doe" TO LAST-NAME.
MOVE FIRST-NAME DELIMITED BY SPACE TO FULL-NAME.
STRING FULL-NAME DELIMITED BY SIZE SPACE
       LAST-NAME DELIMITED BY SIZE
       INTO FULL-NAME.

* Example of comparison:
IF FULL-NAME = "John Doe"
   DISPLAY "Match Found!".

* Example of substring:
MOVE CUSTOMER-NAME (1:5) TO CUSTOMER-CODE.
```

In the concatenation example, we combine FIRST-NAME and LAST-NAME into FULL-NAME. The comparison example illustrates how to check if FULL-NAME matches a specific string. Finally, the substring example shows how to extract the first five characters from CUSTOMER-NAME and store them in CUSTOMER-CODE.

**Usage of SPACES and LOW-VALUES:** Alphanumeric data types can be initialized with special figurative constants such as SPACES and LOW-VALUES. The SPACES constant initializes a data item with spaces, which is particularly useful for clearing an alphanumeric field.

```
MOVE SPACES TO CUSTOMER-NAME.
```

On the other hand, LOW-VALUES fills the data item with the lowest possible value in the collating sequence.

```
MOVE LOW-VALUES TO CUSTOMER-NAME.
```

**Handling Null Termination:** Although COBOL does not natively support null-terminated strings like C or Java, null termination can still be managed through careful use of PIC clauses and manual insertion. Since alphanumeric strings do not end with a null character by default, adding one might look like this:

```
01 CUSTOMER-NAME PIC X(30).
01 NULL-CHARACTER PIC X VALUE LOW-VALUES.
...
STRING CUSTOMER-NAME DELIMITED BY SIZE
       NULL-CHARACTER DELIMITED BY SIZE
       INTO NULL-TERMINATED-NAME.
```

The example concatenates CUSTOMER-NAME with a null character represented by LOW-VALUES, effectively producing a null-terminated string stored in NULL-TERMINATED-NAME.

**Limitations of Alphanumeric Data Types:** One should be aware of the limitations while using alphanumeric data types. For instance, COBOL does not inherently support dynamic string length; all data items are fixed-length as defined by their PIC clauses. Thus, efficient memory usage and boundary checks become critical, especially when working with large datasets or concatenating multiple strings.

Understanding and effectively utilizing alphanumeric data types is critical for robust COBOL programming. Integrating alphanumeric manipulation techniques can significantly enhance the program's ability to handle and process complex data structures efficiently, aiding in the development of sophisticated business applications.

## 4.5 Picture (PIC) Clauses and Their Usage

The Picture (PIC) clause in COBOL is a fundamental element in the definition of data items. It specifies the type and size of the data that a variable can hold. This clause uses a predefined set of characters to represent data types and their respective formats.

The PIC clause syntax is:

```
PIC format
```

Here, format determines the structure, type, and length of the data item. The main characters and their roles are described below:

- **9**: Represents a numeric digit. Each 9 specifies one position for a digit in the data item.
- **X**: Represents an alphanumeric character. Each X specifies one position for an alphanumeric character (letters, digits, or special characters).
- **A**: Used for alphabetic characters. Each A specifies one position for a letter (A-Z, a-z).
- **V**: Represents an implied decimal point. It indicates the position of the decimal point but does not allocate a space.
- **S**: Specifies that the number is signed, i.e., it can hold positive or negative values.
- **P**: Used for zero suppression (packaging zeros). Each P represents an assumed decimal position without consuming physical storage.
- **Z**: Zero suppression for leading zeros.
- **$**: Specifies a currency symbol placeholder.

For example, to define a five-digit numeric variable, one can use:

```
01 NUM-VAR PIC 9(5).
```

This statement declares a variable NUM-VAR that can hold a five-digit numeric value. The use of parentheses (5) is shorthand to represent five occurrences of 9.

Additionally, an alphanumeric variable declaration example is:

```
01 ALPHA-VAR PIC X(10).
```

Here, the variable ALPHA-VAR is capable of holding a string of up to 10 alphanumeric characters.

**Implied Decimal Point and Signed Numbers**

The V character is used to indicate an implied decimal position. For instance:

```
01 SALARY PIC 999V99.
```

In this case, SALARY is a numeric variable with three digits before the decimal point and two digits after the decimal point. Note that V does not occupy any storage space itself.

To include signed numbers, use the S character:

```
01 BALANCE PIC S999V99.
```

With BALANCE, the variable can hold both positive and negative values with three digits before the decimal point and two digits after it.

**Zero Suppression and Currency Symbols**

The Z character suppresses leading zeros, making numeric data more readable. For example:

```
01 ACCOUNT PIC ZZ9.
```

If ACCOUNT holds the value 007, it will be displayed as 7. Zero suppression is particularly useful in financial applications.

For currency formatting, the dollar sign placeholder ($) can be used to represent monetary amounts:

```
01 PRICE PIC \$999.99.
```

The variable PRICE can store a value formatted with a dollar sign, such as $120.50.

Special Considerations

When using PIC clauses, special characters and certain combinations require careful consideration. For instance, X and A cannot be mixed within a single PIC clause. Additionally, the total number of characters specified in the PIC clause should not exceed the maximum allowed length for the data type or storage constraints defined by the compiler or platform.

Moreover, ensure that the correct sequence and placement are adhered to within PIC clauses to prevent errors in data representation and manipulation. For example, the sign character (S) should precede numeric digits, and the implied decimal point (V) should be correctly placed among the digits.

Using these principles, PIC clauses allow for precise and efficient data structure definitions, which are pivotal for the reliable execution of COBOL programs. By understanding and correctly applying these clauses, one ensures accurate data representation and manipulation throughout the program.

## 4.6 Understanding Level Numbers

Level numbers in COBOL are used to define the hierarchy and relationships among data items within a record structure. This layering of data elements is essential in organizing and managing data efficiently. In COBOL, level numbers range from 01 to 49, with additional special level numbers 66, 77, and 88 serving specific purposes.

A record in COBOL is composed of fields that may be elementary or group items. Group items contain subfields forming a hierarchical structure, signified by their level numbers. The hierarchical relationship among data items dictates the data's parent-child association within a record.

- 01 level numbers are typically used to define the highest-level or root data items in a COBOL record.
- 02-49 are used for subordinate data items, with increasing indentation to signify nested levels of hierarchy.
- 66 is used for RENAMES clause to give an alternate name to an existing set of fields.
- 77 are stand-alone items that are not subdivided.
- 88 is used for condition names, representing Boolean conditions associated with other fields.

The following example illustrates the use of these level numbers in defining a COBOL record:

```
01 EMPLOYEE-RECORD.
    02 EMP-ID PIC 9(5).
    02 EMP-NAME.
        03 FIRST-NAME PIC A(12).
        03 LAST-NAME PIC A(15).
    02 JOB-TITLE PIC A(20).
    02 SALARY PIC 9(7)V99.
```

```
    02 DEPARTMENT.
        03 DEPT-ID PIC 9(3).
        03 DEPT-NAME PIC A(10).
```

In this example, EMPLOYEE-RECORD is a group item with a level number 01. Within it, various subordinate data items such as EMP-ID, EMP-NAME, JOB-TITLE, SALARY, and DEPARTMENT are defined with level number 02. Further nested within EMP-NAME and DEPARTMENT are additional fields with level numbers 03. By convention, each nested data item has a level number incremented from its parent, indicating its hierarchical position.

The level number structure not only clarifies the organization of the data but also influences COBOL operations like moving data, performing calculations, and conditional processing.

To further exemplify, below is an illustration involving 77 and 88 level numbers:

```
01 CUSTOMER-RECORD.
    02 CUST-ID PIC 9(5).
    02 CUST-NAME PIC A(30).
    02 CUST-STATUS PIC X.
        88 ACTIVE-CUST VALUE 'A'.
        88 INACTIVE-CUST VALUE 'I'.
77 COMPANY-NAME PIC A(30) VALUE 'XYZ Corporation'.
```

Here, CUSTOMER-RECORD represents a group item at level 01, containing several fields at level 02. The CUST-STATUS field, with a PIC X clause, is further associated with condition names ACTIVE-CUST and INACTIVE-CUST, both defined at level 88. These condition names provide a readable way to check and set the status of a customer. Standalone item COMPANY-NAME with a level number 77 is not part of any group but exists independently within the structure.

The 66 level number is unique and used for the RENAMES clause. An example is shown below:

```
01 BACKGROUND-INFO.
    02 NAME.
        03 FIRST-NAME PIC A(12).
        03 LAST-NAME PIC A(20).
    02 ADDRESS.
        03 STREET PIC A(30).
```

```
        03 CITY PIC A(20).
        03 ZIP PIC 9(5).
    66 FULL-ADDRESS RENAMES ADDRESS.
```

In this example, FULL-ADDRESS is defined using the RENAMES clause, giving a new name to the combination of STREET, CITY, and ZIP under ADDRESS. The 66 level number is essential for such purposes where a subset of an existing structure is renamed for easier reference.

Understanding and effectively leveraging level numbers in COBOL enhances data organization, manipulation, and overall management, ensuring that COBOL programs remain robust and maintainable. Knowledge of these principles is fundamental to mastering data handling within COBOL programming.

## 4.7 Working with Redefines and Renames

The REDEFINES and RENAMES clauses are powerful features in COBOL that facilitate more efficient memory management and flexible data handling. These clauses afford the ability to overlay and reinterpret data structures within the same storage space, providing versatility in manipulating data without needing additional storage allocation.

REDEFINES allows a storage area defined by one data item to be shared by another, lending the capacity to interpret the same memory space in different ways. This is particularly useful when data formats might change during program execution, or when it is needed to view the same data in multiple representations.

The syntax for REDEFINES is as follows:

```
01 original-data-item PIC X(10).
01 redefined-data-item REDEFINES original-data-item PIC 9(10).
```

In this example, redefined-data-item shares the same storage space as original-data-item, but it interprets it as a numeric data type compared to the alphanumeric data type of the original item. To put it into perspective, consider that when a value is stored in original-data-item, it is simultaneously available in redefined-data-item, albeit in its reinterpreted form.

Additionally, REDEFINES can be employed to interpret complex data structures. For instance:

```
01 original-record.
    05 employee-id PIC X(5).
    05 employee-details PIC X(45).

01 redefined-record REDEFINES original-record.
    05 employee-id PIC X(5).
    05 employee-name PIC X(25).
    05 employee-department PIC X(20).
```

In the above scenario, the redefined-record interprets the original-record by splitting the employee-details into two separate fields: employee-name and employee-department. This technique is effective for reading and processing variable or hierarchical data structures.

RENAMES, on the other hand, provides an alternative method for repurposing data fields within COBOL structures, particularly focusing on grouping contiguous fields into a new collective name. The RENAMES clause simplifies the complex data manipulation often required and is particularly useful in record identification or in situations where repetitive access to grouped fields is necessary.

The syntax for RENAMES is used exclusively in the WORKING-STORAGE section and follows this pattern:

```
01 transaction-record.
    05 transaction-id PIC X(10).
    05 transaction-date PIC X(8).
    05 transaction-amount PIC 9(7)V99.
    05 filler PIC X(20).

66 transaction-info RENAMES transaction-id THRU
    transaction-amount.
```

In this context, transaction-info is defined to collectively refer to the fields from transaction-id through transaction-amount. This approach allows the referencing of transaction-id, transaction-date, and transaction-amount as a single data item, providing a streamlined way to access and manipulate related data fields.

The use of REDEFINES and RENAMES requires careful planning and awareness of the underlying memory layout to avoid unintended consequences such as data corruption. For example, understanding that both the redefined and original data items share the same memory means changing one will affect the other, an aspect that needs to be strategically managed within the program logic.

Consider practical implementation constraints and their effects, such as:

- Ensure that redefined data items are correctly typed to appropriately represent the data.
- Confirm that renamed groups span only contiguous fields to avoid access violations.
- Validate that memory space is aptly calculated and managed to prevent overflow errors.

An illustration of a potential pitfall when using REDEFINES might involve inadvertently misaligning data types:

```
01 number-field PIC 9(5).
01 string-field REDEFINES number-field PIC X(5).
```

If number-field holds a numeric value, interpreting it as alphanumeric in string-field might yield unintended results, especially if the memory representation of numbers does not straightforwardly convert to strings. Hence, ensuring the correct context when defining and accessing these fields is paramount for the integrity of the program.

The prudent use of REDEFINES and RENAMES in COBOL programming allows for more compact data storage and versatile data interpretation, essential for optimizing both memory usage and program performance.

## 4.8 Data Initialization and Value Assignment

Data initialization and value assignment are pivotal aspects of data handling in COBOL programming. Accurate initialization ensures that variables hold predictable and meaningful values at the start of their usage, while value assignment allows for the updating and modification of these variables throughout the program.

**Data Initialization** in COBOL typically takes place in the DATA DIVISION. During initialization, variables are assigned initial values when they are declared. This is accomplished using the VALUE clause within the WORKING-STORAGE SECTION or any other data section. The basic syntax for initializing a variable is as follows:

```
01 WS-VARIABLE PIC X(10) VALUE 'INITIALVAL'.
```

In this example, WS-VARIABLE is a data item of alphanumeric type with an initial value of 'INITIALVAL'. The VALUE clause directly follows the PIC clause, specifying the initial value assigned to the variable.

Numeric variables can also be initialized in a similar manner. For example:

```
01 WS-NUMERIC-VAR PIC 9(5) VALUE 12345.
```

Here, WS-NUMERIC-VAR is a numeric field with five digits, initialized to hold the value 12345.

**Value Assignment** in COBOL, on the other hand, is typically performed using the MOVE statement. The MOVE statement copies the value from one field to another and its basic syntax is as follows:

```
MOVE source-item TO destination-item.
```

For instance:

```
MOVE 'NEWTEXT' TO WS-VARIABLE.
MOVE 67890 TO WS-NUMERIC-VAR.
```

In the first MOVE statement, the string 'NEWTEXT' is assigned to WS-VARIABLE, while in the second statement, the numeric value 67890 is assigned to WS-NUMERIC-VAR.

It's important to note that the data type and size of the source-item should be compatible with the destination-item to prevent data truncation or overflow. For alphanumeric types, if the source string is shorter than the destination, the destination will be padded with spaces. Conversely, if the source string is longer, it will be truncated from the right:

```
01 WS-DEST PIC X(5).
MOVE 'LONGTEXT' TO WS-DEST.
```

The content of WS-DEST after the MOVE operation will be 'LONGT' due to truncation.

For numeric types, COBOL will fill any unused positions with leading zeros or spaces, depending on the operation:

```
01 WS-DEST-NUM PIC 9(5).
MOVE 99 TO WS-DEST-NUM.
```

The content of WS-DEST-NUM after the MOVE operation will be 00099.

Numeric items can also be involved in computations before assignment. For example:

```
ADD 5 TO WS-NUMERIC-VAR.
```

If WS-NUMERIC-VAR initially holds the value 12345, after executing the ADD statement, it will hold the value 12350.

Additionally, COBOL supports assigning values to multiple destinations concurrently using the MOVE CORRESPONDING statement, which moves values to identically named sub-fields within different group items:

```
01 GROUP-1.
   05 FIELD-A PIC X(5).
   05 FIELD-B PIC X(5).
01 GROUP-2.
   05 FIELD-A PIC X(5).
   05 FIELD-B PIC X(5).

MOVE CORRESPONDING GROUP-1 TO GROUP-2.
```

In this example, FIELD-A and FIELD-B in GROUP-1 are moved to the corresponding fields in GROUP-2.

To enhance readability and maintainability, initialize variables succinctly and ensure that value assignment is carried out with clear, well-defined logic. This methodical approach minimizes errors and facilitates troubleshooting.

bietern

## 4.9 Using Figurative Constants

A figurative constant in COBOL provides a convenient way to assign well-known and pre-defined values to variables. These constants are essentially a shorthand to bring clarity and reduce the complexity of data initialization and comparison in COBOL programs. This section details the various types of figurative constants available in COBOL along with their practical applications and constraints.

### All Literal and Zero Literal

Two of the most frequently used figurative constants in COBOL are ALL literal and ZERO. Utilizing these constants effectively can streamline many programming tasks.

```
01 FILLER PIC X(10) VALUE ALL '*'.
01 NUM-VAR PIC 9(4) VALUE ZERO.
```

In the above example, FILLER is initialized to ********** (ten asterisks), and NUM-VAR is initialized to 0000 (four zeros).

### Figurative Constants for Numeric Variables

For numeric types, COBOL provides a set of constants that can significantly simplify programming logic, especially in condition evaluations and initializations. These include ZERO, ZEROS, and ZEROES, all referring to the numeric value zero.

```
01 VARIABLE-1 PIC 9(5) VALUE ZEROS.
01 VARIABLE-2 PIC 9(4)V99 VALUE ZEROES.
```

Both VARIABLE-1 and VARIABLE-2 are initialized to zero, differing in their pic clause definition indicating the storage size and precision.

### Blank, Space, and Spaces

When dealing with alphanumeric data, certain figurative constants such as SPACE, SPACES, and BLANK are valuable for initialization and checks. Assigning these constants to a variable essentially fills the variable with blanks or spaces.

```
01 TEXT-FIELD PIC X(15) VALUE SPACES.
01 MESSAGE PIC X(20) VALUE SPACE.
```

These assignments will result in TEXT-FIELD and MESSAGE being filled entirely with spaces. These figurative constants are especially useful when initializing fields meant for textual data and ensuring that unused space is blank.

### High-Value and Low-Value Constants

COBOL also includes the HIGH-VALUE and LOW-VALUE figurative constants. These constants can be particularly useful in scenarios where the highest or lowest possible value for comparison purposes is necessary.

```
01 MAX-VALUE PIC X(1) VALUE HIGH-VALUE.
01 MIN-VALUE PIC X(1) VALUE LOW-VALUE.
```

MAX-VALUE will contain the highest value in the collating sequence, and MIN-VALUE will contain the lowest value. These assignments play a crucial role in sorting, searching, and initializing variables to boundary values.

### Quotations and NULL Constants

Two special sets of figurative constants worth mentioning are QUOTE, QUOTES, and NULL, NULLS. The QUOTE or QUOTES constant is used to represent a double-quote character.

```
01 QUOTE-CHAR PIC X VALUE QUOTE.
01 QUOTES-CHAR PIC XX VALUE QUOTES.
```

Both QUOTE-CHAR and QUOTES-CHAR are initialized with the quotation mark character (").

Similarly, NULL and NULLS are used to represent the null character in certain systems.

```
01 NULL-VAL PIC X VALUE NULL.
01 NULLS-VAL PIC X(2) VALUE NULLS.
```

Usage of NULL or NULLS might depend heavily on the system and compiler being used, and they are often used in interfacing with external systems and ensuring compatibility.

### Examples of Figurative Constants in Practice

To further illustrate the use of these figurative constants, consider the following COBOL program segment that makes use of various constants for initialization and condition checking:

```
DATA DIVISION.
WORKING-STORAGE SECTION.
01 EMP-NAME PIC X(20) VALUE SPACES.
01 EMP-ID PIC 9(5) VALUE ZEROES.
01 SEPARATOR PIC X VALUE QUOTE.
01 HIGH-VALUE-CHAR PIC X VALUE HIGH-VALUE.
```

```
PROCEDURE DIVISION.
INITIALIZE-VARS SECTION.
    IF EMP-ID = ZERO
        MOVE ALL 'N/A' TO EMP-NAME
    END-IF.

DISPLAY-INFO SECTION.
    DISPLAY 'Employee Name: ' EMP-NAME SEPARATOR
    DISPLAY 'Employee ID: ' EMP-ID
    DISPLAY 'High Value Char: ' HIGH-VALUE-CHAR.
```

The INITIALIZE-VARS section uses an IF statement to check if EMP-ID is equal to zero and assigns 'N/A' to EMP-NAME if true. DISPLAY-INFO section demonstrates outputting these values, including the high-value character.

Understanding and utilizing figurative constants efficiently can make a COBOL program more readable and maintainable. These constants not only shorten the code but also imbue it with a self-explanatory quality, as the meaning of SPACES or ZEROES is intuitive and easy to grasp. Deploying such constants appropriately can lead to more resilient and adaptable code structures.

# Chapter 5

# Conditional Statements

**Conditional statements are essential for controlling the flow of a COBOL program. This chapter examines the use of IF...ELSE and nested IF statements, the EVALUATE statement for case-like conditions, and various relational and logical operators. It also covers the combination of conditions, the use of sign and class conditions, and conditional abbreviations, providing a comprehensive understanding of how to implement decision-making logic in COBOL.**

## 5.1 Introduction to Conditional Statements

In COBOL, conditional statements are fundamental constructs that allow a program to execute different code paths based on specific conditions. These statements enhance the decision-making abilities of COBOL programs, enabling them to react dynamically to different scenarios and data inputs. Mastery of conditional statements is crucial for developing robust and flexible programs.

The most basic form of a conditional statement in COBOL is the IF statement. The IF statement assesses a condition and, if the condition evaluates to true, executes a block of code. An optional ELSE clause specifies an alternative block of code to execute when the condition is false. The general syntax of the IF statement is illustrated as follows:

```
IF condition
```

```
    THEN
        imperative-statement-1
    ELSE
        imperative-statement-2
END-IF.
```

In the above syntax, condition represents a Boolean expression that can either be true or false. When condition evaluates to true, imperative-statement-1 is executed. If condition evaluates to false, imperative-statement-2 is executed. The END-IF clause marks the end of the IF statement structure.

Consider a practical application of the IF statement in a banking system to determine an overdraft condition:

```
IF account-balance < 0
    THEN
        DISPLAY "Account is overdrawn"
    ELSE
        DISPLAY "Account is in good standing"
END-IF.
```

Here, we evaluate whether account-balance is less than zero. If the condition is true, the program displays "Account is overdrawn". Otherwise, it displays "Account is in good standing".

For more complex decision-making, COBOL allows for nested IF statements, where an IF statement resides within another IF statement. This nesting permits the evaluation of multiple conditions sequentially. Consider the following nested IF example:

```
IF customer-type = "VIP"
    THEN
        IF account-balance > 1000
            THEN
                DISPLAY "Premium Services Available"
            ELSE
                DISPLAY "Standard Services Available"
        END-IF
    ELSE
        DISPLAY "Regular Customer"
END-IF.
```

In this nested IF structure, the program first checks if the customer-type is "VIP". If true, it performs another check to determine if account-balance exceeds 1000. The program proceeds to display messages accordingly based on the evaluation of these conditions.

Moving beyond traditional IF...ELSE structures, COBOL offers the EVALUATE statement, analogous to switch-case constructs found in other programming languages. The EVALUATE statement provides a more readable and efficient way to handle multiple conditional branches, reducing the complexity of highly nested IF statements. The syntax for the EVALUATE statement is as follows:

```
EVALUATE TRUE
    WHEN condition-1
        imperative-statement-1
    WHEN condition-2
        imperative-statement-2
    WHEN OTHER
        imperative-statement-3
END-EVALUATE.
```

In this structure, each WHEN clause represents a different condition. The imperative-statement associated with the first true condition is executed. If no conditions are met, the WHEN OTHER clause is executed, functioning as a default case.

Consider an example where we set a pricing tier based on customer loyalty points:

```
EVALUATE TRUE
    WHEN loyalty-points >= 1000
        DISPLAY "Platinum Customer"
    WHEN loyalty-points >= 500
        DISPLAY "Gold Customer"
    WHEN loyalty-points >= 100
        DISPLAY "Silver Customer"
    WHEN OTHER
        DISPLAY "Bronze Customer"
END-EVALUATE.
```

Here, based on the loyalty-points, the program assigns different customer tiers. The use of EVALUATE helps in consolidating multiple conditions into a clear and understandable format.

Conditional statements in COBOL also leverage relational operators to evaluate conditions. These operators include $=$, $<>$, $>$, $<$, $>=$, and $<=$. Logical operators, like AND, OR, and NOT, enable the construction of compound conditions that increase the precision and flexibility of decision-making logic. For example:

```
IF (age >= 18 AND age <= 25) OR (age >= 60)
   THEN
      DISPLAY "Eligible for Discount"
   ELSE
      DISPLAY "Not Eligible for Discount"
END-IF.
```

This condition states that an individual is eligible for a discount if they are between 18 and 25 years old or 60 years old and above. Combining conditions using logical operators allows for more sophisticated decision criteria within COBOL programs.

Overall, understanding and effectively utilizing conditional statements are key for developing precise and adaptable COBOL applications. These constructs enable programmers to implement complex operational logics and improve the decision-making capabilities of their programs.

## 5.2 IF...ELSE Statements

The IF...ELSE statement is fundamental in COBOL for directing program execution flow based on boolean conditions. It allows the programmer to execute specific sections of code contingent upon whether the evaluated condition is true or false. In general, IF...ELSE statements enhance the decision-making capabilities within a program, supporting logical branching that governs how different paths in the code are followed.

A basic IF...ELSE statement structure in COBOL is demonstrated below:

```
IF condition
   [statements-1]
ELSE
   [statements-2]
END-IF.
```

Here, condition represents any logical expression that can be evaluated as true or false. If condition is true, statements-1 is executed; otherwise, statements-2 is executed. The END-IF clause marks the termination of the IF...ELSE construct.

### Example of Simple IF...ELSE

Consider the following COBOL program segment that determines if an employee's salary needs adjustment based on a predefined threshold:

```
IF EMPLOYEE-SALARY < 50000
    MOVE 50000 TO EMPLOYEE-SALARY
ELSE
    DISPLAY 'Salary is already sufficient.'
END-IF.
```

In this example, the IF statement checks if EMPLOYEE-SALARY is less than 50,000. If this condition is satisfied, EMPLOYEE-SALARY is adjusted to 50,000. Otherwise, the message "Salary is already sufficient." is displayed.

### IF...ELSE-IF Ladder

The IF...ELSE-IF ladder can be used when multiple conditions need to be evaluated in sequence. The syntax allows for a series of IF conditions to be checked in order, with corresponding branches executed as soon as a true condition is found. The basic structure is shown below:

```
IF condition-1
    [statements-1]
ELSE IF condition-2
    [statements-2]
ELSE IF condition-3
    [statements-3]
ELSE
    [statements-else]
END-IF.
```

### Example of IF...ELSE-IF Ladder

This example demonstrates how to use an IF...ELSE-IF ladder to categorize a numerical score into performance levels:

```
IF SCORE >= 90
    MOVE 'Excellent' TO PERFORMANCE
ELSE IF SCORE >= 75
```

```
    MOVE 'Good' TO PERFORMANCE
ELSE IF SCORE >= 60
    MOVE 'Satisfactory' TO PERFORMANCE
ELSE
    MOVE 'Needs Improvement' TO PERFORMANCE
END-IF.
```

In this case, the score is evaluated against three thresholds. Depending on which condition is met first, the corresponding performance category is assigned. If none of the specified conditions are satisfied, the final ELSE clause assigns the default category "Needs Improvement."

### Nested IF Statements

Nested IF statements involve placing one IF statement within another. This enables more complex decision trees where multiple conditions must be simultaneously evaluated. It is critical to ensure readability and clarity when using nested IF statements to avoid logical errors and improve maintainability.

### Example of Nested IF Statements

The following example demonstrates the use of nested IF statements:

```
IF DEPARTMENT = 'HR'
    IF EMPLOYEE-SALARY < 40000
        MOVE 40000 TO EMPLOYEE-SALARY
    ELSE
        DISPLAY 'HR department salary is adequate.'
    END-IF
ELSE
    IF EMPLOYEE-SALARY < 50000
        MOVE 50000 TO EMPLOYEE-SALARY
    ELSE
        DISPLAY 'Salary is already sufficient.'
    END-IF
END-IF.
```

Here, the program first checks if the DEPARTMENT is "HR." If this condition is true, it then evaluates if the EMPLOYEE-SALARY is less than 40,000, adjusting it accordingly or displaying a message. If the department is not "HR," it evaluates the salary against the 50,000 threshold for other departments.

### Guidelines for Using IF...ELSE Statements

A few best practices can help ensure that IF...ELSE constructs are used effectively:

- Always use clear, descriptive conditions to improve the readability and maintainability of the code.
- Avoid deeply nested IF statements whenever possible; instead, consider restructuring the logic or refactoring portions into smaller, modular procedures.
- Ensure that each logical path is appropriately handled to prevent unintended behavior or logic gaps.
- Use comments to document complex IF...ELSE branches to aid in understanding the intent and flow.

Meticulous implementation of IF...ELSE statements contributes significantly to a COBOL program's robustness and clarity, facilitating effective decision-making logic.

## 5.3 Nested IF Statements

In COBOL, nested IF statements enable complex decision-making processes by allowing multiple level conditions to be evaluated hierarchically. Nested IF statements consist of an IF...ELSE structure placed inside another IF...ELSE structure. This is particularly useful when decisions are contingent upon multiple criteria that must be checked sequentially.

The general structure of nested IF statements in COBOL is as follows:

```
IF condition-1 THEN
    IF condition-2 THEN
        PERFORM action-1
    ELSE
        PERFORM action-2
    END-IF
ELSE
    PERFORM action-3
END-IF
```

Each nested IF statement must be properly terminated with an END-IF to ensure that the program control flows correctly and that the branching is well-defined.

For example, consider a scenario where an organization's payroll system needs to determine the appropriate bonus for employees based on their years of service and department performance. The requirements are such that employees with more than 10 years of service receive a higher bonus if their department has exceeded its targets.

```
IF YEARS-OF-SERVICE > 10 THEN
    IF DEPARTMENT-PERFORMANCE = 'EXCEEDED'
        THEN
        ADD 1000 TO BONUS
    ELSE
        ADD 500 TO BONUS
    END-IF
ELSE
    ADD 200 TO BONUS
END-IF
```

In this example, the outer IF statement checks if the YEARS-OF-SERVICE is greater than 10. If true, the nested IF statement further checks if the DEPARTMENT-PERFORMANCE equals 'EXCEEDED'. Based on the outcome, the bonus is adjusted accordingly.

It is also critical to ensure that nested IF statements do not become excessively deep, as this can make the program difficult to read and maintain. Deeply nested conditions can be simplified by using logical operators or restructuring the code to use EVALUATE statements where applicable.

For instance, consider a more complex example involving multiple nested conditions to determine eligibility for a special employee recognition program. The criteria include years of service, department performance, and individual performance ratings:

```
IF YEARS-OF-SERVICE >= 5 THEN
    IF DEPARTMENT-PERFORMANCE = 'EXCEEDED'
        THEN
        IF INDIVIDUAL-RATING >= 90 THEN
            MOVE 'HIGH' TO ELIGIBILITY-STATUS
        ELSE
            MOVE 'MEDIUM' TO ELIGIBILITY-STATUS
```

```
        END-IF
    ELSE
        IF INDIVIDUAL-RATING >= 80 THEN
            MOVE 'MEDIUM' TO ELIGIBILITY-STATUS
        ELSE
            MOVE 'LOW' TO ELIGIBILITY-STATUS
        END-IF
    END-IF
ELSE
    MOVE 'LOW' TO ELIGIBILITY-STATUS
END-IF
```

Here, the outer IF statement evaluates if the YEARS-OF-SERVICE is greater than or equal to 5. Within this block, it checks the DEPARTMENT-PERFORMANCE and then further checks INDIVIDUAL-RATING to determine ELIGIBILITY-STATUS. This allows for a multi-tier decision-making process that can handle intricate business logic.

To avoid excessive nesting and improve readability, one might consider restructuring the logic or using the EVALUATE statement for more straightforward decision trees. However, nested IF statements remain a fundamental tool in COBOL for handling complex, conditional program flows.

Proper indentation and clear annotation are crucial in nested IF statements to maintain code clarity. It is recommended to use consistent indentation practices to visually distinguish levels of decision-making, and to include comments where necessary to explain decision points within the nested structure.

Understanding nested IF statements and their implementation allows the programmer to write highly contingent business logic into COBOL applications, ensuring that all necessary conditions and rules are evaluated correctly before executing business operations or decisions.

## 5.4 EVALUATE Statements (Case Statements)

The EVALUATE statement in COBOL is a powerful control structure used for multi-way branching, akin to the switch or case statements found in other programming languages. Its ability to handle multiple conditions with clarity makes it indispensable for writing readable and maintainable code. The primary structure of an EVALUATE statement consists of evaluating one or more expressions and executing corresponding actions based on the results.

The general format of the EVALUATE statement is as follows:

```
EVALUATE true|numeric-expression-1|...
    WHEN condition-1
        statement-1
    WHEN condition-2
        statement-2
    ...
    WHEN OTHER
        statement-n
END-EVALUATE
```

Key components include:

- EVALUATE: The initial keyword signalling the start of the statement.
- true or numeric-expression: The value or expression to be evaluated.
- WHEN: Specifies different conditions to be tested against the evaluated value.
- statement: A sequence of COBOL statements to be executed if the associated WHEN condition is met.
- WHEN OTHER: A catch-all for any conditions not explicitly handled by previous WHEN clauses. This is optional but commonly used for completeness.
- END-EVALUATE: Marks the end of the EVALUATE statement.

Consider a scenario where we need to categorize numeric scores into various bands:

```
PROCEDURE DIVISION.
    EVALUATE TRUE
        WHEN score >= 90 AND score <= 100
            DISPLAY 'Grade: A'
```

```
        WHEN score >= 80 AND score < 90
            DISPLAY 'Grade: B'
        WHEN score >= 70 AND score < 80
            DISPLAY 'Grade: C'
        WHEN score >= 60 AND score < 70
            DISPLAY 'Grade: D'
        WHEN OTHER
            DISPLAY 'Grade: F'
    END-EVALUATE.
```

The EVALUATE TRUE construct allows the use of complex conditions within WHEN clauses. Notice the use of relational operators (>=, <=, and <) to specify ranges.

In cases where multiple expressions need to be evaluated, EVALUATE permits handling each one independently. Here is an example where both a numeric grade and a character flag are evaluated:

```
EVALUATE grade, pass-fail-flag
    WHEN 90 THRU 100, 'P'
        DISPLAY 'Excellent and Passed'
    WHEN 80 THRU 89, 'P'
        DISPLAY 'Very Good and Passed'
    WHEN 60 THRU 79, 'F'
        DISPLAY 'Needs Improvement and Failed'
    WHEN OTHER
        DISPLAY 'Consult your instructor'
END-EVALUATE.
```

This example evaluates both grade and pass-fail-flag. Each WHEN clause pairs specific ranges of grade with exact character conditions of pass-fail-flag, thus providing more granular control over the decision-making process.

The versatility of EVALUATE is further underscored by its ability to replace multiple nested IF statements, simplifying complex decision trees. Compare the following nested IF structure:

```
IF season = 'Winter' THEN
    IF weather = 'Snowy' THEN
        DISPLAY 'Wear a heavy coat'
    ELSE
        DISPLAY 'Dress warmly'
    END-IF
```

```
ELSE
    IF season = 'Summer' THEN
        IF temperature > 85 THEN
            DISPLAY 'Stay hydrated'
        ELSE
            DISPLAY 'Light clothing is sufficient'
        END-IF
    ELSE
        DISPLAY 'Check the weather forecast'
    END-IF
END-IF.
```

The same logic can be expressed more clearly using EVALUATE:

```
EVALUATE season ALSO weather ALSO temperature
    WHEN 'Winter' ALSO 'Snowy' ALSO ANY
        DISPLAY 'Wear a heavy coat'
    WHEN 'Winter' ALSO OTHER ALSO ANY
        DISPLAY 'Dress warmly'
    WHEN 'Summer' ALSO ANY ALSO > 85
        DISPLAY 'Stay hydrated'
    WHEN 'Summer' ALSO ANY ALSO <= 85
        DISPLAY 'Light clothing is sufficient'
    WHEN OTHER
        DISPLAY 'Check the weather forecast'
END-EVALUATE.
```

In this example, the EVALUATE statement uses the ALSO keyword to separate multiple expressions, improving readability and maintainability.

The EVALUATE statement is thus integral to modern COBOL programming, providing a robust mechanism for multi-condition logic, reducing complexity, and enhancing code clarity. Its strategic use can yield substantial benefits in program efficiency and ease of understanding.

## 5.5 Conditions and Relational Operators

Conditions and relational operators are fundamental building blocks in COBOL programming, essential for implementing decision-making logic and controlling the flow of a program. This section delves into the various types of conditions and relational operators available in COBOL, providing detailed explanations and practical examples to facilitate a thorough understanding.

In COBOL, a condition is a logical expression that evaluates to either true or false. Conditions are primarily used in conditional statements such as IF and EVALUATE. There are several types of conditions in COBOL:

- Relational Conditions
- Class Conditions
- Sign Conditions
- Condition-Name Conditions

This section focuses on relational conditions, as they are the most commonly used.

Relational conditions compare two operands using relational operators. The result of this comparison is either true or false. In COBOL, the relational operators available are:

- = or IS EQUAL TO,
- < or IS LESS THAN,
- > or IS GREATER THAN,
- <= or IS LESS THAN OR EQUAL TO,
- >= or IS GREATER THAN OR EQUAL TO,
- <> or IS NOT EQUAL TO.

The alternative forms using IS are provided for readability and can make the code more understandable. The syntaxes are interchangeable and can be used according to the programmer's preference.

Consider the following example of a relational condition within an IF statement:

```
IF A > B THEN
    DISPLAY 'A is greater than B'
ELSE
    DISPLAY 'A is not greater than B'.
```

In this example, the condition $A > B$ is evaluated. If A is greater than B, the program executes the first DISPLAY statement; otherwise, it executes the ELSE part.

## Relational Operator Details

Each relational operator has specific functionality:

- **Equality (=, IS EQUAL TO):** Compares if the left operand is equal to the right operand.
- **Inequality (<>, IS NOT EQUAL TO):** Checks if the left operand is not equal to the right operand.
- **Greater Than (>, IS GREATER THAN):** Determines if the left operand is greater than the right operand.
- **Less Than (<, IS LESS THAN):** Evaluates if the left operand is less than the right operand.
- **Greater Than or Equal To (>=, IS GREATER THAN OR EQUAL TO):** Checks if the left operand is greater than or equal to the right operand.
- **Less Than or Equal To (<=, IS LESS THAN OR EQUAL TO):** Determines if the left operand is less than or equal to the right operand.

Consider another example with the IS EQUAL TO relational operator:

```
IF TOTAL-SALES IS EQUAL TO TARGET THEN
    DISPLAY 'Sales target achieved'
ELSE
    DISPLAY 'Sales target not achieved'.
```

Here, TOTAL-SALES is compared to TARGET, and the program displays a message based on whether the sales target has been achieved.

## Complex Condition Examples

Relational operators can be used in more complex conditions by combining them with logical operators (AND, OR, NOT). For instance:

```
IF A < B AND B < C THEN
    DISPLAY 'A is less than B and B is less than C'.
```

This demonstrates a condition where both sub-conditions must be true for the entire condition to be true.

In COBOL, relational conditions can also compare data items of different data categories, such as numeric and alphanumeric, provided they are compatible. Non-numeric data comparisons are performed based on the standard EBCDIC (Extended Binary Coded Decimal Interchange Code) collating sequence.

For practical application, consider a purchasing scenario:

```
IF QUANTITY-ORDERED IS GREATER THAN 100 THEN
    DISPLAY 'Bulk discount applicable'
ELSE
    DISPLAY 'No bulk discount'.
```

Here, a bulk discount is determined based on the quantity ordered. The relational operator IS GREATER THAN facilitates this decision-making process.

It is also important to understand how relational conditions function within the EVALUATE statement, which acts as a switch-case-like structure:

```
EVALUATE TRUE
    WHEN ITEM-COST <= 50
        DISPLAY 'Low cost item'
    WHEN ITEM-COST > 50 AND ITEM-COST <= 100
        DISPLAY 'Medium cost item'
    WHEN ITEM-COST > 100
        DISPLAY 'High cost item'
    WHEN OTHER
        DISPLAY 'Unknown cost category'
END-EVALUATE
```

In this example, different cost categories are determined based on the value of ITEM-COST. The EVALUATE statement allows for efficient evaluation of multiple conditions, reducing the need for multiple IF statements and enhancing code readability.

In COBOL programming, mastering the use of conditions and relational operators is crucial for implementing effective decision-making logic and controlling the program flow.

## 5.6 Logical Operators in COBOL

Logical operators in COBOL allow the combination of multiple conditions to form complex logical expressions. These operators enable the construction of intricate decision-making logic by letting programmers specify multiple criteria that an expression must satisfy. The primary logical operators in COBOL are AND, OR, and NOT.

AND and OR operators connect conditions to produce a compound condition. The NOT operator is used to negate a condition.

**The AND Operator**

The AND operator asserts that both conditions on either side of it must be true for the entire expression to be true. The syntax is straightforward:

```
IF condition-1 AND condition-2
    ...
END-IF.
```

Consider the following example with two conditions combined using the AND operator:

```
IF AGE >= 18 AND AGE <= 65
    DISPLAY 'Eligible for work'.
END-IF.
```

In this instance, the message "Eligible for work" is displayed only if AGE is between 18 and 65, inclusive. Both conditions must be satisfied.

**The OR Operator**

The OR operator is used when at least one of the conditions must be true for the entire expression to be true. This is useful when permitting multiple accepting paths within conditional logic:

```
IF condition-1 OR condition-2
    ...
END-IF.
```

For instance:

```
IF MARITAL-STATUS = 'SINGLE' OR MARITAL-STATUS = '
    DIVORCED'
   DISPLAY 'Marital status is either single or divorced'.
END-IF.
```

The message is displayed if MARITAL-STATUS is either 'SINGLE' or 'DIVORCED'.

**The NOT Operator**

The NOT operator negates the condition that follows it, converting true conditions to false and vice versa. It is often used to check the opposite of a condition:

```
IF NOT condition
   ...
END-IF.
```

Using the NOT operator:

```
IF NOT VALID-USER
   DISPLAY 'Invalid user detected'.
END-IF.
```

This condition checks if VALID-USER is false; if so, it displays "Invalid user detected".

**Combining Logical Operators**

Logical operators can be combined to form more complex conditions. For combined conditions, the order of operations follows a specific precedence: expressions within parentheses are evaluated first, followed by NOT, then AND, and finally OR. It is best practice to use parentheses for clarity and to ensure the correct order of evaluation.

```
IF (condition-1 AND condition-2) OR (condition-3 AND NOT
    condition-4)
   ...
END-IF.
```

An application of combined logical operators can be demonstrated as follows:

```
IF (AGE >= 18 AND AGE <= 65) OR NOT EMPLOYED
```

```
    DISPLAY 'Eligible candidate'.
END-IF.
```

In this case, "Eligible candidate" is displayed if an individual's AGE is between 18 and 65 or if the individual is not employed, making the logic expressive and adaptable to complex scenarios.

**Order of Precedence**

To ensure the accurate interpretation of logical expressions, understanding the order of precedence is essential. The hierarchy is as follows:

- Parentheses: Conditions within parentheses are evaluated first.
- NOT: Negation of conditions comes next.
- AND: Conjunction of conditions is evaluated after negation.
- OR: Disjunction of conditions is evaluated last.

For instance, in the logical expression:

```
IF A OR B AND NOT C
```

NOT C is evaluated first, followed by B AND NOT C, and finally A OR (B AND NOT C).

Maintaining the correct order of operations ensures the intended logic is implemented, preventing logical errors that might arise from misinterpreted condition combinations. In intricate expressions, it is advisable to use parentheses extensively, not only for controlling precedence but also for enhancing readability and maintainability.

Understanding the implementation and nuances of logical operators significantly empowers the creation of robust, error-free, and sophisticated decision-making constructs in COBOL programs.

## 5.7 Combining Conditions

In COBOL programming, it is often necessary to combine multiple conditions to control the program flow precisely. By using combined conditions, the program can make more complex decisions based on multiple criteria. This section delves into the ways conditions can be combined in COBOL, focused on the use of logical operators and the parentheses to structure comprehensive logical statements.

**Logical Operators:**

COBOL supports three primary logical operators for combining conditions:

- AND
- OR
- NOT

These operators are used to form compound conditions that evaluate to either true or false.

**AND Operator:**

The AND operator requires all conditions it combines to be true for the overall condition to be true.

```
IF CONDITION-A AND CONDITION-B THEN
    PERFORM ACTION-1
END-IF.
```

In the example above, ACTION-1 is performed only if both CONDITION-A and CONDITION-B evaluate to true.

**OR Operator:**

The OR operator requires at least one of the conditions it combines to be true for the overall condition to be true.

```
IF CONDITION-A OR CONDITION-B THEN
    PERFORM ACTION-2
END-IF.
```

In this case, ACTION-2 is performed if either CONDITION-A or CONDITION-B, or both, evaluate to true.

**NOT Operator:**

The NOT operator negates the condition it precedes. If the condition is true, NOT makes it false, and vice versa.

```
IF NOT CONDITION-A THEN
    PERFORM ACTION-3
END-IF.
```

Here, ACTION-3 is performed only if CONDITION-A is false.

**Combining Multiple Conditions:**

Multiple conditions can be combined using both AND and OR operators. Parentheses should be used to group conditions and ensure the intended logic is preserved.

```
IF (CONDITION-A AND CONDITION-B) OR (CONDITION-C
    AND CONDITION-D) THEN
    PERFORM ACTION-4
END-IF.
```

In this example, ACTION-4 is performed if either both CONDITION-A and CONDITION-B are true, or both CONDITION-C and CONDITION-D are true.

**Practice Example:**

Consider a practical scenario where an account status must be checked for various conditions: if the account is active, the balance is above a threshold, and there are no recent flags. Below is a combination of conditions to handle this:

```
IF ACCOUNT-STATUS = 'ACTIVE' AND
   BALANCE > MINIMUM-THRESHOLD AND
   NOT HAS-RECENT-FLAGS
THEN
    PERFORM ALLOW-TRANSACTION
ELSE
    MOVE 'DENIED' TO TRANSACTION-STATUS
END-IF.
```

The example evaluates if the account is active, the balance exceeds a minimum threshold, and there are no recent flags. If all conditions are true, ALLOW-TRANSACTION is performed; otherwise, the status is set to 'DENIED'.

**Order of Evaluation:**

When combining conditions, it is crucial to be aware of the order of evaluation. COBOL evaluates conditions from left to right, applying parentheses for precedence similar to arithmetic operations:

- Conditions within parentheses are evaluated first.
- The NOT operator is evaluated next.

- AND conditions are evaluated after NOT.
- OR conditions are evaluated last.

**Example:**

Given the expression:

```
IF A OR B AND NOT C THEN
    PERFORM ACTION-5
END-IF.
```

This evaluates as (A OR (B AND (NOT C))) due to the precedence rules.

A detailed understanding of combining conditions allows a COBOL programmer to construct precise and complex logical expressions, making the program more robust and versatile for real-world applications.

## 5.8 Using Sign and Class Conditions

Sign and class conditions in COBOL provide a mechanism for testing specific properties of data items, which is essential for creating efficient and readable decision-making logic. Sign conditions test whether a numeric value is positive, negative, or zero, while class conditions verify whether a value conforms to a specific set of characters. Together, these conditions facilitate the writing of clear and concise code when dealing with numeric and alphanumeric data.

Sign Conditions are used to determine the arithmetic sign of a numeric item. The general syntax for a sign condition is:

```
IF data-item IS POSITIVE
    ...
ELSE IF data-item IS NEGATIVE
    ...
ELSE IF data-item IS ZERO
    ...
END-IF
```

Here, data-item represents the numeric item whose sign is being tested. The POSITIVE, NEGATIVE, and ZERO keywords are used to specify the sign condition. This construct simplifies checking the sign of a numeric value without manually comparing it to zero.

Consider the following example. A program is designed to process financial transactions and requires an action based on the sign of the balance:

```
IF balance IS POSITIVE
    PERFORM Process-Credit
ELSE IF balance IS NEGATIVE
    PERFORM Process-Debit
ELSE IF balance IS ZERO
    PERFORM Handle-Zero-Balance
END-IF
```

In this example, the procedure Process-Credit is performed if the balance is positive, Process-Debit is performed if the balance is negative, and Handle-Zero-Balance is executed if the balance is zero.

Class Conditions are used to verify whether a data item belongs to certain character classes. The primary classes used in COBOL are ALPHABETIC, NUMERIC, and ALPHABETIC-UPPER. The general syntax for a class condition is:

```
IF data-item IS NUMERIC
    ...
ELSE IF data-item IS ALPHABETIC
    ...
END-IF
```

The NUMERIC class condition checks if all characters in the data-item are digits, while the ALPHABETIC class condition checks if all characters are letters. Additionally, COBOL provides the ALPHABETIC-UPPER and ALPHABETIC-LOWER classes to check for upper-case and lower-case alphabetic characters, respectively.

Consider the following example. A program needs to validate user input, ensuring that account numbers are numeric and customer names are alphabetic:

```
IF account-number IS NUMERIC
    PERFORM Validate-Account-Number
ELSE
    PERFORM Invalid-Account-Error
END-IF

IF customer-name IS ALPHABETIC
```

```
    PERFORM Validate-Customer-Name
ELSE
    PERFORM Invalid-Name-Error
END-IF
```

In this example, Validate-Account-Number is performed if account-number is numeric, while Invalid-Account-Error is executed otherwise. Similarly, Validate-Customer-Name is performed if customer-name is alphabetic, and Invalid-Name-Error is performed otherwise.

By employing sign and class conditions, COBOL programs can effectively manage both numeric and alphanumeric data, ensuring the correct execution of logic based on the properties of data items. These conditions streamline the process of data validation and decision-making, making COBOL code more readable and maintainable.

## 5.9 Conditional Abbreviations

Conditional abbreviations in COBOL streamline the complexity and potential verbosity of conditional statements, enhancing code readability and maintainability. Utilizing abbreviations allows programmers to minimize redundancy and write more concise conditional expressions.

One key feature of COBOL's conditional statements is its ability to abbreviate conditions using the NEXT SENTENCE, AND, and OR operators, as well as negated conditions. These can collectively reduce the size of logical expressions without compromising their clarity. Here we will discuss each of these abbreviations with detailed examples.

**NEXT SENTENCE**

The NEXT SENTENCE statement is often used in conjunction with conditional expressions to direct program control. For instance, given a simple IF statement:

```
IF A GREATER THAN B
    DISPLAY "A is greater than B"
    NEXT SENTENCE
ELSE
    DISPLAY "A is not greater than B".
```

The NEXT SENTENCE operator will move the control to the next executable statement after the terminating period of the IF block. This mechanism helps in skipping over segments of code under specific conditions without explicitly writing GOTO statements.

### AND and OR Operators

The AND and OR operators can be employed to combine multiple conditions in a single logical expression. This is useful in performing complex decision-making while maintaining concise code. Consider the following example:

```
IF (A GREATER THAN B) AND (C LESS THAN D)
    DISPLAY "A is greater than B and C is less than D."
ELSE
    DISPLAY "Either A is not greater than B or C is not less than D.
        ".
```

In this case, the program checks both conditions simultaneously. If both conditions are true, the upper DISPLAY statement executes; otherwise, the ELSE part applies.

### Complex Abbreviated Conditions

Complex logical decisions can often be dissected into smaller, reusable components to make them more understandable and maintainable. With conditional abbreviations, it's possible to split a complex condition, as demonstrated below:

```
IF (A EQUAL TO 1) OR (A EQUAL TO 2) OR (A EQUAL TO 3)
    AND B LESS THAN 5
    DISPLAY "Condition met."
ELSE
    DISPLAY "Condition not met.".
```

This example shows multiple OR conditions followed by an AND condition, forming a combined logical expression evaluated sequentially according to COBOL operator precedents.

### Negated Conditions

COBOL allows the explicit negation of conditions using the NOT operator. Negated conditions are useful for expressing logical complements succinctly. For instance:

```
IF NOT (A GREATER THAN B)
    DISPLAY "A is not greater than B."
ELSE
    DISPLAY "A is greater than B.".
```

In this instance, NOT negates the condition, simplifying the logic without any need to rewrite it redundantly.

### Abbreviated Compound Conditions

For conditions where multiple variables must be compared against a single value or a set of values, abbreviated compound conditions can be used. As an illustration:

```
IF (A OR B OR C) EQUAL TO ZERO
    PERFORM ERROR-ROUTINE
ELSE
    CONTINUE.
```

The expression checks if any of A, B, or C is equal to zero, performing the error handling if true.

**Data:** A, B, C
**Result:** Initiate error handling if A, B, or C equals 0

```
if A == 0 or B == 0 or C == 0 then
    Perform "ERROR-ROUTINE";
else
    Continue to next operation;
```

This algorithm demonstrates how the condition $(\mathrm{A\ OR\ B\ OR\ C}) = 0$ can be operationalized into compact logic instructions using conditional abbreviations to enhance code clarity and efficiency.

Through these principles of conditional abbreviations, COBOL provides robust tools for structuring and simplifying decision-making expressions within a program. This leads to more readable, maintainable, and efficient code—critical aspects of proficient COBOL programming.

# Chapter 6

# Looping and Iteration

**Looping and iteration are critical for executing repetitive tasks in COBOL programs. This chapter details various looping constructs, including simple PERFORM loops, PERFORM VARYING, and PERFORM UNTIL loops. It also covers nested loops, the use of the EXIT statement, and inline PERFORM. Emphasis is placed on best practices to ensure efficient and readable code, enabling programmers to handle repetitive operations effectively.**

## 6.1 Introduction to Looping in COBOL

Looping, or iteration, is a fundamental concept in programming that allows a block of code to be executed repeatedly based on a condition. In COBOL, loops are used to perform repetitive tasks efficiently and concisely. This section introduces the primary looping constructs in COBOL and discusses how they are used to control the flow of execution within a program.

Looping constructs in COBOL can be categorized into several types: PERFORM loops, PERFORM VARYING loops, and PERFORM UNTIL loops. Each of these constructs serves different purposes and offers various levels of control over iterative processes.

**The Simple PERFORM Loop**

The PERFORM loop is the simplest form of iteration in COBOL. This loop is primarily used for invoking a section or paragraph of code a fixed number of times. To illustrate a PERFORM loop, consider the following example:

```
IDENTIFICATION DIVISION.
PROGRAM-ID. SimplePerformExample.
DATA DIVISION.
WORKING-STORAGE SECTION.
01 COUNTER PIC 9(2) VALUE 1.
01 LIMIT PIC 9(2) VALUE 5.

PROCEDURE DIVISION.
    PERFORM Example-Paragraph LIMIT TIMES.
    STOP RUN.

Example-Paragraph.
    DISPLAY "Iteration Number: " COUNTER.
    ADD 1 TO COUNTER.
```

In this example, the paragraph Example-Paragraph is executed five times, as indicated by the LIMIT TIMES clause. The DISPLAY statement outputs the current value of the COUNTER, which is incremented by 1 during each iteration using the ADD statement. The loop terminates after executing the specified number of iterations.

### The PERFORM VARYING Loop

The PERFORM VARYING loop provides more flexibility by allowing iteration over a range of values. This type of loop is especially useful for processing data structures such as arrays. The following example demonstrates a PERFORM VARYING loop:

```
IDENTIFICATION DIVISION.
PROGRAM-ID. PerformVaryingExample.
DATA DIVISION.
WORKING-STORAGE SECTION.
01 INDEX PIC 9(2) VALUE 1.
01 LIMIT PIC 9(2) VALUE 5.
01 NAMES.
    05 NAME-ARRAY OCCURS 5 TIMES.
        10 NAME PIC A(10) VALUE SPACES.

PROCEDURE DIVISION.
    PERFORM VARYING INDEX FROM 1 BY 1 UNTIL
        INDEX > LIMIT
```

```
        MOVE "NAME" TO NAME-ARRAY(INDEX)
        STRING INDEX DELIMITED BY SIZE INTO
            NAME-ARRAY(INDEX)
        DISPLAY NAME-ARRAY(INDEX)
    END-PERFORM.
    STOP RUN.
```

In this example, the PERFORM VARYING loop iterates from 1 to 5, updating the INDEX variable during each cycle. Within the loop, the MOVE and STRING statements populate the NAME-ARRAY with values, and the DISPLAY statement prints the current element of the array. The loop terminates when the INDEX variable exceeds the LIMIT.

**The PERFORM UNTIL Loop**

The PERFORM UNTIL loop allows for condition-based iteration, where the loop continues to execute until a specified condition is met. This form of loop is particularly useful when the number of iterations is not known in advance. Consider the following example:

```
IDENTIFICATION DIVISION.
PROGRAM-ID. PerformUntilExample.
DATA DIVISION.
WORKING-STORAGE SECTION.
01 COUNTER PIC 9(2) VALUE 1.
01 THRESHOLD PIC 9(2) VALUE 10.

PROCEDURE DIVISION.
    PERFORM UNTIL COUNTER > THRESHOLD
        DISPLAY "Counter Value: " COUNTER
        ADD 1 TO COUNTER
    END-PERFORM.
    STOP RUN.
```

In this case, the PERFORM UNTIL loop continues to execute as long as the COUNTER variable is less than or equal to the THRESHOLD. The loop increments the COUNTER variable by 1 during each iteration and displays its current value. The loop terminates when the COUNTER exceeds the THRESHOLD.

These fundamental looping constructs provide a robust framework for implementing iteration in COBOL programs. The examples illustrated above demonstrate the typical use cases for each type of loop, highlighting their respective strengths and applications. By selecting the appropriate looping construct, COBOL programmers can effectively manage repetitive tasks and enhance the readability and maintainability of their code.

## 6.2 Performing Iterative Processes

Understanding how to perform iterative processes is crucial for developing efficient COBOL programs. Iteration allows the execution of a block of code multiple times, enabling solutions to complex problems that require repeated operations. COBOL provides various constructs to implement iteration, each suited for different scenarios. This section will delve into the core iterative processes in COBOL, focusing on their syntax, use cases, and performance considerations.

COBOL primarily employs the PERFORM statement to handle iteration. The PERFORM statement can be executed in various modes such as simple PERFORM, PERFORM UNTIL, and PERFORM VARYING. Each mode allows the programmer to control the loop in different ways.

### The Simple PERFORM Loop

The simplest form of iteration in COBOL is the PERFORM loop, which executes a specified paragraph or section a fixed number of times. The syntax is straightforward:

```
PERFORM Paragraph-Name TIMES
```

Here, Paragraph-Name is the label of the paragraph to be executed. Consider this example:

```
PERFORM 10 TIMES
    DISPLAY "Processing iteration"
END-PERFORM.
```

In this example, the DISPLAY statement within the loop will execute ten times, outputting the string "Processing iteration" each time.

### PERFORM UNTIL Loop

The PERFORM UNTIL loop continues executing until a specified condition is true. This construct is typically used when the number of iterations is not predetermined but depends on a condition evaluated at runtime.

```
PERFORM UNTIL Condition
    Statements
END-PERFORM.
```

For instance:

```
PERFORM UNTIL Counter > 10
    DISPLAY "Counter value: " Counter
    ADD 1 TO Counter
END-PERFORM.
```

In this example, the loop continues executing the statements within it until Counter exceeds 10. Each iteration increments Counter by 1, and the DISPLAY statement outputs its current value.

### PERFORM VARYING Loop

The PERFORM VARYING loop offers a more flexible iteration form by allowing the initial value, increment (or decrement), and the termination condition to be specified. This loop is useful for scenarios requiring variable control over the loop counter.

```
PERFORM VARYING Counter FROM Start BY Increment UNTIL
    Condition
    Statements
END-PERFORM.
```

Consider this example:

```
PERFORM VARYING Index FROM 1 BY 2 UNTIL Index > 10
    DISPLAY "Index value: " Index
END-PERFORM.
```

In this scenario, the loop initializes Index to 1, incrementing it by 2 each iteration until Index exceeds 10. It will execute the DISPLAY statement with Index's current value at each iteration.

## Employing Nested Loops

Nested loops are constructed by placing one PERFORM statement inside another. It's important to manage nested loops carefully to avoid excessive complexity and ensure readability.

```
PERFORM Outer-Loop
    PERFORM Inner-Loop
END-PERFORM.
```

An example with nested PERFORM UNTIL loops:

```
PERFORM UNTIL Outer-Counter > 5
    PERFORM UNTIL Inner-Counter > 3
        DISPLAY "Outer: " Outer-Counter " Inner: " Inner-Counter
        ADD 1 TO Inner-Counter
    END-PERFORM.
    ADD 1 TO Outer-Counter
    MOVE 1 TO Inner-Counter
END-PERFORM.
```

Here, Outer-Counter increments from 1 to 5, and for each value of Outer-Counter, Inner-Counter increments from 1 to 3. This creates a loop within a loop, facilitating operations within a multidimensional scope.

## Performance Considerations

While using the PERFORM statement, it is vital to consider performance implications. Inefficient looping constructs can lead to excessive CPU utilization and slow program execution. It is best practice to initialize and reset counters appropriately, minimize the operations within the loop, and ensure conditions are evaluated correctly to avoid infinite loops.

Utilizing the correct iterative construct based on the problem context is essential. Simple PERFORM is best for known iteration counts, PERFORM UNTIL suits loops with a conditional stop, and PERFORM VARYING is ideal for loops with varying increments or steps.

Adopting best practices for looping not only improves performance but also the maintainability and readability of the COBOL program. Integrating these constructs effectively will enable robust and efficient handling of repetitive tasks in COBOL programming.

## 6.3 Simple Perform Loop

The PERFORM statement is a powerful and flexible tool in COBOL for executing repetitive tasks. The simplest form of this construct is the Simple PERFORM Loop, which allows a specified section or paragraph to be executed a fixed number of times. This form is concise and particularly useful when the number of iterations is known beforehand.

The general syntax for a Simple PERFORM Loop is:

```
PERFORM [procedure-name-1] [NUMBER] TIMES.
```

Here, procedure-name-1 specifies the procedure, such as a section or paragraph, to be executed repeatedly. The NUMBER denotes the integer constant or data item that indicates the number of times the specified procedure should be performed.

To demonstrate a concrete example, consider the following COBOL code snippet:

```
IDENTIFICATION DIVISION.
PROGRAM-ID. SimplePerformDemo.
DATA DIVISION.
WORKING-STORAGE SECTION.
01 COUNTER PIC 9(2) VALUE 0.

PROCEDURE DIVISION.
MAIN-LOGIC.
    PERFORM SIMPLE-LOOP 5 TIMES
    STOP RUN.

SIMPLE-LOOP.
    ADD 1 TO COUNTER
    DISPLAY 'Iteration: ' COUNTER.
```

In this example, the SIMPLE-LOOP paragraph is executed five times. During each iteration, the COUNTER variable is incremented by one, and its value is displayed. This results in the following output when the program is executed:

```
Iteration: 01
Iteration: 02
Iteration: 03
Iteration: 04
Iteration: 05
```

### Conceptual Overview

When the PERFORM statement is encountered, COBOL initiates the execution of the specified procedure. The control is temporarily transferred from the point immediately following the PERFORM statement to the start of the indicated paragraph or section. Upon completion of one cycle, control is returned to the PERFORM statement to check if additional iterations are required. This cycle continues until the specified number of iterations is completed, after which normal program execution resumes immediately following the PERFORM statement.

It is crucial to understand that the PERFORM statement does not create a loop within the code itself but rather dictates the repeated execution of the specified procedure. This looping mechanism ensures that the code in the specified procedure runs repeatedly without the need to rewrite the sequence.

### Data Considerations

In practice, the number of iterations can be determined dynamically. This is achieved by using a data item in place of a literal number in the PERFORM statement. For instance:

```
IDENTIFICATION DIVISION.
PROGRAM-ID. PerformWithVariable.
DATA DIVISION.
WORKING-STORAGE SECTION.
01 ITERATION-COUNT PIC 9(2) VALUE 3.
01 COUNTER PIC 9(2) VALUE 0.

PROCEDURE DIVISION.
MAIN-LOGIC.
    PERFORM VARIABLE-LOOP ITERATION-COUNT
        TIMES
    STOP RUN.

VARIABLE-LOOP.
    ADD 1 TO COUNTER
    DISPLAY 'Count Value: ' COUNTER.
```

In this example, the ITERATION-COUNT variable, which is set to 3, dictates the number of times the VARIABLE-LOOP paragraph is executed. This results in the following displayed output:

```
Count Value: 01
Count Value: 02
Count Value: 03
```

### Edge Cases

### Handling Zero Iterations It is also essential to consider edge cases, such as when the number of specified iterations is zero. In such a scenario, the designated procedure will not execute at all, allowing the program to skip the loop gracefully without errors or unexpected behaviors.

### Conclusion

Understanding and efficiently utilizing Simple PERFORM Loops in COBOL is foundational for mastering iterative processes within the language. The Simple PERFORM Loop is not just limited to fixed integers; it can adapt to dynamic execution counts, providing both flexibility and robustness in program control flows. By leveraging these constructs, developers can ensure clear, concise, and efficient code execution for repetitive tasks.

## 6.4 Perform Varying Loop

The PERFORM VARYING loop in COBOL is a versatile loop structure that allows for precise control over the iteration of code blocks. This looping construct is particularly useful for scenarios where the loop needs to vary the values of one or more index variables, making it analogous to the for loop in many other programming languages. The flexible design of PERFORM VARYING enables the programmer to specify initial values, increments, and termination conditions clearly.

PERFORM VARYING is defined using the following syntax:

```
PERFORM
  VARYING identifier-1 FROM start-value BY increment-value
  UNTIL end-condition
      {statements to be executed}
END-PERFORM.
```

In this structure, identifier-1 is the loop-control variable, start-value is the initial value of the variable, increment-value is the value by which the loop-control variable is incremented after each iteration, and end-condition is the condition that, when met, terminates the loop.

**Example of a Basic PERFORM VARYING Loop:**

```
WORKING-STORAGE SECTION.
01 WS-INDEX PIC 9(02) VALUE 1.
01 WS-LIMIT PIC 9(02) VALUE 10.

PROCEDURE DIVISION.
    PERFORM VARYING WS-INDEX FROM 1 BY 1
        UNTIL WS-INDEX > WS-LIMIT
        DISPLAY "Current value of WS-INDEX: "
            WS-INDEX
    END-PERFORM.
    STOP RUN.
```

In this example, the PERFORM VARYING loop initializes WS-INDEX to 1, increments it by 1 each iteration, and continues until WS-INDEX exceeds the value held in WS-LIMIT (10). The loop body contains a DISPLAY statement that outputs the current value of WS-INDEX.

**Multiple Loop-Control Variables:**

PERFORM VARYING also supports nested variation using multiple loop-control variables. This can be particularly useful for iterating over multi-dimensional arrays or complex data structures.

```
WORKING-STORAGE SECTION.
01 WS-ROW-INDEX PIC 9(02) VALUE 1.
01 WS-COL-INDEX PIC 9(02) VALUE 1.
01 WS-MAX-ROWS PIC 9(02) VALUE 3.
01 WS-MAX-COLS PIC 9(02) VALUE 3.
01 WS-MATRIX PIC X(02) VALUE '00' OCCURS 3 TIMES
        OCCURS 3 TIMES INDEXED BY IDX1, IDX2.

PROCEDURE DIVISION.
    PERFORM VARYING WS-ROW-INDEX FROM 1 BY 1
        UNTIL WS-ROW-INDEX > WS-MAX-ROWS
        PERFORM VARYING WS-COL-INDEX FROM 1
            BY 1
            UNTIL WS-COL-INDEX > WS-MAX-COLS
            SET IDX1 TO WS-ROW-INDEX
            SET IDX2 TO WS-COL-INDEX
```

```
                MOVE FUNCTION NUMVAL-C(
                    WORKING-STORAGE-FILLER)
                  TO WS-MATRIX(IDX1, IDX2)
                DISPLAY "Matrix[" WS-ROW-INDEX ","
                    WS-COL-INDEX "]: "
                  WS-MATRIX(IDX1, IDX2)
            END-PERFORM
        END-PERFORM.
        STOP RUN.
```

This nested loop example uses PERFORM VARYING to iterate over a 3x3 matrix. The outer loop varies WS-ROW-INDEX from 1 to 3, and the inner loop varies WS-COL-INDEX from 1 to 3. Within the inner loop, specific elements of the WS-MATRIX array are accessed and manipulated.

**Advantages of PERFORM VARYING:**

- **Clarity**: The syntax clearly separates initialization, condition, and increment, making the loop intent easy to understand.
- **Flexibility**: Supports multiple loop-control variables, allowing complex iteration over data structures.
- **Readability**: The natural language-like structure improves code readability and maintainability.

By employing the PERFORM VARYING loop correctly, COBOL programmers can write clear, efficient, and maintainable code for a wide range of iterative tasks.

## 6.5 Perform Until Loop

The PERFORM UNTIL loop is a fundamental construct in COBOL that facilitates the execution of a block of code repeatedly until a specified condition is met. This construct is essential for scenarios where the number of iterations is not known beforehand and depends on dynamic runtime conditions.

The syntax for the PERFORM UNTIL loop is as follows:

```
PERFORM UNTIL condition
```

```
    [statements]
END-PERFORM
```

Here, condition is an expression that evaluates to true or false. The statements within the PERFORM UNTIL block will execute repeatedly as long as condition evaluates to false. When condition becomes true, control passes to the statement following the END-PERFORM.

### Example Usage

Consider the following example where a PERFORM UNTIL loop is employed to sum the numbers from 1 to n.

```
IDENTIFICATION DIVISION.
PROGRAM-ID. SumUntilExample.

DATA DIVISION.
WORKING-STORAGE SECTION.
77 WS-SUM PIC 9(4) VALUE 0.
77 WS-COUNTER PIC 9(2) VALUE 1.
77 WS-N PIC 9(2) VALUE 10.

PROCEDURE DIVISION.
    PERFORM UNTIL WS-COUNTER > WS-N
        ADD WS-COUNTER TO WS-SUM
        ADD 1 TO WS-COUNTER
    END-PERFORM
    DISPLAY 'Sum of numbers from 1 to ' WS-N ' is: '
        WS-SUM
    STOP RUN.
```

The execution begins by setting WS-SUM to 0 and WS-COUNTER to 1. The PERFORM UNTIL loop runs as long as WS-COUNTER is less than or equal to WS-N. During each iteration, WS-COUNTER is added to WS-SUM, and WS-COUNTER is incremented by 1. Once WS-COUNTER exceeds WS-N, the loop terminates, and the sum is displayed.

Output:

```
Sum of numbers from 1 to 10 is: 55
```

### Characteristics

- **Initialization and Condition Evaluation:** Initialization of loop variables should be handled prior to entering the loop. The condition is evaluated before entering and after each pass through the loop body. - **Termination:** The loop can terminate in two scenarios: the condition becomes true, or an explicit EXIT statement within the loop is executed. - **Iterations:** Since the condition is checked before each iteration, it is possible for the loop body to never execute if the condition is initially true.

### Nested PERFORM UNTIL Loops

Just like any other loop construct, PERFORM UNTIL loops can be nested inside other loops, enabling more intricate iteration patterns. Careful attention should be given to the management of loop variables and exit conditions to avoid infinite loops or unintended behavior.

Example of nested PERFORM UNTIL loops:

```
IDENTIFICATION DIVISION.
PROGRAM-ID. NestedUntilExample.

DATA DIVISION.
WORKING-STORAGE SECTION.
77 WS-I PIC 9(2) VALUE 1.
77 WS-J PIC 9(2) VALUE 1.
77 WS-ROWS PIC 9(2) VALUE 3.
77 WS-COLUMNS PIC 9(2) VALUE 3.

PROCEDURE DIVISION.
    PERFORM UNTIL WS-I > WS-ROWS
        MOVE 1 TO WS-J
        PERFORM UNTIL WS-J > WS-COLUMNS
            DISPLAY 'Row: ' WS-I ' Column: ' WS-J
            ADD 1 TO WS-J
        END-PERFORM
        ADD 1 TO WS-I
    END-PERFORM
    STOP RUN.
```

Output:

```
Row: 1 Column: 1
Row: 1 Column: 2
Row: 1 Column: 3
Row: 2 Column: 1
Row: 2 Column: 2
Row: 2 Column: 3
Row: 3 Column: 1
Row: 3 Column: 2
Row: 3 Column: 3
```

### Best Practices

- **Clarity:** Ensure that the loop condition is clear and straightforward to avoid logic errors. - **Initialization:** Properly initialize loop control variables outside the loop to avoid unexpected behaviors. - **Update Mechanism:** Ensure that the loop makes progress toward meeting the termination condition within the loop body to prevent infinite loops. - **Resource Management:** When performing resource-intensive operations within a PERFORM UNTIL loop, consider the efficiency and potential optimizations to enhance performance.

Using the PERFORM UNTIL construct effectively in COBOL enhances the readability and maintainability of iteration logic, ensuring that programs execute repetitive tasks accurately and efficiently.

## 6.6 Nested Loops in COBOL

Nested loops in COBOL are a powerful construct for performing multiple levels of iteration, allowing more complex repetitive tasks to be handled efficiently. This section details how to implement nested loops, addresses common pitfalls, and demonstrates best practices for maintaining code readability and performance.

**Implementing Nested Loops**

In COBOL, nested loops are achieved by placing one PERFORM statement inside another. The inner loop is executed completely for each iteration of the outer loop. Here is a basic example of a nested PERFORM VARYING loop:

```
IDENTIFICATION DIVISION.
PROGRAM-ID. NestedLoopExample.
DATA DIVISION.
WORKING-STORAGE SECTION.
01 Outer-Loop-Index PIC 9 VALUE 1.
01 Inner-Loop-Index PIC 9 VALUE 1.

PROCEDURE DIVISION.
    PERFORM VARYING Outer-Loop-Index FROM 1 BY 1
        UNTIL Outer-Loop-Index > 5
        DISPLAY "Outer Loop Index: " Outer-Loop-Index

        PERFORM VARYING Inner-Loop-Index FROM 1 BY
```

```
                    1 UNTIL Inner-Loop-Index > 3
                    DISPLAY " Inner Loop Index: " Inner-Loop-Index
                END-PERFORM

            END-PERFORM.

            STOP RUN.
```

This program will produce the following output:

```
Outer Loop Index: 1
  Inner Loop Index: 1
  Inner Loop Index: 2
  Inner Loop Index: 3
Outer Loop Index: 2
  Inner Loop Index: 1
  Inner Loop Index: 2
  Inner Loop Index: 3
Outer Loop Index: 3
  Inner Loop Index: 1
  Inner Loop Index: 2
  Inner Loop Index: 3
Outer Loop Index: 4
  Inner Loop Index: 1
  Inner Loop Index: 2
  Inner Loop Index: 3
Outer Loop Index: 5
  Inner Loop Index: 1
  Inner Loop Index: 2
  Inner Loop Index: 3
```

The example demonstrates how each value of Outer-Loop-Index triggers a complete cycle of the inner loop.

**Common Pitfalls of Nested Loops**

When working with nested loops, it is important to avoid certain pitfalls:

- **Initialization Issues**: Ensure loop control variables are correctly initialized before the loops begin. Failure to do so can result in infinite loops or incorrect iteration counts.
- **Inefficient Code**: Be mindful of the computational complexity. Nested loops, especially those with high iteration counts, can lead to performance issues. Optimize the loop bodies to minimize the workload within each iteration.
- **Readability**: Deeply nested loops can become difficult to read and understand. Use meaningful variable names and include comments to clarify the purpose and function of each loop.

**Example with Complex Logic**

Consider a scenario where you need to process a table of data, comparing each entry with every other entry. Nested loops are ideal for such tasks. Here's an example that demonstrates comparing elements in a table:

```
IDENTIFICATION DIVISION.
PROGRAM-ID. TableComparison.
DATA DIVISION.
WORKING-STORAGE SECTION.
01 Table.
   05 Table-Entry OCCURS 10 TIMES.
      10 Entry-Value PIC 9(4).
01 Outer-Index PIC 99 VALUE 1.
01 Inner-Index PIC 99 VALUE 1.

PROCEDURE DIVISION.
   MOVE 1000 TO Table-Entry (1) Entry-Value
   MOVE 2000 TO Table-Entry (2) Entry-Value
   MOVE 3000 TO Table-Entry (3) Entry-Value
   MOVE 4000 TO Table-Entry (4) Entry-Value
   MOVE 5000 TO Table-Entry (5) Entry-Value

   PERFORM VARYING Outer-Index FROM 1 BY 1
       UNTIL Outer-Index > 5
      PERFORM VARYING Inner-Index FROM 1 BY 1
          UNTIL Inner-Index > 5
         IF Outer-Index NOT = Inner-Index
            DISPLAY "Comparing " Table-Entry (
                Outer-Index) Entry-Value
            " with " Table-Entry (Inner-Index)
                Entry-Value
         END-IF
      END-PERFORM
   END-PERFORM.

   STOP RUN.
```

This program initializes a table with five entries and then uses nested loops to compare each entry with every other entry, excluding self-comparisons. This results in the following output:

```
Comparing 1000 with 2000
Comparing 1000 with 3000
Comparing 1000 with 4000
Comparing 1000 with 5000
Comparing 2000 with 1000
Comparing 2000 with 3000
Comparing 2000 with 4000
Comparing 2000 with 5000
Comparing 3000 with 1000
Comparing 3000 with 2000
Comparing 3000 with 4000
Comparing 3000 with 5000
Comparing 4000 with 1000
Comparing 4000 with 2000
Comparing 4000 with 3000
Comparing 4000 with 5000
Comparing 5000 with 1000
Comparing 5000 with 2000
Comparing 5000 with 3000
Comparing 5000 with 4000
```

This sophisticated example shows nested loops handling more complex logic, emphasizing the importance of correct initialization, efficiency, and clarity.

**Best Practices**

Utilize the following best practices to ensure effective use of nested loops:

- **Use Meaningful Variable Names**: Clearly differentiate between outer and inner loop indexes.
- **Comment Your Code**: Provide comments that describe the purpose and logic of the loops.
- **Minimize Nesting Depth**: Avoid excessive nesting by breaking complex tasks into subroutines.
- **Optimize Inner Loop Operations**: Perform only necessary calculations inside inner loops to boost efficiency.

Nested loops in COBOL provide a structured way to handle multiple levels of iteration, enabling developers to write clear and efficient code for complex tasks.

## 6.7 Using the EXIT Statement

The EXIT statement in COBOL is employed to provide a controlled exit from a loop or a paragraph. It serves as a powerful mechanism to manage the flow of control within iterative processes. By leveraging the EXIT statement, developers can enhance the readability and efficiency of their code, especially in complex nested loops or when certain conditions warrant an early exit from repetitive execution.

To illustrate the use of the EXIT statement, consider the following example where we exit a PERFORM UNTIL loop before it completes all iterations. This scenario demonstrates how the EXIT statement can be utilized for early termination based on a specific condition.

```
IDENTIFICATION DIVISION.
PROGRAM-ID. ExampleExitLoop.
DATA DIVISION.
WORKING-STORAGE SECTION.
01 Counter PIC 9(2) VALUE 1.
01 ExitCondition PIC X VALUE 'N'.
PROCEDURE DIVISION.
Main-Paragraph.
    PERFORM WITH TEST BEFORE
        VARYING Counter FROM 1 BY 1 UNTIL Counter >
            10
            DISPLAY 'Counter: ' Counter
            IF Counter = 5 THEN
                MOVE 'Y' TO ExitCondition
                EXIT
            END-IF
        END-PERFORM
    DISPLAY 'Exited loop at Counter: ' Counter
    STOP RUN.
```

In this example, the loop is designed to iterate from 1 to 10. However, an exit condition is checked within the loop. When Counter reaches 5, the EXIT statement is executed, resulting in an immediate termination of the loop. The program subsequently displays the exiting value of the Counter.

```
Counter: 1
Counter: 2
Counter: 3
Counter: 4
Counter: 5
Exited loop at Counter: 5
```

The importance of the EXIT statement becomes more apparent in nested loops where terminating the inner loop can lead to more efficient programs. Consider a case where two nested loops are used and the

EXIT statement ensures we break out of the inner loop on a specific condition.

```
IDENTIFICATION DIVISION.
PROGRAM-ID. NestedExitExample.
DATA DIVISION.
WORKING-STORAGE SECTION.
01 OuterCounter PIC 9(2) VALUE 1.
01 InnerCounter PIC 9(2) VALUE 1.
PROCEDURE DIVISION.
Main-Paragraph.
    PERFORM WITH TEST BEFORE
        VARYING OuterCounter FROM 1 BY 1 UNTIL
            OuterCounter > 3
        DISPLAY 'Outer Loop Iteration: ' OuterCounter
        PERFORM WITH TEST BEFORE
            VARYING InnerCounter FROM 1 BY 1 UNTIL
                InnerCounter > 4
            DISPLAY ' Inner Loop Iteration: ' InnerCounter
            IF InnerCounter = 3 THEN
                EXIT
            END-IF
        END-PERFORM
        MOVE 1 TO InnerCounter
    END-PERFORM
    STOP RUN.
```

```
Outer Loop Iteration: 1
  Inner Loop Iteration: 1
  Inner Loop Iteration: 2
  Inner Loop Iteration: 3
Outer Loop Iteration: 2
  Inner Loop Iteration: 1
  Inner Loop Iteration: 2
  Inner Loop Iteration: 3
Outer Loop Iteration: 3
  Inner Loop Iteration: 1
  Inner Loop Iteration: 2
  Inner Loop Iteration: 3
```

In the above example, the inner loop iterates from 1 to 4 for each iteration of the outer loop. However, upon reaching an InnerCounter value of 3, the execution exits the inner loop and proceeds to the next iteration of the outer loop. By employing the EXIT statement, we efficiently control the flow of execution within nested iterations, ensuring that the inner loop does not execute beyond the specified condition.

At this point, it is crucial to understand that the EXIT statement does not terminate the entire program, nor does it transfer control to any other paragraph or section. Its sole purpose is to provide a means to exit from the current loop or procedure, allowing for a controlled and readable structure of the program logic.

Employing the EXIT statement within conditional constructs enhances the maintainability of code, simplifying the understanding and debugging processes. It also minimizes any potential overhead associated with unnecessary iterations, considerably improving efficiency in scenarios with complex logical conditions.

Through the judicious use of the EXIT statement, COBOL programmers can create more adaptive and responsive programs, capable of handling intricate looping scenarios with increased precision and clarity.

## 6.8 Working with Inline Perform

The PERFORM statement in COBOL can be significantly enhanced using the inline method, which allows for greater control and readability within loops. An inline PERFORM executes a block of code placed immediately following the PERFORM statement itself, rather than calling a separately defined paragraph. This can be particularly useful for encapsulating functionality that is only needed in a single place within a program, thereby improving modularization and reducing external dependencies.

To define an inline PERFORM in COBOL, the PERFORM statement is followed by the block of code ending with the END-PERFORM statement. The intrinsic benefit is that it maintains a logical sequence of operations directly in the code flow, as opposed to branching out to a separate block. Two types of inline PERFORM loops are commonly used: fixed iteration loops and conditional loops.

**Inline Fixed Iteration Loop**

A fixed iteration inline loop is used when the number of iterations is known in advance. This is achieved by specifying from which value to start, the step increment, and the end limit within the VARYING clause. Here's an example implementation:

```
WORKING-STORAGE SECTION.
    01 WS-INDEX PIC 9(02) VALUE 1.
```

```
PROCEDURE DIVISION.
    PERFORM VARYING WS-INDEX FROM 1 BY 1 UNTIL
        WS-INDEX > 10
        DISPLAY 'Iteration: ' WS-INDEX
    END-PERFORM.
```

In this example, the inline PERFORM loop runs ten times, incrementing WS-INDEX by 1 each time until it exceeds 10. Each iteration displays the current iteration number.

**Inline Conditional Loop**

Conditional inline loops operate based on a condition rather than a fixed number of iterations. An example of a PERFORM UNTIL loop implemented inline is provided below:

```
WORKING-STORAGE SECTION.
    01 WS-COUNTER PIC 9(02) VALUE 0.

PROCEDURE DIVISION.
    PERFORM UNTIL WS-COUNTER = 5
        ADD 1 TO WS-COUNTER
        DISPLAY 'Counter value: ' WS-COUNTER
    END-PERFORM.
```

This loop continues executing while WS-COUNTER is less than 5. At each iteration, it increments WS-COUNTER by 1 and displays its current value.

**Advantages of Using Inline Perform**

The use of inline PERFORM blocks provides several advantages:

- **Locality of Reference:** Keeping the loop logic close to the point of use improves readability and makes understanding the program flow easier.
- **Reduced Boilerplate:** Inline PERFORM minimizes the need for additional paragraphs strictly defined for looping, reducing the boilerplate code within a COBOL program.
- **Enhanced Maintenance:** With the loop logic embedded within the scope of the main code, maintaining and modifying programs becomes simpler.

- **Improved Performance:** Potentially faster execution due to lesser overhead from not having to branch out to separate paragraphs.

**Considerations and Best Practices**

While the inline PERFORM offers clear benefits, it is essential to use it appropriately:

- **Simplicity:** Inline blocks are best suited for simple looping constructs. For complex logic, consider separating the loop into a named paragraph for better clarity.
- **Indentation and Formatting:** Maintain proper indentation and formatting to ensure the inline loop's readability and distinguishability from the surrounding code easily.
- **Documentation:** Commenting on the purpose of the loop and indicating critical sections within the inline block is crucial, especially in a collaborative environment.
- **Limitation of Scope:** Use inline PERFORM where the loop is specific to a small section of code. Overusing it can lead to clutter in the main procedure, countering the readability it aims to achieve.

Inline PERFORM structures are powerful tools for looping in COBOL. Their effective use can greatly contribute to the modularity, readability, and maintainability of programs. Achieving proficiency with inline PERFORM helps elevate a COBOL programmer's ability to write clean and efficient code tailored to the demands of modern applications.

## 6.9 Best Practices for Looping

When utilizing looping constructs in COBOL, adhering to best practices is critical for creating efficient, maintainable, and readable code. This section delves into a range of strategies and guidelines that can help programmers optimize their use of loops in COBOL programs.

**1. Choosing the Appropriate Loop Type**

Selecting the correct loop type for the task at hand can significantly impact performance and readability. COBOL provides several types of loops, including PERFORM loops, PERFORM VARYING, and PERFORM UNTIL. Understanding the differences and appropriate applications of each loop type can help streamline code execution.

- Use PERFORM loops for simple, predefined iterations where the number of iterations is fixed.
- Opt for PERFORM VARYING when iterating over a range of values or when the loop counter is explicitly manipulated.
- Employ PERFORM UNTIL for scenarios where the loop continues until a specific condition is met.

**2. Minimizing Loop Control Overhead**

When dealing with large datasets or performance-critical applications, minimizing the overhead associated with loop control becomes essential. One effective way to achieve this is by avoiding excessive condition checks or complex expressions within the loop control clauses.

```
PERFORM VARYING idx FROM 1 BY 1 UNTIL idx > max-idx
    * Process code here
END-PERFORM
```

In the above example, the loop control remains simple, making the iteration efficient.

**3. Proper Initialization of Loop Variables**

Ensure that all loop control variables are properly initialized before entering the loop. This prevents unpredictable behavior and logic errors within the loop.

```
MOVE 1 TO idx
PERFORM VARYING idx UNTIL idx > max-idx
    * Process code here
    ADD 1 TO idx
END-PERFORM
```

**4. Minimizing Nesting**

Excessive nesting of loops can make the code hard to read and maintain. It is advisable to minimize the depth of nested loops and to simplify nested logic where possible.

```
PERFORM VARYING idx FROM 1 BY 1 UNTIL idx > max-idx
```

```
    PERFORM VARYING jdx FROM 1 BY 1 UNTIL jdx > max-jdx
        * Process code here
    END-PERFORM
END-PERFORM
```

If deeper nesting is necessary, consider refactoring the code into smaller, more manageable modules.

**5. Using Inline Comments for Clarification**

Documenting the purpose and functionality of loops with inline comments can greatly enhance code readability. Comments should explain the rationale behind the loop and any critical operations performed within its body.

```
PERFORM VARYING idx FROM 1 BY 1 UNTIL idx > max-idx
    * Process each record in the dataset
    CALL 'ProcessRecord' USING idx
END-PERFORM
```

**6. Efficient Data Access within Loops**

Efficiently accessing and modifying data within loops is crucial for maintaining performance. Avoid costly operations such as file I/O or database queries inside the loop body if they can be performed outside and reused within the loop.

```
PERFORM VARYING idx FROM 1 BY 1 UNTIL idx > max-idx
    MOVE dataset(idx) TO ws-record
    * Process ws-record here
END-PERFORM
```

**7. Controlling Loop Execution with the EXIT Statement**

The EXIT statement can be used to provide greater control over loop execution. This is particularly useful when a loop must be terminated prematurely based on a specific condition.

```
PERFORM VARYING idx FROM 1 BY 1 UNTIL idx > max-idx
    IF some-condition THEN
        EXIT PERFORM
    END-IF
    * Process code here
END-PERFORM
```

**8. Avoiding Hard-Coded Values**

Hard-coded values within loop control parameters can make the program inflexible and prone to errors. Use named constants or configuration parameters instead.

```
77 max-idx PIC 9(4) VALUE 100.

PERFORM VARYING idx FROM 1 BY 1 UNTIL idx > max-idx
    * Process code here
END-PERFORM
```

**9. Utilizing PERFORM Blocks for Complex Logic**

For loops encapsulating complex logic, utilize PERFORM blocks to maintain readability and modularity.

```
PERFORM VARYING idx FROM 1 BY 1 UNTIL idx > max-idx
    PERFORM ProcessRecord USING idx
END-PERFORM

ProcessRecord SECTION.
    * Processing logic here
    EXIT.
```

**10. Testing and Debugging Loop Constructs**

Thoroughly test loop constructs to ensure they behave as expected under various scenarios, including edge cases. Debugging tools and logging statements can be valuable in identifying and resolving issues.

```
PERFORM VARYING idx FROM 1 BY 1 UNTIL idx > max-idx
    DISPLAY 'Processing index: ' idx
    * Process code here
END-PERFORM
```

Adhering to these best practices ensures that COBOL looping constructs are robust, efficient, and maintainable. Proper usage of loops can significantly enhance the clarity and performance of COBOL programs, making them easier to understand and manage.

# Chapter 7

# Arrays and Tables

**Arrays and tables are essential for managing collections of data in COBOL. This chapter introduces the definition and use of single-dimensional and multi-dimensional arrays and explores table handling and indexing techniques. It covers the OCCURS clause, dynamic arrays, and SEARCH and SEARCH ALL statements, providing practical insights into effective data manipulation and common use cases for tables in COBOL programming.**

## 7.1 Introduction to Arrays and Tables

Arrays and tables in COBOL facilitate the effective management and manipulation of collections of data. These structures are crucial for organizing data that need to be processed in a repetitive manner, and they simplify the handling of large sets of homogeneous items. The terminology used for arrays and tables in COBOL is often interchangeable as arrays are a type of table structure.

**Arrays** in COBOL are simple, structured data types that allow a programmer to define a collection of similar data elements. Each element in the array is of the same data type and the array elements are accessed by their index or subscript. Arrays can be single-dimensional or multi-dimensional based on the requirements of the program.

**Tables** in COBOL refer to more complex structures that may contain either single or multiple dimensions. Tables can be considered as an extension of arrays. They provide more control over data manipulation through defining data items that occur multiple times.

To define an array or a table in COBOL, the OCCURS clause is used. This clause allows the declaration of a repeated group of similar data items. The syntax for a single-dimensional array using the OCCURS clause is straightforward:

```
01 EMPLOYEE-NAME PIC X(20) OCCURS 10 TIMES.
```

In the above example, EMPLOYEE-NAME is declared as an array of 10 elements, with each element being able to hold a character string of up to 20 characters.

When it comes to multi-dimensional arrays, the structure expands to include multiple OCCURS clauses. Each dimension adds another layer of data repetition. The following example demonstrates a two-dimensional array:

```
01 SALES-TABLE.
    05 REGION OCCURS 5 TIMES.
        10 DEPARTMENT OCCURS 4 TIMES.
            15 SALES-AMOUNT PIC 9(6)V99.
```

In this multi-dimensional array example, SALES-TABLE contains regions, and each region contains departments with sales amounts. This establishes the structure where each region is divided into multiple departments, and for each department, sales data is recorded.

Tables in COBOL are manipulated using indices and subscripts. A subscript is a simple numeric value, whereas an index is a more sophisticated construct. Subscripts can be directly used to reference the positions within the array, albeit less efficiently than indices. The following examples illustrate this:

```
MOVE "John Doe" TO EMPLOYEE-NAME(1).
DISPLAY EMPLOYEE-NAME(1).
```

In the above code snippet, EMPLOYEE-NAME(1) refers to the first element in the EMPLOYEE-NAME array.

To work with table handling more efficiently, indices are preferred. An index is declared using the INDEXED BY phrase. Consider the following example:

```
01 EMPLOYEE-NAME PIC X(20) OCCURS 10 TIMES
```

```
        INDEXED BY EMP-IDX.
```

Here, EMP-IDX is an index used to navigate through EMPLOYEE-NAME entries. Operations using indices are executed more efficiently since indices allow COBOL to perform address arithmetic.

Initializing and setting values to arrays and tables efficiently is a key activity. The move statement can be used, in a loop, to initialize an entire array or table. Consideration must be given to the initialization of multi-dimensional arrays.

```
PERFORM VARYING REGION-INDEX FROM 1 BY 1 UNTIL
    REGION-INDEX > 5
  PERFORM VARYING DEPARTMENT-INDEX FROM 1 BY 1
      UNTIL DEPARTMENT-INDEX > 4
    MOVE 0 TO SALES-TABLE(REGION-INDEX,
        DEPARTMENT-INDEX)
  END-PERFORM
END-PERFORM
```

Effective management of arrays and tables not only involves defining and initializing them but also includes aspects of searching, sorting, and dynamic management which are covered in subsequent sections. Arrays and tables in COBOL enhance the ability to handle large sets of structured data, thereby playing a pivotal role in various types of data processing applications.

## 7.2 Defining Single-Dimensional Arrays

In COBOL, arrays are commonly known as tables. Defining a single-dimensional array requires the use of the OCCURS clause within the DATA DIVISION. The OCCURS clause specifies the number of times an elementary or group item is repeated. By effectively using this clause, we can address and manipulate large sets of homogeneous data elements efficiently.

To define a single-dimensional array, you must declare it in the WORKING-STORAGE SECTION of the DATA DIVISION. Each element in the array is identified by an index. Below is a standard example of defining a single-dimensional array in COBOL:

```
DATA DIVISION.
```

```
WORKING-STORAGE SECTION.
01 STUDENT-NAMES.
   05 STUDENT-NAME OCCURS 10 TIMES.
      10 FIRST-NAME PIC X(10).
      10 LAST-NAME PIC X(15).
```

In this example, STUDENT-NAMES is an array composed of group items, which occur 10 times. Each occurrence includes two elementary items: FIRST-NAME with a picture clause of X(10), indicating a 10-character alphanumeric field, and LAST-NAME with a picture clause of X(15), indicating a 15-character alphanumeric field.

### Key Characteristics of Single-Dimensional Arrays in COBOL:

- **Flat Structure:** Each item within the array has the same structure and data type as defined by the OCCURS clause.
- **Sequential Access:** By default, COBOL allows sequential access to array elements.
- **Indexing:** The index in COBOL typically starts at 1, not 0, which is a differentiator from many other programming languages.

### Memory Allocation

COBOL assigns memory for all occurrences of the items defined with the OCCURS clause when the program begins execution. Thus, understanding the memory footprint before declaring large arrays is essential for optimal program performance.

### Using the OCCURS Clause

The OCCURS clause is versatile and can be applied to both elementary and group items. Here is an example that demonstrates using OCCURS with an elementary item:

```
DATA DIVISION.
WORKING-STORAGE SECTION.
01 MONTHLY-SALES.
   05 SALES-AMOUNT PIC 9(7)V99 OCCURS 12 TIMES.
```

In this example, SALES-AMOUNT is an elementary item that occurs 12 times, each having a PIC clause 9(7)V99 which defines a numeric field with 7 digits and 2 decimals.

### Accessing Array Elements

To access and manipulate elements of a single-dimensional array, you use subscript notation. Here's an example:

```
PROCEDURE DIVISION.
    MOVE 'John' TO FIRST-NAME (1).
    MOVE 'Doe' TO LAST-NAME (1).
    DISPLAY FIRST-NAME (1) LAST-NAME (1).
```

The above code moves the string 'John' to the first occurrence of FIRST-NAME and 'Doe' to the first occurrence of LAST-NAME. The displayed output would be:

John Doe

### Initialization

Arrays can be initialized in COBOL either through value clauses within the DATA DIVISION or by explicit moves within the PROCEDURE DIVISION. For instance:

```
01 NUMBERS.
    05 NUMBER PIC 9(3) OCCURS 5 TIMES
        VALUE 100.
```

This initialization sets all occurrences of NUMBER to 100 by default.

### Boundary Considerations

A significant consideration when working with arrays is avoiding boundary errors. Accessing an element outside the declared range will cause run-time errors. It is prudent to perform boundary checks in the code:

```
IF WS-SUB > 0 AND WS-SUB <= 10 THEN
    PERFORM PROCESS-ELEMENT
ELSE
    DISPLAY 'Subscript out of bounds'.
```

Here WS-SUB is validated to ensure it falls within the appropriate boundaries before proceeding with further operations.

### Practical Example

Below is a practical program example demonstrating defining, initializing, and accessing a single-dimensional array:

```
IDENTIFICATION DIVISION.
PROGRAM-ID. STUDENT-PROG.
```

```
DATA DIVISION.
WORKING-STORAGE SECTION.
01 STUDENTS.
   05 STUDENT-NAME PIC X(20) OCCURS 5 TIMES
                        VALUE 'STUDENT-1', 'STUDENT-2', '
                           STUDENT-3', 'STUDENT-4', '
                           STUDENT-5'.

PROCEDURE DIVISION.
   PERFORM VARYING WS-INDEX FROM 1 BY 1 UNTIL
      WS-INDEX > 5
     DISPLAY 'Name: ' STUDENT-NAME (WS-INDEX)
   END-PERFORM.
   STOP RUN.
```

The output of the above code would be:

```
Name: STUDENT-1
Name: STUDENT-2
Name: STUDENT-3
Name: STUDENT-4
Name: STUDENT-5
```

Understanding how to define single-dimensional arrays in COBOL equips you with the capability to manage structured data collections efficiently. These principles lay the foundation for more advanced array operations and table handling techniques in subsequent sections.

## 7.3 Accessing and Modifying Array Elements

In the context of COBOL, accessing and modifying array elements is fundamental for data manipulation and computations. Utilizing single-dimensional and multi-dimensional arrays, programmers can efficiently store and process collections of data. The following guidelines will provide an in-depth understanding of the mechanisms involved.

To start, consider a single-dimensional array defined with the OCCURS clause. For example, suppose we have an array that stores monthly sales.

```
01 SALES-MONTHLY.
   05 SALES-AMT PIC 9(6)V99 OCCURS 12 TIMES.
```

Here, SALES-AMT is a single-dimensional array that holds 12 elements, each accommodating a sales amount for a month. Each element can be accessed with an appropriate index ranging from 1 to 12.

To access an element within this array, we use the subscript notation. For instance, to access and display the sales amount for March, which is the third element, the following code can be utilized:

```
MOVE SALES-AMT (3) TO DISPLAY-VALUE.
DISPLAY "Sales for March: " DISPLAY-VALUE.
```

Similarly, we can modify the element by assigning a new value to the specified position:

```
MOVE 15000.50 TO SALES-AMT (3).
```

This command updates the sales amount for March to 15000.50.

When working with multi-dimensional arrays, the complexity increases slightly. Consider a two-dimensional array that stores sales data for 4 quarters over 3 years, defined as follows:

```
01 QUARTERLY-SALES.
    05 YEAR-MONTHLY-SALES OCCURS 3 TIMES.
        10 SALES-AMT PIC 9(6)V99 OCCURS 4 TIMES.
```

In this instance, QUARTERLY-SALES is a two-dimensional array. The first dimension represents the year (3 years), and the second dimension represents the sales by quarter (4 quarters).

To access an element in this array, two subscripts are required. For example, to retrieve the sales amount for the second quarter of the first year, we use:

```
MOVE SALES-AMT (1, 2) TO DISPLAY-VALUE.
DISPLAY "Sales for Q2, Year 1: " DISPLAY-VALUE.
```

Modifying an element within a two-dimensional array follows the same principle. For instance:

```
MOVE 20000.75 TO SALES-AMT (1, 2).
```

This command updates the sales amount for the second quarter of the first year to 20000.75.

Arrays can also be dynamically modified in COBOL. Consider the case where the number of active elements changes. Suppose we have an array of employees:

```
01 EMPLOYEES.
    05 EMP-NAME PIC X(30) OCCURS 100 TIMES.
```

If only the first 10 elements are active initially and we want to set the 11th employee's name:

```
MOVE "JOHN DOE" TO EMP-NAME (11).
```

When working with dynamic arrays, effective use of the PERFORM statement is often required to iterate and manipulate the elements. Here's an example of summing the sales amounts for a specific year in the QUARTERLY-SALES array:

```
01 TOTAL-SALES PIC 9(8)V99.

PERFORM VARYING I FROM 1 BY 1 UNTIL I > 4
    ADD SALES-AMT (2, I) TO TOTAL-SALES
END-PERFORM.
DISPLAY "Total Sales for Year 2: " TOTAL-SALES.
```

In this code: - I is used as the index to iterate through the quarters. - ADD operation accumulates the sales amounts into TOTAL-SALES. - The PERFORM loop continues until all four quarters for the specified year (second year) are summed.

Efficient manipulation of array elements is pivotal for optimizing COBOL programs. Both ACCESS and MODIFY operations ensure arrays reflect accurate data states, crucial for subsequent processing tasks.

Here is a coherent application of the aforementioned principles involving dynamic arrays and SEARCH statements to locate a specific element:

```
01 TARGET-NAME PIC X(30) VALUE "MARTIN LUTHER".
01 INDEX PIC 9(3) VALUE 0.
01 FOUND PIC X VALUE "N".

PERFORM VARYING INDEX FROM 1 BY 1 UNTIL INDEX > 100
    IF EMP-NAME (INDEX) = TARGET-NAME
        MOVE "Y" TO FOUND
        EXIT PERFORM
    END-IF
```

```
END-PERFORM.

IF FOUND = "Y"
    DISPLAY "Employee " TARGET-NAME " found at position "
        INDEX
ELSE
    DISPLAY "Employee " TARGET-NAME " not found."
END-IF.
```

This code dynamically searches through the EMP-NAME array for a specific name, demonstrating how to adapt array operations for real-world scenarios. Accurate and efficient use of dynamic and multi-dimensional array operations ensures optimal data management in COBOL programs.

## 7.4 Working with Multi-Dimensional Arrays

Multi-dimensional arrays in COBOL are a powerful tool for handling more complex data structures. These arrays allow for the representation of data that cannot be easily organized within a single dimension. A typical use case for multi-dimensional arrays is to represent tables or grids where data is aligned both horizontally and vertically. For instance, consider a table of sales data where rows correspond to different products and columns to different time periods (e.g., months).

In COBOL, multi-dimensional arrays are defined using multiple OCCURS clauses. The definition syntax for these arrays extends the single-dimensional structure by nesting additional OCCURS clauses within each level.

```
01 SALES-DATA.
    05 PRODUCT-LINE OCCURS 10 TIMES.
        10 MONTHLY-SALES OCCURS 12 TIMES
            PIC 9(5)V99.
```

In the example above, SALES-DATA is a two-dimensional array. PRODUCT-LINE occurs 10 times, and for each product line, there is a nested MONTHLY-SALES which occurs 12 times. Each element in MONTHLY-SALES represents the sales for one month for a specific product.

Accessing elements in a multi-dimensional array requires specifying indices for each dimension. The index of each level is provided in the order of its hierarchy. For example, to access the sales data for the third product in the sixth month, the notation would be:

```
MOVE SALES-DATA (3, 6) TO WS-SALES.
```

Here, WS-SALES is a working storage variable used to hold the value retrieved from the array.

```
01 WS-SALES PIC 9(5)V99.
```

Modifying elements in a multi-dimensional array follows a similar approach. You first need to reference the specific element using its indices and then assign a new value to it.

```
MOVE 12345.67 TO SALES-DATA (3, 6).
```

Iterating over multi-dimensional arrays can be done using nested PERFORM loops. Each loop controls one level of the hierarchy.

```
PERFORM VARYING WS-PRODUCT-INDEX FROM 1 BY
    1 UNTIL WS-PRODUCT-INDEX > 10
    PERFORM VARYING WS-MONTH-INDEX FROM 1
        BY 1 UNTIL WS-MONTH-INDEX > 12
        DISPLAY "SALES FOR PRODUCT "
            WS-PRODUCT-INDEX " AND MONTH "
            WS-MONTH-INDEX " IS "
                SALES-DATA (WS-PRODUCT-INDEX,
                    WS-MONTH-INDEX)
    END-PERFORM
END-PERFORM.
```

The code above initializes two loop index variables, WS-PRODUCT-INDEX and WS-MONTH-INDEX, for iterating through products and months, respectively. It displays the sales data for each product and each month.

A common operation with multi-dimensional arrays is to search for a specific element. COBOL's SEARCH and SEARCH ALL statements, usually associated with single-dimensional arrays, can be used within nested loops to traverse multi-dimensional arrays effectively.

```
PERFORM VARYING WS-PRODUCT-INDEX FROM 1 BY
    1 UNTIL WS-PRODUCT-INDEX > 10
```

```
        SEARCH SALES-DATA (WS-PRODUCT-INDEX)
            AT END DISPLAY "No sales data available."
            WHEN SALES-DATA (WS-PRODUCT-INDEX,
                SOME-MONTH) = 99999.99
                DISPLAY "High sales data found for product "
                    WS-PRODUCT-INDEX
        END-SEARCH
    END-PERFORM.
```

To elaborate, the SEARCH command traverses the SALES-DATA array corresponding to the specific product indexed by WS-PRODUCT-INDEX. It checks each month's sales data for a particular value, here exemplified as 99999.99.

Working with multi-dimensional arrays in COBOL allows for organized and efficient data handling, which is essential for large and complex datasets. The flexibility of defining multiple levels of arrays via multiple OCCURS clauses and accessing or modifying these elements through indexed operations makes these structures integral for sophisticated COBOL applications.

## 7.5 Table Handling and Indexing

Tables in COBOL serve as a fundamental tool for organizing and manipulating collections of data. The effective management of data within tables requires an understanding of both the data structure and the methods employed to access and modify the data efficiently. This section delves into the intricacies of table handling and indexing in COBOL, highlighting the necessary concepts and providing detailed examples to illustrate their practical application.

Tables in COBOL are defined using the OCCURS clause. This clause specifies the number of times a particular data item (or group of items) is repeated, forming a structured collection—also known as an array or table. Efficient table handling involves not only defining and initializing tables but also accessing, searching, and modifying elements within these tables using various indexing techniques.

The following example defines a single-dimensional table that stores employee names:

```
01 EMPLOYEE-TABLE.
```

```
    05 EMPLOYEE-NAME PIC X(20) OCCURS 10 TIMES.
```

In this example, the EMPLOYEE-NAME item is repeated 10 times, creating an array with 10 slots capable of holding 20-character names.

To work with these table elements, COBOL provides two primary ways to access and manipulate the data: direct subscripting and indexing.

**Direct Subscripting**

Subscripting involves specifying the occurrence number directly to access a table element. The occurrence number, or subscript, must be a positive integer and is enclosed in parentheses. Here is an example of setting values in a table using direct subscripting:

```
MOVE "JOHN SMITH" TO EMPLOYEE-NAME (1).
MOVE "SARA JONES" TO EMPLOYEE-NAME (2).
MOVE "ALICE BROWN" TO EMPLOYEE-NAME (3).
```

To retrieve values from the table, you can similarly use subscripting:

```
DISPLAY EMPLOYEE-NAME (1). *> Displays "JOHN SMITH"
DISPLAY EMPLOYEE-NAME (2). *> Displays "SARA JONES"
```

While straightforward, direct subscripting can be less efficient when dealing with larger tables or when performing complex data manipulations. This is where indexing provides significant advantages.

**Indexing**

Indexes in COBOL are special data items used explicitly for accessing elements of a table. Unlike subscripts, which are numeric and can be used in arithmetic operations, indexes are maintained internally by COBOL to point to specific occurrences within a table, providing faster access due to their direct reference capability.

To use indexing, you need to define an INDEXED BY clause when specifying the table:

```
01 EMPLOYEE-TABLE.
    05 EMPLOYEE-NAME PIC X(20) OCCURS 10 TIMES
        INDEXED BY EMP-IDX.
```

Here, EMP-IDX is an index defined to enable indexed access to the EMPLOYEE-NAME table. Operations using the SET, PERFORM, and SEARCH statements can then be utilized to manage table access more efficiently.

### Setting and Accessing Indexes

The SET statement positions an index to a specific occurrence:

```
SET EMP-IDX TO 1. *> Sets index to the first entry
SET EMP-IDX UP BY 1. *> Moves index up by one
```

You can access table elements pointed to by an index like this:

```
DISPLAY EMPLOYEE-NAME (EMP-IDX). *> Displays the
    employee name at the index position
```

### Performing Indexed Operations

To iterate over table elements, the PERFORM VARYING construct can be employed with indexes:

```
PERFORM VARYING EMP-IDX FROM 1 BY 1 UNTIL EMP-IDX
    > 10
    DISPLAY EMPLOYEE-NAME (EMP-IDX)
END-PERFORM.
```

This loop will display all employee names in the table from the first to the tenth element.

### SEARCH Statement

The SEARCH statement is used for searching through tables based on specific conditions, particularly beneficial when the table is indexed. The SEARCH statement iterates over the table until the condition is met or the end is reached.

Consider the following example of a table of employee records with a search operation:

```
01 EMPLOYEE-TABLE.
   05 EMPLOYEE-RECORD OCCURS 10 TIMES
      INDEXED BY EMP-IDX.
      10 EMPLOYEE-ID PIC 9(4).
      10 EMPLOYEE-NAME PIC X(20).

01 SEARCH-ID PIC 9(4) VALUE 1001.
01 FOUND PIC X VALUE 'N'.
...
SET EMP-IDX TO 1.
```

```
SEARCH EMPLOYEE-RECORD
    AT END
        DISPLAY "Employee not found"
    WHEN EMPLOYEE-ID (EMP-IDX) = SEARCH-ID
        MOVE 'Y' TO FOUND
        DISPLAY EMPLOYEE-NAME (EMP-IDX)
END-SEARCH.
```

In this example, the SEARCH statement navigates through EMPLOYEE-RECORD to find an entry matching SEARCH-ID. Upon finding a match, it sets FOUND to 'Y' and displays the corresponding employee name.

Proper utilization of tables and indexes in COBOL enhances the efficiency of data handling operations, allowing for rapid access and manipulation of data stored in structured formats. By leveraging the power of indexed arrays, programs can achieve optimized performance, especially in scenarios that require frequent and complex data processing.

## 7.6 Using the OCCURS Clause

The OCCURS clause in COBOL is a fundamental construct that simplifies the definition of arrays or tables by allowing the specification of repeated data items. This clause empowers programmers to create efficient and manageable data structures by defining repetitive elements within a group. We will examine the syntax, various uses of the OCCURS clause, along with practical examples and best practices for utilizing this feature in COBOL programming.

The OCCURS clause is primarily used within the DATA DIVISION and is enclosed within a group or elementary item declaration. By including the OCCURS clause, a programmer can indicate how many times a particular data item repeats consecutively. The syntax for the OCCURS clause is straightforward:

```
01 GROUP-ITEM.
    05 ELEMENTARY-ITEM PIC X(10) OCCURS 10 TIMES.
```

In this example, ELEMENTARY-ITEM is declared with a PIC (picture) clause of X(10), indicating that it holds a string of 10 characters. The OCCURS 10 TIMES clause signifies that ELEMENTARY-ITEM will repeat 10 times within GROUP-ITEM.

### Nested OCCURS

The OCCURS clause is not limited to single-level arrays. It supports nested structures, facilitating the creation of multi-dimensional arrays. For instance:

```
01 CLASS-RECORD.
    05 STUDENT-RECORD OCCURS 30 TIMES.
        10 STUDENT-ID PIC 9(5).
        10 STUDENT-NAME PIC X(20).
        10 GRADES OCCURS 6 TIMES.
            15 SUBJECT PIC X(10).
            15 SCORE PIC 99.
```

In this sample, CLASS-RECORD contains STUDENT-RECORD, which occurs 30 times, representing 30 students. Each STUDENT-RECORD comprises STUDENT-ID, STUDENT-NAME, and another nested array GRADES that occurs 6 times, representing grades in 6 subjects. Each GRADE entry contains SUBJECT and SCORE.

### Dynamic Arrays Using OCCURS DEPENDING ON

COBOL provides the capability to define dynamic arrays with the OCCURS DEPENDING ON clause, which allows an array to have a variable number of occurrences based on a control variable. This approach is particularly useful when the number of elements cannot be determined at compile time. The syntax is as follows:

```
01 STUDENT-CLASS.
    05 STUDENT-COUNT PIC 9(2).
    05 STUDENT-RECORD OCCURS 1 TO 30 TIMES
        DEPENDING ON STUDENT-COUNT.
        10 STUDENT-ID PIC 9(5).
        10 STUDENT-NAME PIC X(20).
```

In this example, STUDENT-RECORD will occur from 1 to 30 times, based on the value of STUDENT-COUNT. This dynamic array functionality allows for more flexible data handling and memory usage.

### Indexing in OCCURS Clause

Indexing is an essential feature when working with arrays. COBOL allows the use of index names with the OCCURS ... INDEXED BY clause, providing a technique for efficient element access and traversal. For example:

```
01 EMPLOYEE-DATA.
   05 EMPLOYEE-RECORD OCCURS 100 TIMES
      INDEXED BY EMP-IDX.
      10 EMPLOYEE-ID PIC 9(5).
      10 EMPLOYEE-NAME PIC X(20).
```

The INDEXED BY EMP-IDX declaration introduces an index, EMP-IDX, used to reference elements in the EMPLOYEE-RECORD array. You can use this index in COBOL's procedural code for array manipulation:

```
SET EMP-IDX TO 1.
PERFORM VARYING EMP-IDX FROM 1 BY 1 UNTIL
    EMP-IDX > 100
   DISPLAY EMPLOYEE-RECORD (EMP-IDX).
END-PERFORM.
```

This loop iterates over the EMPLOYEE-RECORD array from 1 to 100, using EMP-IDX to access and display each record.

### Practical Considerations

Several factors should be considered to maximize the OCCURS clause's effectiveness:

- Ensure the control variables defined for OCCURS DEPENDING ON have values within specified limits to avoid run-time errors.
- Use indexing and subscript notations correctly to reduce logical errors and enhance program readability.
- Initialize arrays appropriately to prevent accessing undefined data, which could lead to unpredictable program behavior.

Careful use of the OCCURS clause results in more organized and readable code, facilitating effective memory management and enhancing performance in data processing tasks.

## 7.7 Dynamic Arrays in COBOL

Dynamic arrays in COBOL provide the flexibility to allocate memory for array elements at runtime, rather than at compile time. This functionality proves particularly useful when the size of the data set is not known until the program is executed. This section delves into the mechanisms and syntax used to define and manipulate dynamic arrays in COBOL, emphasizing how they differ from static arrays.

To create a dynamic array in COBOL, we primarily use the ALLOCATE and FREE verbs, available in the COBOL language extensions. The example below illustrates a basic implementation:

```
IDENTIFICATION DIVISION.
PROGRAM-ID. DynamicArrayExample.

DATA DIVISION.
WORKING-STORAGE SECTION.
01 NumberOfElements PIC 9(4) VALUE 0.
01 ArrayPointer POINTER.
01 DynamicArray.
   05 Element OCCURS 0 TO 1000 TIMES DEPENDING ON
        NumberOfElements.
      10 ArrayElement PIC X(10).

PROCEDURE DIVISION.
   DISPLAY "Enter the number of elements: " WITH NO
        ADVANCING.
   ACCEPT NumberOfElements.

   ALLOCATE DYNAMICArray OF Element TO ArrayPointer.

   IF ArrayPointer = NULL
      DISPLAY "Memory allocation failed."
      STOP RUN
   END-IF.

* Populate the array with some data
   PERFORM VARYING i FROM 1 BY 1 UNTIL i GREATER
        THAN NumberOfElements
      MOVE "Data-" TO ArrayElement (i)
      STRING i DELIMITED BY SIZE INTO ArrayElement(i)
   END-PERFORM.

* Display the array elements
   PERFORM VARYING i FROM 1 BY 1 UNTIL i GREATER
        THAN NumberOfElements
      DISPLAY "Element " i ":" ArrayElement(i)
```

```
    END-PERFORM.

 * Free the allocated memory
    FREE DYNAMICArray OF Element FROM ArrayPointer.

    STOP RUN.

END PROGRAM DynamicArrayExample.
```

The example program above accomplishes the following tasks:

- Prompts the user to input the desired number of array elements.
- Utilizes the ALLOCATE verb to allocate memory dynamically for the array based on the user's input.
- Populates the array with sample data.
- Displays the content of the dynamic array.
- Frees the allocated memory using the FREE verb.

The guidance given in the example program is fundamental for effectively working with dynamic arrays in COBOL. Let's further dissect the specific aspects of dynamic allocation:

**Defining Dynamic Arrays** In COBOL, dynamic arrays are defined similar to traditional ones. However, the OCCURS clause is specified with a range, including OCCURS 0 TO N TIMES DEPENDING ON followed by a variable that determines the current subscript bounds at runtime.

**Memory Allocation** The ALLOCATE verb plays a crucial role in initializing dynamic arrays. This operation assigns memory space for the number of elements specified by the variable. The allocated space is referenced by a pointer (e.g., ArrayPointer). If memory allocation fails, ensuring proper error handling mechanisms, such as verifying against NULL pointers, is critical.

**Access and Manipulation** Accessing and manipulating elements in a dynamically allocated array follow the same procedures as with static arrays. The array can be populated or modified via loops or direct indexing.

**Memory Deallocation** Deallocating memory with the FREE verb is a necessary step to avoid memory leaks, particularly in environments where memory resources are limited. The FREE operation releases the memory previously allocated through the pointer, ensuring the system's resources are appropriately managed.

In COBOL environments supporting dynamic array features, leveraging such arrays enhances program efficiency and flexibility, accommodating varying data set sizes and optimizing memory usage at runtime. This makes dynamic arrays an invaluable tool for robust and adaptive COBOL programming.

## 7.8 SEARCH and SEARCH ALL Statements

The SEARCH and SEARCH ALL statements in COBOL are powerful tools used for searching within arrays or tables. These statements facilitate locating specific data elements based on given criteria and are essential for efficient data management.

SEARCH is typically used with sequential tables, where each element is examined one-by-one until the desired element is found. Conversely, SEARCH ALL is utilized for binary searching of sorted tables, leveraging the efficiency of divide-and-conquer principles to rapidly locate elements.

### SEARCH Statement

The SEARCH statement performs a serial search of the table elements. The process begins at the first element of the table and proceeds sequentially until a match is found, or the end of the table is reached. The generalized form of the SEARCH statement is as follows:

```
SEARCH identifier-1
    {AT END imperative-statement-1}
    WHEN condition-1 imperative-statement-2
    {WHEN condition-2 imperative-statement-3}...
```

Here, identifier-1 must be an INDEXED BY data item of an OCCURS clause, and the condition specifies the criteria used to find the desired element.

- AT END clause is optional and executes imperative-statement-1 if no match is found in the table.

- WHEN condition is evaluated for each element. When the condition is true, imperative-statement-2, imperative-statement-3, etc., execute sequentially.

A practical example of the SEARCH statement:

```
INDEXED BY IDX.

01 CUSTOMERS.
    05 CUSTOMER-DETAILS OCCURS 10 TIMES
        INDEXED BY IDX.
        10 CUSTOMER-ID PIC X(5).
        10 CUSTOMER-NAME PIC X(30).

    PERFORM VARYING IDX FROM 1 BY 1 UNTIL IDX > 10
        SEARCH CUSTOMER-DETAILS
            AT END DISPLAY "Customer not found."
            WHEN CUSTOMER-ID(IDX) = "C1234"
                DISPLAY "Customer found: " CUSTOMER-NAME(
                    IDX)
        END-SEARCH
    END-PERFORM.
```

This program segment searches the CUSTOMER-DETAILS table for a customer with CUSTOMER-ID “C1234” and displays the CUSTOMER-NAME.

## SEARCH ALL Statement

The SEARCH ALL statement employs a binary search algorithm, requiring the table to be sorted in ascending or descending order based on the key being searched. The syntax for SEARCH ALL is provided below:

```
SEARCH ALL identifier-1
    {AT END imperative-statement-1}
    WHEN condition-1 imperative-statement-2
    {WHEN condition-2 imperative-statement-3}...
```

Several critical constraints must be satisfied:

- The table must be sorted on the key you are searching for.

- Key must be defined with the OCCURS clause.
- SEARCH ALL results in undefined behavior if the table is not sorted.
- The WHEN condition must include comparisons using the key.

An example of SEARCH ALL:

```
PROCEDURE DIVISION.
...
SEARCH ALL CUSTOMER-DETAILS
    AT END DISPLAY "Customer not found."
    WHEN CUSTOMER-ID = "C1234"
        DISPLAY "Customer found: " CUSTOMER-NAME
END-SEARCH.
```

The key differences between SEARCH and SEARCH ALL lie in their respective applicabilities and performance characteristics. SEARCH offers versatility for unsorted tables and cases where sequential examination of elements is acceptable. In contrast, SEARCH ALL leverages binary search for significant performance gains but requires prior table sorting. Understanding the nuances of these statements ensures more effective and efficient COBOL table handling.

Beyond syntactic accuracy is the importance of maintaining a sorted condition with SEARCH ALL. Automated sorting mechanisms should precede this search for assured accuracy. Together, SEARCH and SEARCH ALL empower comprehensive data retrieval methodologies within COBOL's expansive data management framework.

## 7.9 Common Use Cases for Tables

Tables in COBOL are versatile structures used extensively in business and scientific applications to manage and manipulate collections of data efficiently. Understanding common use cases for tables can significantly improve a programmer's ability to write effective and maintainable COBOL code.

**1. Processing Payroll Data**

One of the most common enterprise applications for tables in COBOL is processing payroll data. Typically, a table can be used to store employee records, including details such as employee ID, hours worked, hourly rate, and total pay.

```
IDENTIFICATION DIVISION.
PROGRAM-ID. PayrollProcessing.

DATA DIVISION.
WORKING-STORAGE SECTION.
01 EMPLOYEE-TABLE.
    05 EMPLOYEE-RECORD OCCURS 100 TIMES.
        10 EMPLOYEE-ID PIC 9(5).
        10 HOURS-WORKED PIC 99V99.
        10 HOURLY-RATE PIC 99V99.
        10 TOTAL-PAY PIC 9(6)V99.
```

In the code above, EMPLOYEE-TABLE is used to store records for up to 100 employees. Each EMPLOYEE-RECORD contains the necessary payroll details. By iterating over this table, payroll processing such as calculating total pay can be automated.

```
PROCEDURE DIVISION.
    PERFORM VARYING EMP-INDEX FROM 1 BY 1
         UNTIL EMP-INDEX > 100
        COMPUTE TOTAL-PAY OF EMPLOYEE-RECORD
              (EMP-INDEX)
             = HOURS-WORKED OF
                  EMPLOYEE-RECORD (EMP-INDEX) *
               HOURLY-RATE OF EMPLOYEE-RECORD (
                    EMP-INDEX)
    END-PERFORM.
    STOP RUN.
```

**2. Handling Inventory Data**

Managing inventory data is another common use case for tables in COBOL, particularly in retail and manufacturing sectors. Tables can track items, their quantities, and costs, simplifying the management of large inventories.

```
IDENTIFICATION DIVISION.
PROGRAM-ID. InventoryManagement.

DATA DIVISION.
WORKING-STORAGE SECTION.
```

```
01 INVENTORY-TABLE.
    05 ITEM-RECORD OCCURS 1000 TIMES.
        10 ITEM-ID PIC X(10).
        10 ITEM-NAME PIC X(30).
        10 ITEM-QUANTITY PIC 9(4).
        10 ITEM-COST PIC 9(6)V99.
```

Here, INVENTORY-TABLE is used to maintain an inventory of up to 1000 items. The structure stores unique identifiers, item names, quantities, and costs.

To update the quantity of an item after a sale:

```
PROCEDURE DIVISION.
    PERFORM VARYING ITEM-INDEX FROM 1 BY 1
         UNTIL ITEM-INDEX > 1000
        IF ITEM-ID OF ITEM-RECORD (ITEM-INDEX) = '
            A12345'
            SUBTRACT 1 FROM ITEM-QUANTITY OF
                ITEM-RECORD (ITEM-INDEX)
        END-IF
    END-PERFORM.
    STOP RUN.
```

**3. Customer Data Management**

Tables are also effective for managing customer data in customer relationship management (CRM) systems. They can store information such as customer IDs, names, contact details, and transaction histories.

```
IDENTIFICATION DIVISION.
PROGRAM-ID. CustomerDataManagement.

DATA DIVISION.
WORKING-STORAGE SECTION.
01 CUSTOMER-TABLE.
    05 CUSTOMER-RECORD OCCURS 500 TIMES.
        10 CUSTOMER-ID PIC 9(5).
        10 CUSTOMER-NAME PIC X(30).
        10 CUSTOMER-PHONE PIC X(12).
        10 LAST-TRANSACTION PIC 9(8).
```

CUSTOMER-TABLE equips a system to manage up to 500 customer

records effectively. One can easily search, update, and process customer transactions.

To find a customer by ID and update their phone number:

```
PROCEDURE DIVISION.
    PERFORM VARYING CUST-INDEX FROM 1 BY 1
        UNTIL CUST-INDEX > 500
        IF CUSTOMER-ID OF CUSTOMER-RECORD (
            CUST-INDEX) = 12345
            MOVE '555-1234' TO CUSTOMER-PHONE OF
                CUSTOMER-RECORD (CUST-INDEX)
        END-IF
    END-PERFORM.
    STOP RUN.
```

**4. Managing Sales Data**

For businesses focusing on sales data such as order tracking and revenue analysis, tables in COBOL can provide organized and efficient ways to handle such information.

```
IDENTIFICATION DIVISION.
PROGRAM-ID. SalesManagement.

DATA DIVISION.
WORKING-STORAGE SECTION.
01 SALES-TABLE.
    05 SALES-RECORD OCCURS 2000 TIMES.
        10 ORDER-ID PIC 9(10).
        10 CUSTOMER-ID PIC 9(5).
        10 ORDER-AMOUNT PIC 9(7)V99.
        10 ORDER-DATE PIC 9(8).
```

By organizing sales data into a table, businesses can efficiently process orders, track customer purchases, and analyze revenue patterns.

To calculate total sales for a particular day:

```
PROCEDURE DIVISION.
WORKING-STORAGE SECTION.
01 TOTAL-SALES PIC 9(7)V99 VALUE 0.

    PERFORM VARYING SALES-INDEX FROM 1 BY 1
        UNTIL SALES-INDEX > 2000
```

```
        IF ORDER-DATE OF SALES-RECORD (
            SALES-INDEX)= 20230101
            ADD ORDER-AMOUNT OF SALES-RECORD (
                SALES-INDEX) TO TOTAL-SALES
        END-IF
    END-PERFORM.
    DISPLAY 'TOTAL SALES FOR 20230101: '
        TOTAL-SALES.
    STOP RUN.
```

**5. Managing Product Catalogs**

In e-commerce platforms, tables can be used to manage product catalogs, including product IDs, descriptions, prices, and stock status.

```
IDENTIFICATION DIVISION.
PROGRAM-ID. ProductCatalogManagement.

DATA DIVISION.
WORKING-STORAGE SECTION.
01 PRODUCT-TABLE.
    05 PRODUCT-RECORD OCCURS 1000 TIMES.
        10 PRODUCT-ID PIC X(10).
        10 PRODUCT-DESCRIPTION PIC X(50).
        10 PRODUCT-PRICE PIC 9(5)V99.
```

This implementation helps to manage various product attributes effectively. Updates to the catalog can be efficiently performed using table manipulation.

To update the price of a product:

```
PROCEDURE DIVISION.
    PERFORM VARYING PROD-INDEX FROM 1 BY 1
        UNTIL PROD-INDEX > 1000
        IF PRODUCT-ID OF PRODUCT-RECORD (
            PROD-INDEX) = 'PRD0001'
            MOVE 99.99 TO PRODUCT-PRICE OF
                PRODUCT-RECORD (PROD-INDEX)
        END-IF
    END-PERFORM.
    STOP RUN.
```

These common use cases demonstrate the utility and flexibility of tables in COBOL for handling various types of data. Tables are indispensable for efficiently managing and manipulating collections of structured data, making them a fundamental concept in COBOL programming.

# Chapter 8

# File Handling in COBOL

**File handling is a fundamental aspect of COBOL for managing data storage and retrieval. This chapter explores the different types of files—sequential, indexed, and relative—and details how to define files within a COBOL program. It covers file operations such as OPEN, CLOSE, READ, WRITE, REWRITE, and DELETE, along with error handling specific to file operations, equipping programmers with the skills needed to perform essential data management tasks efficiently.**

## 8.1 Introduction to File Handling

File handling in COBOL is a crucial aspect of managing persistent data. Files are utilized to store and retrieve data, enabling COBOL programs to maintain and process information over time. Understanding how files operate and how to efficiently implement file handling commands is essential for a proficient COBOL programmer.

In COBOL, files are classified into three main types: sequential, indexed, and relative. Each type serves different use cases and has unique characteristics in terms of data access and organization. Files are defined in the File-Control and File Section of the COBOL program, and specific operations are applied to them using COBOL's comprehensive set of file-handling statements.

To start with, file handling involves understanding the basic file operations, which include:

- OPEN: Prepares the file for processing by the program.
- CLOSE: Ends the use of the file in the program.
- READ: Retrieves data from the file.
- WRITE: Adds data to the file.
- REWRITE: Updates existing data within the file.
- DELETE: Removes data from the file.

**File-Control and File Section:** The File-Control paragraph within the Environment Division indicates how files are connected to specific storage mediums. It includes essential information, such as file names and the mode of file access. The following COBOL code snippet demonstrates a typical File-Control entry:

```
ENVIRONMENT DIVISION.
INPUT-OUTPUT SECTION.
FILE-CONTROL.
    SELECT EMPLOYEE-FILE
        ASSIGN TO 'employee.dat'
        ORGANIZATION IS SEQUENTIAL.
```

Here, SELECT associates the logical file name, EMPLOYEE-FILE, with the physical storage, 'employee.dat', and specifies that the file uses sequential organization.

The File Section in the Data Division defines the structure of the files. For the EMPLOYEE-FILE defined in the File-Control paragraph, the following definition in the File Section specifies its structure:

```
DATA DIVISION.
FILE SECTION.
FD EMPLOYEE-FILE.
01 EMPLOYEE-RECORD.
    05 EMP-ID PIC X(6).
    05 EMP-NAME PIC X(20).
    05 EMP-SALARY PIC 9(5)V99.
```

This definition declares the file descriptor (FD) for the EMPLOYEE-FILE and describes the layout of the EMPLOYEE-RECORD, including the employee ID, name, and salary fields.

**Basic File Operations:**

- OPEN: The OPEN statement is used to make files available for processing. The specific mode, such as INPUT, OUTPUT, I-O, or EXTEND, determines the type of operations allowed. For instance:

  ```
  OPEN INPUT EMPLOYEE-FILE.
  ```

  This statement opens the EMPLOYEE-FILE for reading.

- CLOSE: The CLOSE statement is used to close files after processing:

  ```
  CLOSE EMPLOYEE-FILE.
  ```

  This closes EMPLOYEE-FILE, ensuring that all buffers are flushed, and the file is properly finalized.

- READ: The READ statement retrieves records from the file. When reading a sequential file, the next record in order is read:

  ```
  READ EMPLOYEE-FILE INTO
      EMPLOYEE-RECORD
      AT END
          DISPLAY 'End of file reached.'
  END-READ.
  ```

  The above example reads a record into EMPLOYEE-RECORD and handles the AT END condition, which occurs when no more records are available.

- WRITE: The WRITE statement adds records to the file:

  ```
  MOVE '123456' TO EMP-ID.
  MOVE 'John Doe' TO EMP-NAME.
  MOVE 50000 TO EMP-SALARY.
  WRITE EMPLOYEE-RECORD.
  ```

  This sequence of statements assigns values to the EMPLOYEE-RECORD fields and writes the record to the file.

- REWRITE: The REWRITE statement updates existing records. It is used after positioning the file to the desired record, typically with a READ:

```
MOVE '123456' TO EMP-ID.
MOVE 'John Smith' TO EMP-NAME.
READ EMPLOYEE-FILE INTO
    EMPLOYEE-RECORD KEY IS EMP-ID.
IF EMP-ID = '123456'
   MOVE 55000 TO EMP-SALARY
   REWRITE EMPLOYEE-RECORD.
```

This updates the salary of an employee with EMP-ID '123456'.

- DELETE: The DELETE statement is used to remove records in indexed and relative records, but not in sequential files:

```
DELETE EMPLOYEE-RECORD.
```

This statement removes the specified record from the file.

The appropriate use of these file operations allows COBOL applications to effectively manage data within various file structures, providing both flexibility and precision in data handling tasks. Understanding and properly implementing these operations forms the foundation of proficient COBOL file handling.

## 8.2 Types of Files in COBOL

COBOL facilitates the handling of several types of files, each suited for specific data storage and retrieval scenarios. The primary file types in COBOL are sequential files, indexed files, and relative files. Each of these has distinct characteristics and uses, which are discussed in detail below.

**Sequential Files:** Sequential files store data records in a linear order, one after another, akin to lines in a book. This format is often used for simple data processing tasks where all records must be read or written in sequence. The records in a sequential file are organized logically, as the name suggests, one record directly after the other. This type of file is simple to implement but lacks flexibility—searching for a specific record requires reading through all preceding records.

Defining a sequential file in COBOL involves specifying the ORGANIZATION IS SEQUENTIAL clause within the FILE-CONTROL paragraph of the ENVIRONMENT DIVISION. Below is an example of how to define a sequential file:

```
SELECT INFILE ASSIGN TO "input.dat"
    ORGANIZATION IS SEQUENTIAL.
```

Typical operations performed on sequential files include reading all records sequentially starting from the first record, writing new records at the end of the file, and rarely rewriting records due to inefficiency in locating specific records.

**Indexed Files:** Indexed files feature a more complex structure where each record is associated with a unique key that allows for rapid access and manipulation. These files are organized with an index that maintains the keys in sorted order, facilitating faster search operations. Indexed files are advantageous for applications needing random access to records based on key values. Defining an indexed file requires the ORGANIZATION IS INDEXED clause and specifying the RECORD KEY IS clause.

Example of defining an indexed file:

```
SELECT INDFILE ASSIGN TO "index.dat"
    ORGANIZATION IS INDEXED
    RECORD KEY IS IN-REC-KEY.
```

With indexed files, operations such as reading, writing, rewriting, and deleting can be performed efficiently using the record key. COBOL ensures that the index remains consistent and updated with each operation, providing reliable and quick data access.

**Relative Files:** Relative files utilize a relative record number (RRN) to access records. The RRN serves as a direct address to a record's position within the file, allowing for rapid access similar to indexed files but typically implemented with less overhead. This type of file organization is suitable for fixed-size records where the position of a record can be easily computed.

To define a relative file in COBOL, use the ORGANIZATION IS RELATIVE clause along with RELATIVE KEY IS:

```
SELECT RELFILE ASSIGN TO "relative.dat"
    ORGANIZATION IS RELATIVE
    RELATIVE KEY IS REL-REC-NO.
```

Relative files support efficient access patterns, including direct reads and writes using the relative record number, making them ideal for scenarios where record order is non-sequential and direct access is critical.

Each file type in COBOL is tailored to different data processing needs. Understanding the operational and structural differences between sequential, indexed, and relative files is crucial for selecting the appropriate file organization for specific applications. The following sections will delve into the implementation of various file operations, providing practical examples and detailed use cases.

## 8.3 Defining Files in COBOL Programs

In COBOL, defining files within a program is a critical step to ensure proper file handling and to facilitate various file operations like reading, writing, and updating data. Files are defined using specific entries in the Data Division of a COBOL program, primarily within the FILE-CONTROL and FILE SECTION entries. These definitions must align with the type of file being accessed and the operations that need to be performed.

To define a file in a COBOL program, three main elements must be considered: the file's logical name, the physical storage location, and the record structure. Below is a detailed explanation of each component and associated syntax, followed by an example that contextualizes these concepts.

- **Logical Name**: The logical name is a symbolic name used within the program to refer to a file. This is specified in the SELECT clause of the FILE-CONTROL paragraph.
- **Physical Storage**: The physical storage identification includes the external name and the environment where the file resides, specified using the ASSIGN clause.
- **Record Structure**: This specifies the format and structure of the records within the file and is defined in the FILE SECTION of the Data Division.

```
DATA DIVISION.
FILE-CONTROL.
```

```
SELECT file-logical-name ASSIGN TO external-file-name
    [ORGANIZATION IS {SEQUENTIAL | INDEXED |
        RELATIVE}]
    [ACCESS MODE IS {SEQUENTIAL | RANDOM |
        DYNAMIC}]
    [FILE STATUS IS data-name-1 data-name-2].
```

**Explanation of the Components:**

- SELECT clause: Associates the logical file name used in the program with the external file name.
- ASSIGN clause: Specifies the name by which the operating system or UNIX environment knows the file.
- ORGANIZATION clause (Optional): Defines the organization of the file, which can be SEQUENTIAL, INDEXED, or RELATIVE.
- ACCESS MODE clause (Optional): Defines how the records within the file are to be accessed – either SEQUENTIAL, RANDOM, or DYNAMIC.
- FILE STATUS clause (Optional): Provides variables for capturing the status code after file operations for error handling purposes.

```
DATA DIVISION.
FILE SECTION.

FD file-logical-name
   LABEL RECORDS ARE STANDARD
   BLOCK CONTAINS 0 RECORDS
   RECORD CONTAINS n CHARACTERS
   DATA RECORD IS record-name.

01 record-name.
   05 field-1 PIC X(n).
   05 field-2 PIC 9(n).
   ...
```

**Explanation of the Components:**

- FD (File Description) entry: Begins the description of the file. file-logical-name should match the logical name specified in the FILE-CONTROL entry.

- LABEL RECORDS clause: Indicates whether there are any label records for the file. STANDARD would be the typical choice.
- BLOCK CONTAINS clause: Specifies the blocking factor, e.g., how many records make up a block.
- RECORD CONTAINS clause: Indicates the size (in characters) of each record within the file.
- DATA RECORD clause: Names the record. This should be consistent with how the records will be referred to in the PROCEDURE DIVISION.
- 01 Level number: Contains the actual record structure. It is a high-level definition that holds various fields within the record.
- Field definitions: These define the actual fields within the record, each with its own Picture (PIC) clause, which specifies the data type and length.

**Example: Defining a Sequential File for Customer Records**

Below is a practical example of how to define a sequential file named CUSTOMER-FILE, where each record contains customer details such as CUSTOMER-ID, CUSTOMER-NAME, and CUSTOMER-AGE.

```
DATA DIVISION.
FILE-CONTROL.
    SELECT CUSTOMER-FILE ASSIGN TO 'customer.dat'
        ORGANIZATION IS SEQUENTIAL
        ACCESS MODE IS SEQUENTIAL
        FILE STATUS IS file-status.

FILE SECTION.
FD CUSTOMER-FILE
   LABEL RECORDS ARE STANDARD
   RECORD CONTAINS 100 CHARACTERS
   DATA RECORD IS CUSTOMER-RECORD.

01 CUSTOMER-RECORD.
   05 CUSTOMER-ID PIC X(10).
   05 CUSTOMER-NAME PIC X(50).
   05 CUSTOMER-AGE PIC 9(2).
END DATA DIVISION.
```

**Breakdown of Example Code:**

- The SELECT clause links CUSTOMER-FILE logical name with the physical file name 'customer.dat'.
- The file is managed as a sequential file, defined through the ORGANIZATION IS SEQUENTIAL clause.
- The ACCESS MODE IS SEQUENTIAL indicates that records will be accessed in a sequential manner.
- The FILE STATUS IS file-status clause is included to capture the file status after each operation.
- In the FILE SECTION, FD CUSTOMER-FILE defines the file details, including the record structure.
- 01 CUSTOMER-RECORD outlines the fields involved, detailing the Picture clause for each field. CUSTOMER-ID is a 10-character field, CUSTOMER-NAME is a 50-character field, and CUSTOMER-AGE is a 2-digit numeric field.

When constructing the definitions, it is essential to ensure that the logical and physical names, alongside the record structures, are coherent and align with the expected data format. This allows the program to correctly interpret and manipulate the file, facilitating seamless file operations across various use case scenarios.

## 8.4 File-Control and File Section

The FILE-CONTROL paragraph and the FILE SECTION are vital components of a COBOL program, designed to manage and specify the characteristics of files to be used. Understanding their structure and function is essential for effective file handling in COBOL.

FILE-CONTROL **Paragraph**

The FILE-CONTROL paragraph resides in the ENVIRONMENT DIVISION of a COBOL program. It is used to associate a logical file name (also known as a file variable) with the actual physical file on the storage device. Here is a sample FILE-CONTROL paragraph:

```
ENVIRONMENT DIVISION.
INPUT-OUTPUT SECTION.
```

```
FILE-CONTROL.
    SELECT input-file ASSIGN TO "input.dat"
        ORGANIZATION IS SEQUENTIAL.
    SELECT output-file ASSIGN TO "output.dat"
        ORGANIZATION IS SEQUENTIAL.
```

In this example, input-file and output-file are logical names used within the COBOL program. They are associated with the physical files "input.dat" and "output.dat" respectively. The ORGANIZATION clause specifies the type of file, indicating that both files are sequential.

SELECT **Clause**

The SELECT clause assigns a logical file name to a specific physical file. The syntax is as follows:

```
SELECT file-name ASSIGN TO external-file-name
    ORGANIZATION IS [SEQUENTIAL | INDEXED | RELATIVE];
```

- file-name: Represents the logical name of the file within the COBOL program. - external-file-name: Specifies the name of the actual external file. - ORGANIZATION IS: Indicates the file organization type, which can be SEQUENTIAL, INDEXED, or RELATIVE.

ASSIGN **Clause**

The ASSIGN clause maps the logical file name to its corresponding physical file name or path. It supports different methods depending on the system in use. For instance:

- Literal Strings: Directly specifies the file name (e.g., "input.dat").
- Environment Variables: Utilizes environmental variables to specify the file.

### Advanced Options in File-Control

Other advanced options can be specified in the FILE-CONTROL paragraph to control file access and locking. Examples include the ACCESS MODE and FILE STATUS clauses:

```
SELECT indexed-file ASSIGN TO "datafile.dat"
    ORGANIZATION IS INDEXED
    ACCESS MODE IS RANDOM
    FILE STATUS IS file-status-variable.
```

- ACCESS MODE: Determines how the file will be accessed (e.g., SEQUENTIAL, RANDOM, DYNAMIC). - FILE STATUS: Specifies a PIC X(02) variable to hold the status code for file operations.

FILE SECTION

The FILE SECTION is located in the DATA DIVISION of a COBOL program. It declares the structure and organization of records within a file. Here is an example:

```
DATA DIVISION.
FILE SECTION.
FD input-file.
01 input-record.
    05 customer-id PIC X(05).
    05 customer-name PIC X(30).
    05 customer-balance PIC 9(7)V99.

FD output-file.
01 output-record.
    05 customer-id-out PIC X(05).
    05 customer-name-out PIC X(30).
    05 customer-balance-out PIC 9(7)V99.
```

In this example: - The FD (File Description) entry, FD input-file, corresponds to the logical name defined in the FILE-CONTROL paragraph. - The 01 level entry, input-record, defines the record structure for the input file. - The 05 level entries define the fields within the record, specifying their data types and lengths.

### FD **and** SD **Entries**

The FD (File Description) and SD (Sort Description) entries describe the structure of files and sort files, respectively. The syntax for these entries is:

```
FD file-name
    [RECORD CONTAINS integer-1 TO integer-2 CHARACTERS]
    [BLOCK CONTAINS integer-3 TO integer-4 RECORDS]
    [RECORDING MODE IS {F | V}]
    [DATA RECORD IS record-name-1 [, ...]].
```

- RECORD CONTAINS: Specifies the minimum and maximum record size. - BLOCK CONTAINS: Defines the number of records per block. - RECORDING MODE: Indicates the recording mode (F for fixed, V for variable). - DATA RECORD: Lists the record names associated with the file.

WORKING-STORAGE **Section**

Associated variables for file status and error handling are typically declared in the WORKING-STORAGE section. For example:

```
WORKING-STORAGE SECTION.
01 file-status-variable PIC X(02).
01 error-message PIC X(50).
```

These variables track the status of file operations and store error messages, facilitating robust error handling and debugging.

Combined, the FILE-CONTROL and FILE SECTION paragraphs serve as the backbone for file manipulation in COBOL, providing the necessary infrastructure to manage file interactions effectively and efficiently. Understanding the nuanced flexibility of these sections enhances a programmer's ability to handle complex data processing tasks.

## 8.5 File Operations: OPEN, CLOSE

File operations in COBOL are executed through specific commands, primarily OPEN and CLOSE. These operations are essential for accessing and managing the status of files within a COBOL program. Understanding their syntax and usage is crucial for robust file handling.

**OPEN Command**

The OPEN command is used to prepare a file for reading, writing, or updating. The mode in which a file is opened determines the permissible operations. The most common modes are INPUT, OUTPUT, I-O, and EXTEND. Each mode serves a distinct purpose:

- INPUT: Opens the file for reading. When a file is opened in INPUT mode, data can be read from the file but cannot be altered. The file must exist before opening.

- OUTPUT: Opens the file for writing. If the file exists, it is truncated to zero length. If it does not exist, it is created. Data can be written to the file, but reading is not allowed.

- I-O: Opens the file for both reading and writing. This mode requires the file to exist and permits both modification and retrieval of data.
- EXTEND: Opens the file for writing, appending data to the end of the file. If the file does not exist, it is created.

The syntax for the OPEN statement is straightforward:

```
OPEN {INPUT | OUTPUT | I-O | EXTEND} file-name-1 [,
    file-name-2]...
```

Example:

```
OPEN INPUT CUSTOMER-FILE.
OPEN OUTPUT NEW-RECORDS-FILE.
OPEN I-O TRANSACTION-FILE.
OPEN EXTEND LOG-FILE.
```

It is important to note that multiple files can be opened with a single OPEN statement by separating the file names with commas.

Error handling during the OPEN operation can be managed using the FILE STATUS clause in the FD (File Description) entry. The file status code should be checked after an OPEN operation to ensure successful execution.

**CLOSE Command**

The CLOSE command terminates the association of a file with its storage medium, ensuring that all buffers are flushed and that the integrity of the data is maintained. It is a good practice to close files when they are no longer needed, which releases system resources and maintains data integrity.

The syntax for the CLOSE statement is:

```
CLOSE file-name-1 [, file-name-2]...
```

Example:

```
CLOSE CUSTOMER-FILE.
CLOSE NEW-RECORDS-FILE.
```

Like the OPEN statement, multiple files can be closed in a single CLOSE statement by separating the file names with commas.

It is essential to check the file status after attempting to close a file to ensure that the operation was completed successfully. Here is an example showing the OPEN and CLOSE operations including file status checking:

```
DATA DIVISION.
FILE SECTION.
FD CUSTOMER-FILE.
01 CUSTOMER-RECORD.
    05 CUST-NAME PIC X(30).
    05 CUST-ID PIC 9(5).

WORKING-STORAGE SECTION.
01 FILE-STATUS-CODE PIC XX.

PROCEDURE DIVISION.
OPEN-FILES.
    OPEN INPUT CUSTOMER-FILE.
    IF FILE-STATUS-CODE NOT = '00'
        DISPLAY "Error opening CUSTOMER-FILE."
        STOP RUN
    END-IF.

CLOSE-FILES.
    CLOSE CUSTOMER-FILE.
    IF FILE-STATUS-CODE NOT = '00'
        DISPLAY "Error closing CUSTOMER-FILE."
        STOP RUN
    END-IF.
    STOP RUN.
```

In this example, after each OPEN and CLOSE operation, the file status code is checked. If any error occurs, an appropriate message is displayed, and the program terminates.

Properly managing the OPEN and CLOSE operations ensures efficient file handling and data integrity within a COBOL program.

## 8.6 Reading Data from Files

Reading data from files in COBOL involves a set of precise steps designed to ensure data integrity and proper file handling. COBOL provides robust file handling capabilities, and understanding these operations is critical for achieving efficient data management.

The fundamental syntax for reading a record from a file involves the READ statement. Here is the typical pattern for reading data from a sequential file:

```
READ file-name NEXT RECORD INTO identifier
   AT END imperative-statement
   NOT AT END imperative-statement
   END-READ
```

In this syntax:

- file-name is the name of the file declared in the FILE SECTION.
- NEXT RECORD directs COBOL to read the next logical record in the file.
- identifier is the target location where the data will be stored.
- AT END specifies the actions to take when the end of the file is reached.
- NOT AT END specifies the actions to take when there are more records to read.

A typical COBOL program snippet for reading data from a sequential file might look like the following:

```
IDENTIFICATION DIVISION.
PROGRAM-ID. ReadData.
DATA DIVISION.
FILE SECTION.
FD INPUT-FILE
      LABEL RECORDS ARE STANDARD
      BLOCK CONTAINS 0 RECORDS
      RECORD CONTAINS 80 CHARACTERS.
01 INPUT-RECORD.
      05 FIELD-1 PIC X(10).
```

```
    05 FIELD-2 PIC X(30).
    05 FIELD-3 PIC X(40).

WORKING-STORAGE SECTION.
01 WS-EOF PIC X VALUE 'N'.

PROCEDURE DIVISION.
OPEN INPUT INPUT-FILE.
PERFORM UNTIL WS-EOF = 'Y'
    READ INPUT-FILE INTO INPUT-RECORD
        AT END
            MOVE 'Y' TO WS-EOF
        NOT AT END
            PERFORM PROCESS-RECORD
    END-READ
END-PERFORM.
CLOSE INPUT-FILE.
STOP RUN.

PROCESS-RECORD.
    DISPLAY 'Field 1: ' FIELD-1
    DISPLAY 'Field 2: ' FIELD-2
    DISPLAY 'Field 3: ' FIELD-3.
```

Key considerations in reading data from files include:

- Always checking the AT END condition to handle the end-of-file scenario gracefully.
- Ensuring that the file is properly opened before attempting to read from it.
- Using structured programs, often involving PERFORM loops, to manage reading operations effectively.

When reading indexed files, the process involves slightly more complexity due to the need to handle keys. The read operation can be directed by specifying a KEY clause to locate a particular record directly.

```
READ file-name RECORD [INTO identifier]
  [KEY IS data-name]
  AT END imperative-statement
  NOT AT END imperative-statement
```

```
END-READ
```

For example, the following code demonstrates reading specific records from an indexed file based on the primary key:

```
IDENTIFICATION DIVISION.
PROGRAM-ID. ReadIndexedFile.
DATA DIVISION.
FILE SECTION.
FD INDEXED-FILE
    LABEL RECORDS ARE STANDARD
    RECORD CONTAINS 80 CHARACTERS
    BLOCK CONTAINS 0 RECORDS.
01 INDEXED-RECORD.
    05 FIELD-1 PIC X(10).
    05 FIELD-2 PIC X(30).
    05 FIELD-3 PIC X(40).

WORKING-STORAGE SECTION.
01 WS-KEY PIC X(10) VALUE ' '.

PROCEDURE DIVISION.
OPEN I-O INDEXED-FILE.
MOVE '1234567890' TO WS-KEY.
READ INDEXED-FILE RECORD KEY IS WS-KEY
   AT END
      DISPLAY 'Record not found.'
   NOT AT END
      DISPLAY 'Record found.'
      DISPLAY 'Field 1: ' FIELD-1
      DISPLAY 'Field 2: ' FIELD-2
      DISPLAY 'Field 3: ' FIELD-3.
CLOSE INDEXED-FILE.
STOP RUN.
```

In the case of relative files, it is essential to correctly manage and locate records based on their relative record number (RRN). The syntax involves specifying the RELATIVE KEY clause which indicates the target record's location.

```
READ file-name RECORD [INTO identifier]
    RELATIVE KEY IS data-name
    AT END imperative-statement
```

```
    NOT AT END imperative-statement
    END-READ
```

An example of reading a relative file is given below:

```
IDENTIFICATION DIVISION.
PROGRAM-ID. ReadRelativeFile.
DATA DIVISION.
FILE SECTION.
FD RELATIVE-FILE
    LABEL RECORDS ARE STANDARD
    RECORD CONTAINS 80 CHARACTERS
    BLOCK CONTAINS 0 RECORDS.
01 RELATIVE-RECORD.
    05 FIELD-1 PIC X(10).
    05 FIELD-2 PIC X(30).
    05 FIELD-3 PIC X(40).

WORKING-STORAGE SECTION.
01 WS-REC-NUM PIC 9(4) VALUE 1.

PROCEDURE DIVISION.
OPEN I-O RELATIVE-FILE.
READ RELATIVE-FILE RECORD RELATIVE KEY IS
     WS-REC-NUM
   AT END
      DISPLAY 'Record not found.'
   NOT AT END
      DISPLAY 'Record found.'
      DISPLAY 'Field 1: ' FIELD-1
      DISPLAY 'Field 2: ' FIELD-2
      DISPLAY 'Field 3: ' FIELD-3.
CLOSE RELATIVE-FILE.
STOP RUN.
```

When performing read operations in COBOL, it is crucial to handle possible exceptions and implement error-checking mechanisms. Depending on the file organization type, the read syntax and considerations differ slightly but maintaining a structured approach and thorough error checks is universally beneficial across all types of files.

Understanding and implementing these read operations correctly enable robust data processing capabilities, essential for any COBOL-based application that depends on accurate data retrieval.

## 8.7 Writing Data to Files

Writing data to files in COBOL involves several critical steps, starting from file definition to the actual data writing process. This section provides an exhaustive guide on how to write data to files, considering different file types and ensuring accurate data storage.

Firstly, the SELECT and FD (File Description) entries must be properly defined. These entries link logical file names used in the COBOL program to physical files on the system.

```
SELECT EMPLOYEE-FILE ASSIGN TO 'EMPLOYEE.DAT'
    ORGANIZATION IS SEQUENTIAL
    ACCESS MODE IS SEQUENTIAL.

FD EMPLOYEE-FILE
    LABEL RECORDS ARE STANDARD
    BLOCK CONTAINS 0 RECORDS
    RECORD CONTAINS 80 CHARACTERS
    DATA RECORD IS EMPLOYEE-RECORD.

01 EMPLOYEE-RECORD.
    05 EMP-ID PIC X(10).
    05 EMP-NAME PIC X(30).
    05 EMP-DEPT PIC X(20).
    05 EMP-SALARY PIC 9(8)V99.
```

After defining the file structure, it is essential to open the file in OUTPUT mode. This mode is specifically designed for writing data to a file.

```
OPEN OUTPUT EMPLOYEE-FILE.
```

In the subsequent steps, data is moved into the data record defined in the FD section. Using the MOVE statement, the program populates the fields in the EMPLOYEE-RECORD.

```
MOVE "1234567890" TO EMP-ID.
MOVE "John Doe" TO EMP-NAME.
MOVE "Accounting" TO EMP-DEPT.
MOVE 55000.75 TO EMP-SALARY.
```

Once the data fields are populated, the WRITE statement is used to write the EMPLOYEE-RECORD to the file.

```
WRITE EMPLOYEE-RECORD.
```

To write multiple records, the program typically uses a loop structure. For instance, if data is read from a user input or another file, the program would iterate over each record, perform the MOVE operations, and write each record sequentially.

```
PERFORM UNTIL EOF-FLAG = 'Y'
    MOVE "1234567890" TO EMP-ID
    MOVE "John Doe" TO EMP-NAME
    MOVE "Accounting" TO EMP-DEPT
    MOVE 55000.75 TO EMP-SALARY
    WRITE EMPLOYEE-RECORD
END-PERFORM.
```

Upon completion of writing operations, it is crucial to close the file to ensure all buffers are flushed and data is correctly saved.

```
CLOSE EMPLOYEE-FILE.
```

For indexed or relative files, writing operations must account for additional parameters such as the key values. Indexed files require a similar approach but incorporate key fields in the record format:

```
SELECT EMPLOYEE-FILE ASSIGN TO 'EMPLOYEE.IDX'
    ORGANIZATION IS INDEXED
    ACCESS MODE IS DYNAMIC
    RECORD KEY IS EMP-ID.

FD EMPLOYEE-FILE
    LABEL RECORDS ARE STANDARD
    BLOCK CONTAINS 0 RECORDS
    RECORD CONTAINS 80 CHARACTERS
    DATA RECORD IS EMPLOYEE-RECORD.

01 EMPLOYEE-RECORD.
    05 EMP-ID PIC X(10).
    05 EMP-NAME PIC X(30).
    05 EMP-DEPT PIC X(20).
    05 EMP-SALARY PIC 9(8)V99.
```

With indexed files, writing data involves ensuring the unique EMP-ID:

```
OPEN OUTPUT EMPLOYEE-FILE.

MOVE "1234567890" TO EMP-ID.
MOVE "John Doe" TO EMP-NAME.
MOVE "Accounting" TO EMP-DEPT.
MOVE 55000.75 TO EMP-SALARY.

WRITE EMPLOYEE-RECORD.
CLOSE EMPLOYEE-FILE.
```

Handling error conditions is pivotal when writing records. The INVALID KEY phrase is used for indexed files to catch scenarios where a record cannot be written.

```
WRITE EMPLOYEE-RECORD INVALID KEY
    DISPLAY "ERROR: Unable to write record"
END-WRITE.
```

Similarly, for relative files, the file layout and write operations include a relative key:

```
SELECT EMPLOYEE-FILE ASSIGN TO 'EMPLOYEE.REL'
    ORGANIZATION IS RELATIVE
    ACCESS MODE IS SEQUENTIAL
    RELATIVE KEY IS EMP-REL-KEY.

FD EMPLOYEE-FILE
    LABEL RECORDS ARE STANDARD
    BLOCK CONTAINS 0 RECORDS
    RECORD CONTAINS 80 CHARACTERS
    DATA RECORD IS EMPLOYEE-RECORD.

01 EMPLOYEE-RECORD.
    05 EMP-REL-KEY PIC 9(4).
    05 EMP-ID PIC X(10).
    05 EMP-NAME PIC X(30).
    05 EMP-DEPT PIC X(20).
    05 EMP-SALARY PIC 9(8)V99.
```

For relative files, it is essential to set the EMP-REL-KEY before writing the record:

```
OPEN I-O EMPLOYEE-FILE.

MOVE 1001 TO EMP-REL-KEY.
MOVE "1234567890" TO EMP-ID.
MOVE "John Doe" TO EMP-NAME.
MOVE "Accounting" TO EMP-DEPT.
MOVE 55000.75 TO EMP-SALARY.

WRITE EMPLOYEE-RECORD INVALID KEY
    DISPLAY "ERROR: Unable to write record"
END-WRITE.

CLOSE EMPLOYEE-FILE.
```

Efficient and correct data writing to various file types in COBOL necessitates understanding these specific instructions and implementing them meticulously within the program's logic.

## 8.8 Rewriting and Deleting Records

In the context of COBOL programming, the ability to modify existing records and delete records within a file is essential for maintaining and updating data sets effectively. This section precisely covers the usage of the REWRITE and DELETE statements, with examples to illustrate how these operations are implemented.

The REWRITE statement is utilized to update the content of a record that has been previously read. This operation requires an active file and works differently depending on the type of file being handled—sequential, indexed, or relative.

**Rewriting Records in Sequential Files**

For sequential files, the REWRITE operation is straightforward. The file must be opened in the I-O mode, as both reading and writing operations are needed. When using REWRITE, the following steps are generally followed:

- Open the sequential file in I-O mode.
- Read the record that needs to be updated.

- Modify the fields of the record as needed.
- Use the REWRITE statement to update the record in the file.
- Close the file to save the changes.

Here is an example program that updates a record in a sequential file:

```
IDENTIFICATION DIVISION.
PROGRAM-ID. UpdateSequentialRecord.

ENVIRONMENT DIVISION.
INPUT-OUTPUT SECTION.
FILE-CONTROL.
    SELECT SeqFile ASSIGN TO 'SequentialFile.dat'
        ORGANIZATION IS SEQUENTIAL.

DATA DIVISION.
FILE SECTION.
FD SeqFile.
01 SeqRecord.
        05 SeqID PIC 9(4).
        05 SeqName PIC X(20).

WORKING-STORAGE SECTION.
01 UpdateID PIC 9(4) VALUE 1001.
01 NewName PIC X(20) VALUE 'UpdatedName'.

PROCEDURE DIVISION.
BEGIN.
    OPEN I-O SeqFile.
    READ SeqFile INTO SeqRecord
        AT END DISPLAY 'End of File.'
        NOT AT END
            IF SeqID = UpdateID THEN
                MOVE NewName TO SeqName
                REWRITE SeqRecord
            END-IF.
    CLOSE SeqFile.
    STOP RUN.
```

### Rewriting Records in Indexed Files

For indexed files, the record to be rewritten should be identified using its key. The steps are similar but require the key to locate the precise record:

- Open the indexed file in I-O mode.
- Read the record using its unique key.
- Modify the necessary fields.
- Use the REWRITE statement to update the record.
- Close the file to save the changes.

Example for updating a record in an indexed file:

```
IDENTIFICATION DIVISION.
PROGRAM-ID. UpdateIndexedRecord.

ENVIRONMENT DIVISION.
INPUT-OUTPUT SECTION.
FILE-CONTROL.
    SELECT IdxFile ASSIGN TO 'IndexedFile.dat'
        ORGANIZATION IS INDEXED
        ACCESS MODE IS DYNAMIC
        RECORD KEY IS IdxID.

DATA DIVISION.
FILE SECTION.
FD IdxFile.
01 IdxRecord.
        05 IdxID PIC 9(4).
        05 IdxName PIC X(20).

WORKING-STORAGE SECTION.
01 UpdateID PIC 9(4) VALUE 1002.
01 NewName PIC X(20) VALUE 'UpdatedIndexName'.

PROCEDURE DIVISION.
BEGIN.
    OPEN I-O IdxFile.
    READ IdxFile KEY IS UpdateID INTO IdxRecord
        INVALID KEY DISPLAY 'Record not found.'
        NOT INVALID KEY
            MOVE NewName TO IdxName
```

```
        REWRITE IdxRecord.
    CLOSE IdxFile.
    STOP RUN.
```

### Rewriting Records in Relative Files

Relative files use the relative record number (RRN) to locate and rewrite records. The process is similar but involves specifying the RRN during file operations:

- Open the relative file in I-O mode.
- Read the record using its RRN.
- Modify the desired fields.
- Use the REWRITE statement with the corresponding RRN.
- Close the file to save the changes.

Example of updating a record in a relative file:

```
IDENTIFICATION DIVISION.
PROGRAM-ID. UpdateRelativeRecord.

ENVIRONMENT DIVISION.
INPUT-OUTPUT SECTION.
FILE-CONTROL.
    SELECT RelFile ASSIGN TO 'RelativeFile.dat'
        ORGANIZATION IS RELATIVE
        ACCESS MODE IS DYNAMIC
        RELATIVE KEY IS RelKey.

DATA DIVISION.
FILE SECTION.
FD RelFile.
01 RelRecord.
        05 RelKey PIC 9(4).
        05 RelName PIC X(20).

WORKING-STORAGE SECTION.
01 UpdateKey PIC 9(4) VALUE 1003.
01 NewName PIC X(20) VALUE 'UpdatedRelRecord'.
```

```
PROCEDURE DIVISION.
BEGIN.
    OPEN I-O RelFile.
    READ RelFile RELATIVE KEY UpdateKey INTO RelRecord
        INVALID KEY DISPLAY 'Record not found.'
        NOT INVALID KEY
            MOVE NewName TO RelName
            REWRITE RelRecord.
    CLOSE RelFile.
    STOP RUN.
```

### Deleting Records

Deleting records can only be performed on indexed and relative files. Sequential files do not support direct deletion of records. Instead, for sequential files, a new file is usually created with the required records copied, excluding the one to be deleted.

For indexed files, use the DELETE statement to remove the record identified by its key:

- Open the indexed file in I-O mode.
- Read the record using the key.
- Use the DELETE statement to remove the record.
- Close the file to save the changes.

Example of deleting a record in an indexed file:

```
IDENTIFICATION DIVISION.
PROGRAM-ID. DeleteIndexedRecord.

ENVIRONMENT DIVISION.
INPUT-OUTPUT SECTION.
FILE-CONTROL.
    SELECT IdxFile ASSIGN TO 'IndexedFile.dat'
        ORGANIZATION IS INDEXED
        ACCESS MODE IS DYNAMIC
        RECORD KEY IS IdxID.

DATA DIVISION.
FILE SECTION.
```

```
FD IdxFile.
01 IdxRecord.
      05 IdxID PIC 9(4).
      05 IdxName PIC X(20).

WORKING-STORAGE SECTION.
01 DeleteID PIC 9(4) VALUE 1002.

PROCEDURE DIVISION.
BEGIN.
   OPEN I-O IdxFile.
   READ IdxFile KEY IS DeleteID INTO IdxRecord
      INVALID KEY DISPLAY 'Record not found.'
      NOT INVALID KEY
         DELETE IdxRecord.
   CLOSE IdxFile.
   STOP RUN.
```

Relative files also use the DELETE statement, but records are identified by their RRN:

- Open the relative file in I-O mode.
- Read the record using its RRN.
- Use the DELETE statement with the corresponding RRN.
- Close the file to save the changes.

Example of deleting a record in a relative file:

```
IDENTIFICATION DIVISION.
PROGRAM-ID. DeleteRelativeRecord.

ENVIRONMENT DIVISION.
INPUT-OUTPUT SECTION.
FILE-CONTROL.
   SELECT RelFile ASSIGN TO 'RelativeFile.dat'
      ORGANIZATION IS RELATIVE
      ACCESS MODE IS DYNAMIC
      RELATIVE KEY IS RelKey.

DATA DIVISION.
```

```
FILE SECTION.
FD RelFile.
01 RelRecord.
    05 RelKey PIC 9(4).
    05 RelName PIC X(20).

WORKING-STORAGE SECTION.
01 DeleteKey PIC 9(4) VALUE 1003.

PROCEDURE DIVISION.
BEGIN.
  OPEN I-O RelFile.
  READ RelFile RELATIVE KEY DeleteKey INTO RelRecord
    INVALID KEY DISPLAY 'Record not found.'
    NOT INVALID KEY
      DELETE RelRecord.
  CLOSE RelFile.
  STOP RUN.
```

Through the REWRITE and DELETE operations, COBOL programmers can effectively maintain and update data in various types of files, ensuring that records are accurately modified or removed as needed. Proper usage of these statements is critical for precise file manipulation in any COBOL application.

## 8.9 Handling Sequential Files

In COBOL, sequential files are a basic construct for data storage where records are stored in a specified order, typically based on the sequence of their addition. These files are especially useful for processes where the access pattern is strictly sequential read or write operations. This section provides a precise understanding of how to handle sequential files, leveraging the capabilities that COBOL offers.

To begin with, a sequential file in COBOL is defined in the FILE-CONTROL paragraph and the FILE SECTION of the DATA DIVISION. The SELECT statement associated with the file in the FILE-CONTROL assigns a logical name to the file and specifies its mode of access.

```
SELECT optional-file-name ASSIGN TO file-name
```

```
[ORGANIZATION IS SEQUENTIAL]
[ACCESS MODE IS SEQUENTIAL]
[FILE STATUS IS file-status-variable].
```

Here, optional-file-name is a logical name within the COBOL program, and file-name represents the actual external file name. The ORGANIZATION IS SEQUENTIAL clause specifies that the file organization is sequential. The ACCESS MODE IS SEQUENTIAL clause, while optional, underscores that the access mode for this file is sequential. The FILE STATUS clause is used for storing the status code returned by file operations.

Once the file is properly defined in the FILE-CONTROL paragraph, the next step is to describe its internal record structure in the FILE SECTION of the DATA DIVISION.

```
FILE SECTION.
FD optional-file-name.
01 record-description.
    05 field-1 PIC X(10).
    05 field-2 PIC 9(5).
    05 field-3 PIC X(20).
```

Here, record-description represents the layout of a single record within the file. Each 05-level item defines a field within the record using PICTURE clauses that specify the data format.

Handling operations on sequential files typically involves opening the file in the required mode using the OPEN statement, performing read or write operations, and then closing the file using the CLOSE statement.

**Opening the Sequential File:**

```
OPEN INPUT optional-file-name.
```

The OPEN statement here opens the file for reading. If you wish to write to the file, you can use:

```
OPEN OUTPUT optional-file-name.
```

In cases where the program needs to append data to an existing sequential file, the file must be opened in EXTEND mode:

```
OPEN EXTEND optional-file-name.
```

**Reading from a Sequential File:**

Reading records from a sequential file is performed using the READ statement. The syntax is as follows:

```
READ optional-file-name
    INTO read-buffer
    AT END MOVE 'YES' TO eof-flag
END-READ.
```

read-buffer is the data area where the read record is stored. The AT END clause specifies the action to be taken when the end of the file is reached. The eof-flag can be any variable indicating the end-of-file condition.

**Writing to a Sequential File:**

Writing records to a sequential file uses the WRITE statement:

```
WRITE record-description FROM write-buffer.
```

write-buffer contains the data to be written into the file. Each WRITE statement appends a new record at the end of the file if the file is opened in OUTPUT or EXTEND mode.

**Closing the Sequential File:**

To close the file after operations are complete, use the CLOSE statement:

```
CLOSE optional-file-name.
```

Ensuring the file is properly closed is critical to preserving data integrity and avoiding file corruption.

**Example of Sequential File Handling in a COBOL Program:**

The following example demonstrates a complete scenario of handling a sequential file in COBOL, encompassing file definition, opening, reading, writing, and closing operations.

```
IDENTIFICATION DIVISION.
PROGRAM-ID. SequentialExample.

ENVIRONMENT DIVISION.
INPUT-OUTPUT SECTION.
FILE-CONTROL.
    SELECT seq-file ASSIGN TO 'SEQFILE.DAT'
```

```
        ORGANIZATION IS SEQUENTIAL
        FILE STATUS IS file-status.

DATA DIVISION.
FILE SECTION.
FD seq-file.
01 seq-record.
    05 name PIC X(20).
    05 age PIC 99.
    05 address PIC X(50).

WORKING-STORAGE SECTION.
77 file-status PIC XX.
77 eof-flag PIC X VALUE 'NO'.
77 read-buffer PIC X(72).

PROCEDURE DIVISION.
    OPEN INPUT seq-file
    IF file-status NOT = '00'
        DISPLAY 'Error opening file'
        STOP RUN
    END-IF.

    PERFORM UNTIL eof-flag = 'YES'
        READ seq-file INTO read-buffer
        AT END MOVE 'YES' TO eof-flag
        END-READ
        IF eof-flag = 'NO'
            DISPLAY read-buffer
        END-IF
    END-PERFORM.

    CLOSE seq-file.
    STOP RUN.
```

In this example, the SELECT statement assigns the external file SEQ-FILE.DAT to the logical file name seq-file. The FILE SECTION defines the structure of each record within the sequential file. The program opens the file in INPUT mode, reads each record into a buffer, displays its contents, and closes the file upon completion. The file-status variable is used for error handling to detect any issues during the file operations.

Understanding how to manipulate sequential files in COBOL is fundamental. Each operation contributes to efficient and accurate data management, essential in many computational tasks.

## 8.10 Handling Indexed Files

Indexed files in COBOL provide a powerful and efficient way to access records through keys, allowing for prompt retrieval and modification operations. These files consist of data records and an index that maintains the relation between key values and the corresponding record locations in the file. Indexed files are particularly suited for applications that require frequent updates and quick access to specific records.

Creating and defining indexed files in COBOL necessitates a comprehensive understanding of the FILE-CONTROL and DATA DIVISION aspects. The following sub-sections systematically explore the steps and syntax involved in handling indexed files.

**Defining Indexed Files:**

To define an indexed file in a COBOL program, specify the SELECT statement within the FILE-CONTROL paragraph of the INPUT-OUTPUT SECTION. It is followed by defining the file description in the FILE SECTION of the DATA DIVISION. The syntax for defining an indexed file is as follows:

```
SELECT optional-file-name ASSIGN TO 'index-file-name'
    ORGANIZATION IS INDEXED
    ACCESS MODE IS RANDOM [| SEQUENTIAL | DYNAMIC]
    RECORD KEY IS key-name
    [ALTERNATE RECORD KEY IS alt-key-name [WITH
        DUPLICATES]].
```

Here, ASSIGN TO specifies the physical filename, ORGANIZATION IS INDEXED designates the file type, ACCESS MODE defines how records are accessed, and RECORD KEY IS determines the primary key for indexing. ALTERNATE RECORD KEY can introduce secondary keys with optional duplicates.

**Defining the File in the FILE SECTION:**

After the SELECT statement, define the file structure in the FILE SECTION:

```
FD indexed-file-name
    [RECORD CONTAINS number CHARACTERS]
    [BLOCK CONTAINS number RECORDS]
    LABEL RECORDS ARE STANDARD
    DATA RECORD IS data-record-name.

01 data-record-name.
    05 key-name PIC X(len).
    [05 alt-key-name PIC X(len).]
    05 other-fields.
```

Ensure that key-name and alt-key-name match the definitions set in the FILE-CONTROL paragraph.

**Opening Indexed Files:**

Use the OPEN statement to open an indexed file before performing any I/O operations. Indexed files can be opened in various modes:

```
OPEN INPUT indexed-file-name.
OPEN OUTPUT indexed-file-name.
OPEN I-O indexed-file-name.
```

The INPUT mode is for reading, OUTPUT is for writing, and I-O allows reading and updating.

**Reading Records from Indexed Files:**

Indexed files allow access to records either sequentially or randomly using keys. To read a record:

```
READ indexed-file-name
    NEXT RECORD
    INTO data-record-name
    [KEY IS key-name]
    [INVALID KEY imperative-statement]
    [NOT INVALID KEY imperative-statement].
```

For random access, specify the key in the KEY IS clause.

**Writing Records to Indexed Files:**

To add a new record to an indexed file, use the WRITE statement:

```
WRITE data-record-name
    [FROM source-record-name]
```

```
    [INVALID KEY imperative-statement]
    [NOT INVALID KEY imperative-statement].
```

Each record must have a unique key unless specified otherwise via alternate keys permitting duplicates.

**Rewriting and Deleting Records:**

The REWRITE statement updates an existing record:

```
REWRITE data-record-name
    [FROM source-record-name]
    [INVALID KEY imperative-statement]
    [NOT INVALID KEY imperative-statement].
```

To remove a record:

```
DELETE indexed-file-name
    [KEY IS key-name]
    [INVALID KEY imperative-statement]
    [NOT INVALID KEY imperative-statement].
```

**Error Handling:**

Handling errors in indexed file operations ensures robustness. The INVALID KEY clause traps errors when the specified key does not exist or duplicates occur. The format allows tailoring responses to these errors effectively.

```
INVALID KEY DISPLAY 'Error: Record not found or key duplication.'.
```

Understanding the intrinsic structure and operations of indexed files in COBOL equips the programmer to leverage the efficiency of indexed access, leading to optimized data handling setups.

## 8.11 Handling Relative Files

Relative files in COBOL provide a method for direct access to records based on their relative record number (RRN). A relative record number specifies the position of a record within the file, enabling efficient access to data. This section delves into the specifics of defining, accessing, and manipulating relative files within COBOL programs.

**Defining a Relative File:**

To define a relative file, we specify the ORGANIZATION IS RELATIVE clause in the FD (File Description) entry and relate it to the SELECT statement in the FILE-CONTROL paragraph. Consider the following example which defines a relative file:

```
FD RELATIVE-FILE
   LABEL RECORDS ARE STANDARD
   BLOCK CONTAINS 0 RECORDS
   RECORDING MODE IS F
   RECORD CONTAINS 80 CHARACTERS.

01 RELATIVE-RECORD.
   05 REL-RECORD-KEY PIC 9(4).
   05 REL-RECORD-DATA PIC X(76).

SELECT RELATIVE-FILE
   ASSIGN TO 'RELFILE.DAT'
   ORGANIZATION IS RELATIVE.
```

The FD entry defines the structure of the relative file RELATIVE-FILE, describing its record format and size. The 01 level number defines RELATIVE-RECORD, which consists of a key field (REL-RECORD-KEY) and a data portion (REL-RECORD-DATA).

**Opening a Relative File:**

As with other file types, the relative file must be opened before performing any operations. The file can be opened in various modes: INPUT, OUTPUT, I-O, or EXTEND. The following example demonstrates opening the file for I-O (input-output) operations:

```
OPEN I-O RELATIVE-FILE.
IF FILE-STATUS IS NOT '00'
   DISPLAY 'ERROR: Unable to open relative file.'
   STOP RUN.
```

Here, the OPEN statement opens RELATIVE-FILE for reading and writing. Error checking with FILE-STATUS ensures the program handles any issues encountered during the open operation.

**Reading a Record:**

Reading from a relative file depends on the RRN. We use the READ statement with the INVALID KEY clause to handle errors when the specified RRN does not exist:

```
MOVE 10 TO REL-RECORD-KEY.
READ RELATIVE-FILE
    RECORD KEY IS REL-RECORD-KEY
    INVALID KEY
        DISPLAY 'ERROR: Record not found.'.
```

The READ statement retrieves the record with REL-RECORD-KEY equal to 10. If the record is not found, the INVALID KEY clause executes, and an error message displays.

**Writing a Record:**

Writing to a relative file involves specifying the RRN where the new record should be placed. The WRITE statement includes an INVALID KEY clause for error handling if the record already exists:

```
MOVE 15 TO REL-RECORD-KEY.
MOVE 'Sample Data for Record 15' TO REL-RECORD-DATA.
WRITE RELATIVE-RECORD
    INVALID KEY
        DISPLAY 'ERROR: Record already exists.'.
```

The WRITE statement attempts to place a record at position 15. If a record is already present at that position, an error message displays.

**Rewriting a Record:**

Rewriting a record in a relative file updates the specified RRN without changing its position. The REWRITE statement is utilized as follows:

```
MOVE 15 TO REL-RECORD-KEY.
MOVE 'Updated Data for Record 15' TO REL-RECORD-DATA.
REWRITE RELATIVE-RECORD
    INVALID KEY
        DISPLAY 'ERROR: Record not found.'.
```

Here, the REWRITE statement updates the data of the record at RRN 15. If the record does not exist, the INVALID KEY clause handles the error.

**Deleting a Record:**

Deleting a record from a relative file marks the RRN as available. The DELETE statement removes the record at the specified RRN:

```
MOVE 20 TO REL-RECORD-KEY.
```

```
DELETE RELATIVE-RECORD
    RECORD KEY IS REL-RECORD-KEY
    INVALID KEY
        DISPLAY 'ERROR: Record not found.'.
```

The DELETE statement removes the record at RRN 20. If the record does not exist, the INVALID KEY clause manages the error appropriately.

**Error Handling:**

Handling errors in relative file operations is crucial. The FILE STATUS clause provides a mechanism to check the status after each file operation. Use comprehensive error codes for detailed error information:

```
FILE-CONTROL.
    SELECT RELATIVE-FILE
        ASSIGN TO 'RELFILE.DAT'
        ORGANIZATION IS RELATIVE
        FILE STATUS IS WS-STATUS.

WORKING-STORAGE SECTION.
01 WS-STATUS PIC XX.

PROCEDURE DIVISION.
OPEN I-O RELATIVE-FILE.
IF WS-STATUS NOT = '00'
    DISPLAY 'ERROR: File open status: ' WS-STATUS.
```

Here, WS-STATUS captures the file status, allowing the program to display meaningful messages corresponding to different error codes.

This detailed overview of handling relative files in COBOL underscores the efficient data manipulation capabilities associated with relative record numbers. Understanding these operations is fundamental for proficient data management in COBOL applications.

## 8.12 Error Handling in File Operations

Error handling is a critical aspect of file operations in COBOL programs. Proper error management ensures that the program can handle unexpected situations effectively, maintaining data integrity and enabling robust operations. In COBOL, file status codes provide a mechanism for detecting and responding to errors during file handling tasks.

**File Status Codes**: File status codes are returned by the operating system to indicate the success or failure of a file operation. Each code corresponds to a specific condition, which aids in diagnosing the nature of the error. The FILE STATUS clause in the SELECT statement is used to specify a two-character data item that will store the file status code.

```
SELECT FILE-NAME ASSIGN TO 'filename'
    ORGANIZATION IS SEQUENTIAL
    ACCESS MODE IS SEQUENTIAL
    FILE STATUS IS WS-FILE-STATUS.
```

Here, WS-FILE-STATUS is a working-storage field that captures the status code after each file operation.

**Common File Status Codes**:

- "00" - Successful operation.
- "02" - Indexed files: Duplicate key, Random or Dynamic access; re-read.
- "10" - End of file (EOF).
- "21" - Key sequence error (Indexed files).
- "22" - Duplicate key (Indexed files).
- "23" - Record not found (Indexed and Relative files).
- "30" - Permanent error (disk I/O error).
- "41" - File already open.
- "42" - File not open.
- "43" - File not found.

**Checking and Handling Errors in COBOL Programs**: To handle errors efficiently, it is essential to check the file status code after each file operation. The IF statement is typically used for this purpose.

Consider the following example where we open a file and check for errors:

```
OPEN INPUT FILE-NAME
IF WS-FILE-STATUS NOT = "00"
   DISPLAY "Error on opening file: " WS-FILE-STATUS
   GO TO CLOSE-FILE.

...

CLOSE FILE-NAME.

CLOSE-FILE.
.
```

**Detailed Example of Error Handling in File Operations**: To illustrate comprehensive error handling, we examine a scenario involving reading from a file. Below is a COBOL program segment demonstrating this:

```
WORKING-STORAGE SECTION.
01 WS-FILE-STATUS PIC XX.
01 WS-FILE-RECORD PIC X(80).
PROCEDURE DIVISION.

INIT-PROCEDURE.
OPEN INPUT FILE-NAME
IF WS-FILE-STATUS NOT = "00"
   DISPLAY "Error opening file: " WS-FILE-STATUS
   PERFORM ERROR-ROUTINE
   GO TO END-PROGRAM.

READ-FILE.
READ FILE-NAME INTO WS-FILE-RECORD
   AT END
      MOVE "10" TO WS-FILE-STATUS
   NOT AT END
      IF WS-FILE-STATUS NOT = "00"
         DISPLAY "Read error: " WS-FILE-STATUS
         PERFORM ERROR-ROUTINE
         GO TO CLOSE-FILE.

PROCESS-FILE.
DISPLAY "Record: " WS-FILE-RECORD
```

```
PERFORM READ-FILE.

CLOSE-FILE.
CLOSE FILE-NAME
IF WS-FILE-STATUS NOT = "00"
   DISPLAY "Error closing file: " WS-FILE-STATUS
   PERFORM ERROR-ROUTINE.

ERROR-ROUTINE.
DISPLAY "Handling error with status: " WS-FILE-STATUS.

END-PROGRAM.
STOP RUN.
```

In this example, the file is initially opened for reading, and any error during this operation is detected and displayed. The READ statement is subject to error checking as well—if an error occurs, the ERROR-ROUTINE is performed. The file is also checked for potential errors upon closing. These checks ensure the program handles erroneous situations reliably.

**Advanced Error Handling Using Condition Names**: Condition names can make error handling more readable and maintainable. Condition names are user-defined names associated with specific values of a data item.

```
77 WS-FILE-STATUS PIC XX.
   88 FILE-OK VALUE "00".
   88 FILE-EOF VALUE "10".
   88 FILE-ERROR VALUE "30" THRU "49".

SELECT FILE-ASSIGN TO 'filename'
       ORGANIZATION IS SEQUENTIAL
       FILE STATUS IS WS-FILE-STATUS.
```

In the procedure division:

```
OPEN INPUT FILE-NAME
IF NOT FILE-OK
   DISPLAY "Error on opening file"
   PERFORM ERROR-ROUTINE
```

```
    GO TO END-PROGRAM.
```

Using condition names simplifies the understanding of the program's logic, distinguishing the types of status codes effectively.

Attention to error handling is paramount in COBOL file operations to ensure data safety and program reliability. End-program error management encapsulates multiple scenarios to safeguard against unforeseen conditions, preserving the integrity of COBOL applications.

# Chapter 9

# Subroutines and Functions

**Subroutines and functions facilitate modular programming in COBOL, promoting code reuse and maintainability. This chapter covers creating subroutines, using the CALL statement, and passing parameters. It delves into the use of COPY and INCLUDE statements, writing intrinsic functions, and calling subroutines from other programs. Additionally, it addresses error handling within subroutines and best practices for developing modular and maintainable COBOL applications.**

## 9.1 Introduction to Subroutines and Functions

Subroutines and functions are fundamental components in COBOL programming that support the concept of modularity. Modularity allows developers to break down complex programs into smaller, manageable units which can then be developed, tested, and maintained independently. By promoting code reuse and maintainability, subroutines and functions facilitate the development of robust and efficient COBOL applications.

A subroutine in COBOL is a block of code that performs a specific task and can be invoked from different points within a program or even from different programs. Subroutines are commonly used to encapsulate repetitive tasks, such as arithmetic operations, data validation, or input/output processing, thereby enhancing the readability and maintainability of the code.

Functions in COBOL are similar to subroutines but fundamentally different in purpose and usage. While a subroutine may not necessarily return a value, functions are specifically designed to compute and return a result based on the input parameters. COBOL provides intrinsic functions, which are built-in functions that perform various operations such as mathematical calculations, string manipulations, and date and time computations.

Subroutines and functions not only make the program structure more logical and organized but also enable collaboration among multiple developers. This modular approach allows different team members to work on different subroutines or functions concurrently, thus improving development efficiency.

CALL Statement:

```
CALL Subroutine-Name USING Parameter-List
```

The basic syntax of the CALL statement includes the keyword CALL, followed by the name of the subroutine and an optional list of parameters that are passed to the subroutine. The parameters can be literals, variables, or data structures. The USING clause specifies the arguments that are being sent to the subroutine.

Example of calling a subroutine:

```
CALL 'COMPUTE-TAX' USING TAX-AMOUNT,
    GROSS-INCOME
```

In this example, the subroutine COMPUTE-TAX is invoked with TAX-AMOUNT and GROSS-INCOME as parameters. Subroutines can be either internal, defined within the same program, or external, residing in separate program files. The linkage section of the subroutine definition is where parameters passed by the calling program are declared.

To elucidate further:

```
IDENTIFICATION DIVISION.
PROGRAM-ID. COMPUTE.
DATA DIVISION.
WORKING-STORAGE SECTION.
```

```
01 TAX-AMOUNT PIC 9(5)V99 VALUE 0.
01 GROSS-INCOME PIC 9(7)V99 VALUE 0.
...
PROCEDURE DIVISION.
CALL 'COMPUTE-TAX' USING TAX-AMOUNT,
    GROSS-INCOME.
...
END PROGRAM COMPUTE.
```

The subroutine COMPUTE-TAX would be defined as follows:

```
IDENTIFICATION DIVISION.
PROGRAM-ID. COMPUTE-TAX.
DATA DIVISION.
LINKAGE SECTION.
01 TAX-AMOUNT PIC 9(5)V99.
01 GROSS-INCOME PIC 9(7)V99.
PROCEDURE DIVISION USING TAX-AMOUNT,
    GROSS-INCOME.
...
END PROGRAM COMPUTE-TAX.
```

The use of the LINKAGE SECTION enables the subroutine to access and manipulate the parameters passed by the calling program. The PROCEDURE DIVISION USING clause explicitly specifies the parameters to be used by the subroutine.

Functions work similarly but are defined within the context of the program and invoked in expressions. COBOL provides a rich set of intrinsic functions which can be used for operations like mathematical calculations, formatting strings, and handling dates. The syntax for calling an intrinsic function is straightforward:

```
COMPUTE RESULT = FUNCTION-NAME (argument-1,
    argument-2, ...)
```

For example:

```
COMPUTE TOTAL-AMOUNT = FUNCTION SUM (PRICE-1,
    PRICE-2, PRICE-3)
```

In this case, the intrinsic function SUM is used to calculate the total amount of prices.

By understanding and effectively utilizing subroutines and functions, developers can significantly enhance the modularity, efficiency, and maintainability of their COBOL programs. The forthcoming sections will delve into detailed methodologies for creating subroutines, exploring the CALL statement and its variants, and leveraging intrinsic functions in COBOL.

## 9.2 Creating Subroutines

In COBOL, subroutines are an essential tool for creating modular, reusable, and maintainable code. A subroutine in COBOL is commonly defined using the PROGRAM-ID and PROCEDURE DIVISION statements. Subroutines can either be internal, defined within the same program, or external, defined in separate programs and called using the CALL statement.

When creating a subroutine, you need to define a separate program that includes the following key sections:

- IDENTIFICATION DIVISION
- ENVIRONMENT DIVISION
- DATA DIVISION
- PROCEDURE DIVISION

The IDENTIFICATION DIVISION contains the PROGRAM-ID, which is the identifier for the subroutine. The ENVIRONMENT DIVISION specifies the environment in which the program runs. The DATA DIVISION is where you declare the variables and constants used by the subroutine. Finally, the PROCEDURE DIVISION contains the executable COBOL code.

```
IDENTIFICATION DIVISION.
PROGRAM-ID. CALCULATE-INTEREST.
AUTHOR. JOHN DOE.

ENVIRONMENT DIVISION.

DATA DIVISION.
WORKING-STORAGE SECTION.
01 PRINCIPAL-AMOUNT PIC 9(9)V99.
```

```
01 INTEREST-RATE PIC 9V99.
01 TIME-PERIOD PIC 9(2).
01 INTEREST-AMOUNT PIC 9(9)V99.

PROCEDURE DIVISION USING PRINCIPAL-AMOUNT
     INTEREST-RATE TIME-PERIOD.
BEGIN-CALCULATION.
    COMPUTE INTEREST-AMOUNT = PRINCIPAL-AMOUNT *
        INTEREST-RATE * TIME-PERIOD / 100.
    DISPLAY 'INTEREST AMOUNT: ' INTEREST-AMOUNT.
    STOP RUN.
```

In this example, the subroutine CALCULATE-INTEREST calculates the interest amount based on the principal amount, interest rate, and time period provided as parameters.

A subroutine is invoked from another COBOL program using the CALL statement. Ensure the parameters passed match the data types declared in the subroutine. COBOL uses positional parameter passing, which means the order in which parameters are listed in the CALL statement must match the order of parameters in the subroutine's PROCEDURE DIVISION heading.

The calling program might look like this:

```
IDENTIFICATION DIVISION.
PROGRAM-ID. MAIN-PROGRAM.
AUTHOR. JOHN DOE.

ENVIRONMENT DIVISION.

DATA DIVISION.
WORKING-STORAGE SECTION.
01 PRINCIPAL-AMOUNT PIC 9(9)V99 VALUE 1000.00.
01 INTEREST-RATE PIC 9V99 VALUE 5.0.
01 TIME-PERIOD PIC 9(2) VALUE 2.

PROCEDURE DIVISION.
CALL-CALCULATE-INTEREST.
    CALL 'CALCULATE-INTEREST' USING
        PRINCIPAL-AMOUNT INTEREST-RATE TIME-PERIOD.
    STOP RUN.
```

In the calling program, the CALL statement specifies the name of the subroutine (in quotes) followed by the USING clause to pass the parameters.

To ensure proper modular programming, document each subroutine with clear comments describing its purpose, arguments, and expected behavior. This practice aids in maintainability and code readability. Debugging and testing individual subroutines separately before integrating them into larger systems can prevent many issues.

Error handling within a subroutine requires careful attention. Any potential errors should be managed within the subroutine itself to avoid unexpected behaviors in the calling program. Use the RETURN-CODE special register to communicate error conditions. For instance, setting RETURN-CODE to zero indicates success, while non-zero values indicate different types of errors that the calling program can interpret and handle accordingly.

Implementing modular subroutines ensures that code is clean, comprehensible, and more accessible to maintain or extend in the future. Modular programming also promotes reusability, allowing subroutines to be employed in various parts of the program or even different programs.

## 9.3 CALL Statement and Its Variants

The CALL statement in COBOL is a pivotal construct for invoking subroutines, enabling modular and reusable code. Understanding its syntax and its variants is essential for effective COBOL programming. This section elucidates the CALL statement's various forms, parameter passing methods, and conditional calls.

```
CALL subroutine-name USING parameter-1 [, parameter-2, ...].
```

The basic syntax of the CALL statement consists of the CALL keyword followed by the subroutine-name and the USING clause, which is used to pass parameters. The subroutine-name is usually defined in the LINKAGE SECTION of the called subroutine and prefixed with SUB- to indicate it is a subprogram.

Consider the following example where a subroutine SUB-MYROUTINE is called from a main program:

```
CALL 'SUB-MYROUTINE' USING var1, var2.
```

### Static and Dynamic CALLs

There are two primary types of CALL statements in COBOL: static and dynamic. Understanding the differences is crucial for deciding which type to implement, as they offer different performance and flexibility characteristics.

**Static CALL:**

In a static call, the subroutine name is specified directly in the program and remains unchanged at runtime. Static calls are resolved at compile time, resulting in better performance but less flexibility.

```
CALL 'MYROUTINE' USING var1, var2.
```

Here, 'MYROUTINE' is statically linked, meaning the called subroutine must be available at compile time.

**Dynamic CALL:**

Dynamic calls, on the other hand, use a variable to specify the subroutine name, allowing the actual subroutine to be determined at runtime. This approach is more flexible but might incur a performance overhead due to the runtime resolution.

```
CALL subroutine-name-variable USING var1, var2.
```

In the above format, subroutine-name-variable is defined as a PIC X(n) variable that holds the name of the subroutine to be called.

**Example:**

```
01 routine-name PIC X(20).
MOVE 'SUB-MYROUTINE' TO routine-name.
CALL routine-name USING var1, var2.
```

By defining the subroutine name in a variable, the program can call different subroutines based on runtime conditions.

### Conditional CALL

Utilizing conditional calls can add robustness to the program, allowing for error handling and conditional execution. This can be handled using the ON EXCEPTION phrase.

```
CALL 'SUB-MYROUTINE' USING var1, var2
     ON EXCEPTION
          DISPLAY 'Error calling subroutine'
```

```
    NOT ON EXCEPTION
        DISPLAY 'Subroutine called successfully'.
```

In this example, the ON EXCEPTION clause captures any issues encountered during the CALL statement execution, enabling appropriate error handling.

### Passing Parameters by Reference and by Content

Parameters can be passed to subroutines by reference or by content.

**By Reference:**

When parameters are passed by reference, the called subroutine operates directly on the argument's address in the calling program's memory space. This is the default method of passing parameters and is suitable for large data structures.

```
CALL 'SUB-MYROUTINE' USING BY REFERENCE var1, var2.
```

**By Content:**

Passing parameters by content means the called subroutine works with a copy of the argument, ensuring the original data in the calling program remains unaltered. This approach is useful when the subroutine does not need to modify the passed data.

```
CALL 'SUB-MYROUTINE' USING BY CONTENT var1, var2.
```

### Example: Complete CALL Statement

Let's solidify these concepts with a complete example. Consider a main program calling a subroutine that calculates the sum of two numbers.

Main Program:

```
IDENTIFICATION DIVISION.
PROGRAM-ID. MAINPROG.
DATA DIVISION.
WORKING-STORAGE SECTION.
01 number1 PIC 9(4).
01 number2 PIC 9(4).
01 sum PIC 9(4).

PROCEDURE DIVISION.
    MOVE 10 TO number1.
    MOVE 20 TO number2.
```

```
    CALL 'SUB-CALCSUM' USING number1, number2, sum
        ON EXCEPTION
            DISPLAY 'Error calling subroutine.'
        NOT ON EXCEPTION
            DISPLAY 'Sum is: ' sum.
    STOP RUN.
```

Subroutine:

```
IDENTIFICATION DIVISION.
PROGRAM-ID. SUB-CALCSUM.
DATA DIVISION.
LINKAGE SECTION.
01 lnk-number1 PIC 9(4).
01 lnk-number2 PIC 9(4).
01 lnk-sum PIC 9(4).

PROCEDURE DIVISION USING lnk-number1, lnk-number2,
    lnk-sum.
    ADD lnk-number1 TO lnk-number2 GIVING lnk-sum.
    EXIT PROGRAM.
```

### Conclusion

The CALL statement and its variants provide powerful mechanisms for creating modular, maintainable, and reusable COBOL programs. Understanding when and how to use static versus dynamic calls, as well as various parameter passing mechanisms, allows for greater flexibility and robustness in COBOL application development.

## 9.4 Passing Parameters to Subroutines

Passing parameters to subroutines is a fundamental aspect of COBOL programming, as it enables data to be shared and manipulated by different parts of the program. This section meticulously details the mechanisms and practices for passing parameters to subroutines in COBOL, ensuring that data is accurately and efficiently handled.

COBOL subroutines can receive parameters through the USING clause of the CALL statement. The caller supplies the parameters, and the subroutine receives them in the specified order. The passing of parameters in COBOL can be accomplished by reference or by content, each with its specific implications and use cases.

```
CALL 'SUBROUTINE-NAME' USING BY REFERENCE var1
                             BY CONTENT var2
                             BY REFERENCE var3.
```

In the above example, var1 and var3 are passed by reference, while var2 is passed by content. To understand these mechanisms, it is essential to delve into what occurs during each method of parameter passing.

#### Passing by Reference

When a parameter is passed by reference, the subroutine receives a reference (or pointer) to the original data item. Any modification of this parameter within the subroutine directly affects the original data item. This method is efficient regarding memory usage since no additional copies of the data are created. However, it requires careful handling to avoid unintended side effects.

```
SUBROUTINE-NAME.
    PROCEDURE DIVISION USING BY REFERENCE p-var1
                             BY REFERENCE p-var3.
```

#### Passing by Content

Passing by content involves transferring a copy of the data to the subroutine. Throughout the subroutine's execution, this copy is used, and any changes made do not affect the original data item in the caller program. This method isolates the subroutine from the caller's data, thus avoiding unintended modifications but potentially increasing memory usage due to the copy operation.

```
SUBROUTINE-NAME.
    PROCEDURE DIVISION USING BY CONTENT p-var2.
```

#### Defining Data Items in the Subroutine

The parameters expected by a subroutine must be defined in the LINKAGE SECTION of the subroutine's data division. This section declares the data items that are passed to the subroutine.

```
LINKAGE SECTION.
01 p-var1 PIC X(10).
01 p-var2 PIC 9(5)V99.
01 p-var3 PIC S9(4) COMP.
```

In this example, p-var1 is a string of 10 characters, p-var2 is a numeric field with five digits and two decimal places, and p-var3 is a signed binary number.

### Loading Parameters into Subroutines

To load parameters into a subroutine, the PROCEDURE DIVISION header specifies the using clause, aligning with how parameters are defined in the LINKAGE SECTION.

```
PROCEDURE DIVISION USING p-var1
                         p-var2
                         p-var3.
```

This setup ensures that the subroutine's working storage receives the appropriate data items from the caller.

### Practical Example

Consider a practical example where a main program calls a subroutine to update customer records. The main program passes the customer's name, account balance, and status indicator to the subroutine.

```
IDENTIFICATION DIVISION.
PROGRAM-ID. MAIN-PROGRAM.

DATA DIVISION.
WORKING-STORAGE SECTION.
01 WS-NAME PIC X(30).
01 WS-BALANCE PIC 9(7)V99.
01 WS-STATUS PIC X(1).

PROCEDURE DIVISION.
    MOVE 'John Doe' TO WS-NAME.
    MOVE 12345.67 TO WS-BALANCE.
    MOVE 'A' TO WS-STATUS.

    CALL 'UPDATE-CUSTOMER' USING BY REFERENCE
        WS-NAME
                                  BY REFERENCE WS-BALANCE
                                  BY REFERENCE WS-STATUS.
    STOP RUN.
```

The subroutine processes these parameters:

```
IDENTIFICATION DIVISION.
PROGRAM-ID. UPDATE-CUSTOMER.

DATA DIVISION.
LINKAGE SECTION.
01 LINKAGE-NAME PIC X(30).
01 LINKAGE-BALANCE PIC 9(7)V99.
01 LINKAGE-STATUS PIC X(1).

PROCEDURE DIVISION USING LINKAGE-NAME
                         LINKAGE-BALANCE
                         LINKAGE-STATUS.
    DISPLAY 'Processing customer: ' LINKAGE-NAME.
    DISPLAY 'Balance: ' LINKAGE-BALANCE.
    DISPLAY 'Status: ' LINKAGE-STATUS.

    EXIT PROGRAM.
```

When executed, the main program will call the subroutine, which then processes the customer's information. The DISPLAY statements show the received data, demonstrating that the subroutine correctly received and handled the parameters.

```
Processing customer: John Doe
Balance: 12345.67
Status: A
```

Correct parameter passing is crucial for the proper operation of modular programs, avoiding issues like data corruption and ensuring maintainability. Each method, by reference or by content, has its advantages and trade-offs, and choosing the appropriate method depends on the specific requirements of the task.

## 9.5 Using COPY and INCLUDE Statements

COPY and INCLUDE statements in COBOL facilitate the inclusion of common code blocks or configuration data across multiple programs or program units, fostering code reuse and maintainability. While both commands are used for similar purposes, they have distinct applications and benefits. Understanding these differences and knowing when to use each statement is crucial for developing efficient, modular COBOL programs.

The COPY statement is used to include code stored in a separate copybook file (.CPY). Copybooks typically contain commonly used data definitions, file control entries, or procedural code segments. The COPY statement can be placed in the WORKING-STORAGE SECTION, LINKAGE SECTION, or PROCEDURE DIVISION.

Here is an example of using the COPY statement:

```
WORKING-STORAGE SECTION.
01 COMMON-DATA.
    COPY COMMON-DATA-DEF.

PROCEDURE DIVISION.
    COPY COMMON-PROCEDURE.
    ...
```

In the above example, COMMON-DATA-DEF and COMMON-PROCEDURE are external copybook files. The COPY statement will include the contents of these files into the program at the specified locations.

The COPY statement also supports the REPLACING clause, which enables the substitution of text within the copybook during the inclusion process. This feature is particularly useful when including generic templates that need customization in different contexts.

```
COPY TEMPLATE
    REPLACING ==:TOKEN1:== BY ==Specific-Value==,
              ==:TOKEN2:== BY ==Another-Value==.
```

In this example, the tokens :TOKEN1: and :TOKEN2: in the copybook TEMPLATE will be replaced by Specific-Value and Another-Value, respectively.

The INCLUDE statement, on the other hand, is a compiler directive that instructs the preprocessor to include the contents of a specified file at the location where the INCLUDE statement appears. Unlike the COPY statement, INCLUDE is not intrinsic to standard COBOL but is often available and used in many COBOL compilers.

```
INCLUDE 'LIBRARY/INCLFILE'.
```

The filepath 'LIBRARY/INCLFILE' denotes the file to be included.

INCLUDE statements are typically more flexible than COPY statements and are often used to include various types of source files, including configuration files and environment-specific parameters, which might not be strictly COBOL source code.

Both statements provide significant benefits:

- Encouraging **code reuse** by enabling common code to be maintained in a single location.
- Enhancing **maintainability** by reducing the chances of code duplication and inconsistencies.
- Improving **module independence** by isolating configuration and standard procedures in separate files.

Effective use of COPY and INCLUDE statements can greatly improve the organization and efficiency of COBOL codebases. It allows developers to manage changes more efficiently, as updating a shared copybook or include file automatically propagates the changes to all programs that reference it. This aligns with best practices in modular programming, which emphasize consistency, readability, and ease of maintenance.

## 9.6 Writing Functions in COBOL

In COBOL, functions allow for more modular and reusable code by encapsulating operations into callable units. These functions can be intrinsic or user-defined. Intrinsic functions are built into the COBOL language, providing out-of-the-box capabilities. User-defined functions, on the other hand, are written by programmers to meet specific application needs.

To begin writing functions in COBOL, we use the PROCEDURE DIVISION to define the logic of the function. Below is a simple example of a user-defined function:

```
IDENTIFICATION DIVISION.
PROGRAM-ID. MyFunctionProgram.

DATA DIVISION.
WORKING-STORAGE SECTION.
01 Result PIC 9(4). * Result of the function
```

```
PROCEDURE DIVISION.
    CALL 'MyFunction' USING BY VALUE 2 BY VALUE 3
        RETURNING Result.
    DISPLAY 'Result is: ' Result.
    STOP RUN.

MyFunction SECTION.
    * Parameters should follow standard linkage conventions
    LINKAGE SECTION.
    01 ParA PIC 9(4) COMP-5.
    01 ParB PIC 9(4) COMP-5.

    PROCEDURE DIVISION USING ParA ParB RETURNING
        Result.
    COMPUTE Result = FUNCTION MOD (ParA + ParB, 10).
    EXIT.
```

This simple example demonstrates how to define a COBOL function and call it from the PROCEDURE DIVISION. The function, MyFunction, adds two numbers and returns the modulus of the sum with 10.

When parameter passing is involved, the LINKAGE SECTION and the USING clause are crucial. The LINKAGE SECTION defines the parameters that are passed to the function. In the above example, ParA and ParB are used as input values for the function.

An important feature of COBOL functions is their ability to leverage intrinsic functions. These are predefined in the language and cover a wide range of operations from mathematical to string manipulation functions. For instance, the FUNCTION MOD used in the example calculates the remainder of dividing ParA + ParB by 10.

To explore another intrinsic function, consider an example that makes use of the FUNCTION NUMVAL-C intrinsic function. This function converts a formatted numeric string into its numeric equivalent.

```
IDENTIFICATION DIVISION.
PROGRAM-ID. ConvertFunction.

DATA DIVISION.
WORKING-STORAGE SECTION.
01 NumericString PIC X(5) VALUE '12345'.
01 NumericValue PIC 9(5).
```

```
PROCEDURE DIVISION.
    PERFORM ConvertStringToNumber.
    DISPLAY 'Numeric Value is: ' NumericValue.
    STOP RUN.

ConvertStringToNumber SECTION.
    COMPUTE NumericValue = FUNCTION NUMVAL-C (
        NumericString).
    EXIT.
```

In this example, the intrinsic function NUMVAL-C is used to convert a numeric string NumericString to a numeric value NumericValue. The function ensures that formatted numeric strings are correctly interpreted as numerical data types for subsequent calculations.

User-defined functions often require more sophisticated logic. The following example demonstrates a user-defined function to calculate the factorial of a given number.

```
IDENTIFICATION DIVISION.
PROGRAM-ID. FactorialProgram.

DATA DIVISION.
WORKING-STORAGE SECTION.
01 FactorialResult PIC 9(10).
01 InputNumber PIC 9(2) VALUE 5.

PROCEDURE DIVISION.
    CALL 'CalculateFactorial' USING BY VALUE InputNumber
        RETURNING FactorialResult.
    DISPLAY 'Factorial of ' InputNumber ' is: ' FactorialResult.
    STOP RUN.

CalculateFactorial SECTION.
    LINKAGE SECTION.
    01 Input PIC 9(2).
    01 Output PIC 9(10).

    PROCEDURE DIVISION USING Input RETURNING Output.
    IF Input = 0 THEN
        MOVE 1 TO Output
    ELSE
        CALL 'CalculateFactorial' USING BY VALUE Input - 1
```

```
                                        RETURNING Output.
        MULTIPLY Input BY Output
    END-IF.
    EXIT.
```

In the factorial calculation function, CalculateFactorial, recursion is employed. COBOL allows for recursive calls by invoking the same function within its body until a base condition is met (here, when the input is zero). The result is accumulated through successive multiplications.

Properly handling error conditions is crucial while writing robust functions. Consider a scenario where the function performs division, which needs to guard against division by zero:

```
IDENTIFICATION DIVISION.
PROGRAM-ID. SafeDivisionProgram.

DATA DIVISION.
WORKING-STORAGE SECTION.
01 Numerator PIC 9(4) VALUE 100.
01 Denominator PIC 9(4) VALUE 0.
01 DivisionResult PIC 9(10).
01 ErrorIndicator PIC X VALUE 'N'. * N for No Error, Y for Error

PROCEDURE DIVISION.
    CALL 'SafeDivide' USING BY VALUE Numerator
                                BY VALUE Denominator
                          RETURNING DivisionResult.

    IF ErrorIndicator = 'Y' THEN
        DISPLAY 'Error in division operation. Denominator is zero.'
    ELSE
        DISPLAY 'Division Result is: ' DivisionResult
    END-IF.
    STOP RUN.

SafeDivide SECTION.
    LINKAGE SECTION.
    01 Num PIC 9(4).
    01 Denom PIC 9(4).
    01 Result PIC 9(10).

    PROCEDURE DIVISION USING Num Denom RETURNING
```

```
        Result.
    IF Denom = 0 THEN
        MOVE 'Y' TO ErrorIndicator
    ELSE
        COMPUTE Result = Num / Denom
        MOVE 'N' TO ErrorIndicator
    END-IF.
    EXIT.
```

The SafeDivide function includes an error-checking mechanism to verify if the denominator is zero before performing the division. If the denominator is zero, an error indicator (ErrorIndicator) is set to 'Y', and a corresponding error message is displayed.

By comprehensively understanding how to write functions in COBOL, programmers can significantly enhance the modularity and maintainability of their code. Practical use of both intrinsic and user-defined functions contributes to the creation of efficient and readable COBOL programs.

## 9.7 Intrinsic Functions in COBOL

COBOL includes a number of built-in or intrinsic functions that perform various operations on data without the need for separate subroutine calls. These functions can be employed to handle arithmetic calculations, string manipulations, date and time operations, and other common programming tasks efficiently. Utilizing intrinsic functions can greatly enhance the readability and maintainability of the code by encapsulating frequently used operations into concise, standard routines.

An intrinsic function in COBOL is invoked using the FUNCTION keyword followed by the name of the function and any required arguments. Arguments are enclosed within parentheses and separated by commas. The general syntax for calling an intrinsic function is as follows:

```
COMPUTE result-field = FUNCTION function-name (argument-1
    , argument-2, ...).
```

The next sections illustrate various categories of intrinsic functions, providing detailed explanations and examples for each.

**String Handling Functions**

String handling intrinsic functions are crucial for managing and manipulating text data. Commonly used string functions include LENGTH, NUMVAL, INSPECT, and REVERSE.

```
DATA DIVISION.
WORKING-STORAGE SECTION.
01 WS-STRING PIC X(50) VALUE 'Hello World'.
01 WS-LENGTH PIC 9(2).

PROCEDURE DIVISION.
    COMPUTE WS-LENGTH = FUNCTION LENGTH(
        WS-STRING)
    DISPLAY 'The length of WS-STRING is: ' WS-LENGTH
    STOP RUN.
```

In this example, the FUNCTION LENGTH() calculates the length of the variable WS-STRING.

NUMVAL and NUMVAL-C convert string representations of numbers to actual numeric values. These functions are especially useful when working with data inputs that require conversion for arithmetic operations.

```
DATA DIVISION.
WORKING-STORAGE SECTION.
01 WS-VAR-STRING PIC X(10) VALUE '12345'.
01 WS-VAR-NUMERIC PIC 9(5).

PROCEDURE DIVISION.
    COMPUTE WS-VAR-NUMERIC = FUNCTION NUMVAL(
        WS-VAR-STRING)
    DISPLAY 'The numeric value is: ' WS-VAR-NUMERIC
    STOP RUN.
```

### Arithmetic Functions

Arithmetic intrinsic functions simplify complex mathematical operations, such as exponentiation, absolute value, and modular division. Examples include ABS, SQRT, EXP, and MOD.

```
DATA DIVISION.
WORKING-STORAGE SECTION.
01 WS-NUMBER1 PIC S9(5)V9(2) VALUE -123.45.
01 WS-NUMBER2 PIC 9(5)V9(2) VALUE 25.00.
```

```
01 WS-RESULT PIC 9(5)V9(2).

PROCEDURE DIVISION.
    COMPUTE WS-RESULT = FUNCTION ABS(WS-NUMBER1)
    DISPLAY 'Absolute value is: ' WS-RESULT

    COMPUTE WS-RESULT = FUNCTION SQRT(WS-NUMBER2)
    DISPLAY 'Square root is: ' WS-RESULT

    COMPUTE WS-RESULT = FUNCTION EXP(1)
    DISPLAY 'Exponential of 1 is: ' WS-RESULT

    COMPUTE WS-RESULT = FUNCTION MOD(100, 30)
    DISPLAY 'Modular division result is: ' WS-RESULT
    STOP RUN.
```

### Date and Time Functions

Date and time intrinsic functions are essential for handling temporal operations within COBOL programs. Common functions include FUNCTION CURRENT-DATE, DATE-OF-INTEGER, and INTEGER-OF-DATE.

FUNCTION CURRENT-DATE retrieves the current system date and time, formatted as YYYYMMDDHHMISS0000+HHMM. Parsing and using distinct parts of this value simplifies many date-related operations.

```
DATA DIVISION.
WORKING-STORAGE SECTION.
01 WS-CURRENT-DATE PIC X(20).
01 WS-YEAR PIC 9(4).
01 WS-MONTH PIC 9(2).
01 WS-DAY PIC 9(2).

PROCEDURE DIVISION.
    MOVE FUNCTION CURRENT-DATE TO
        WS-CURRENT-DATE
    MOVE WS-CURRENT-DATE(1:4) TO WS-YEAR
    MOVE WS-CURRENT-DATE(5:2) TO WS-MONTH
    MOVE WS-CURRENT-DATE(7:2) TO WS-DAY

    DISPLAY 'Today''s date is: ' WS-YEAR '-' WS-MONTH '-'
```

```
    WS-DAY
STOP RUN.
```

For converting dates to integers and vice versa, DATE-OF-INTEGER and INTEGER-OF-DATE functions are highly useful.

```
DATA DIVISION.
WORKING-STORAGE SECTION.
01 WS-DATE PIC 9(8).
01 WS-INTEGER-DATE PIC 9(9).

PROCEDURE DIVISION.
    MOVE 20230315 TO WS-DATE
    COMPUTE WS-INTEGER-DATE = FUNCTION
        INTEGER-OF-DATE(WS-DATE)
    DISPLAY 'Integer date is: ' WS-INTEGER-DATE

    COMPUTE WS-DATE = FUNCTION DATE-OF-INTEGER(
        WS-INTEGER-DATE)
    DISPLAY 'Date is: ' WS-DATE
    STOP RUN.
```

### Other Useful Functions

Additional intrinsic functions provide utility for specialized tasks. Examples are MAX and MIN for finding the maximum and minimum values from a list of arguments, respectively.

```
DATA DIVISION.
WORKING-STORAGE SECTION.
01 WS-VALUE1 PIC 9(3) VALUE 100.
01 WS-VALUE2 PIC 9(3) VALUE 200.
01 WS-VALUE3 PIC 9(3) VALUE 50.
01 WS-RESULT PIC 9(3).

PROCEDURE DIVISION.
    COMPUTE WS-RESULT = FUNCTION MAX(WS-VALUE1,
        WS-VALUE2, WS-VALUE3)
    DISPLAY 'The maximum value is: ' WS-RESULT

    COMPUTE WS-RESULT = FUNCTION MIN(WS-VALUE1,
        WS-VALUE2, WS-VALUE3)
    DISPLAY 'The minimum value is: ' WS-RESULT
```

```
STOP RUN.
```

By integrating intrinsic functions, COBOL programs can be made more efficient and easier to maintain. Understanding and adeptly utilizing these built-in operations enriches the programming toolkit available to COBOL developers and fosters the creation of robust and streamlined code.

## 9.8 Calling Subroutines from Other Programs

In the context of COBOL, it is essential to understand how subroutines, written in one program, can be called and utilized by other programs. This technique is crucial for promoting code reusability and enabling a modular approach to large-scale software development.

When calling subroutines from other programs, the primary statement used is the CALL statement. The CALL statement can be used to invoke both static and dynamic subroutines, allowing a high degree of flexibility in the program's structure. Below is an example illustrating how a subroutine can be statically and dynamically called from a different COBOL program.

```
IDENTIFICATION DIVISION.
PROGRAM-ID. MAINPROG.

DATA DIVISION.
WORKING-STORAGE SECTION.
01 WS-PARAM.
    05 WS-PARAM-VALUE PIC X(10).

PROCEDURE DIVISION.
0000-START.
    MOVE "Hello" TO WS-PARAM-VALUE.
    CALL 'SUBROUTINE' USING WS-PARAM-VALUE.
    STOP RUN.
```

In this example, the main program MAINPROG calls a subroutine named SUBROUTINE, passing a parameter WS-PARAM-VALUE. The SUBROUTINE program is executed with this passed parameter.

Next, we present the subroutine program SUBROUTINE that interacts with MAINPROG.

```
IDENTIFICATION DIVISION.
PROGRAM-ID. SUBROUTINE.

DATA DIVISION.
LINKAGE SECTION.
01 LK-PARAM.
    05 LK-PARAM-VALUE PIC X(10).

PROCEDURE DIVISION USING LK-PARAM.
0000-START.
    DISPLAY "Received from MAINPROG: "
        LK-PARAM-VALUE
    EXIT PROGRAM.
```

This example exhibits the essential aspects, including how the subroutine receives parameters via the LINKAGE SECTION and how it utilizes the parameter within its PROCEDURE DIVISION. The linkage between the programs is facilitated via the CALL statement and the defined LINKAGE SECTION.

A dynamic subroutine call employs a variable or expression instead of a literal program name. Here's an adapted version of MAINPROG that demonstrates dynamic calling:

```
IDENTIFICATION DIVISION.
PROGRAM-ID. MAINPROG.

DATA DIVISION.
WORKING-STORAGE SECTION.
01 WS-PARAM.
    05 WS-PARAM-VALUE PIC X(10).
01 WS-SUB-NAME PIC X(10) VALUE 'SUBROUTINE'.

PROCEDURE DIVISION.
0000-START.
    MOVE "Hello" TO WS-PARAM-VALUE.
    CALL WS-SUB-NAME USING WS-PARAM-VALUE.
    STOP RUN.
```

In this case, WS-SUB-NAME holds the name of the subroutine to be called, allowing the subroutine being called to potentially be determined at runtime dynamically.

When calling subroutines across different programs, it is also vital to consider error handling. Proper error handling ensures that the calling program can gracefully handle situations in which the called subroutine does not execute as expected. COBOL provides several mechanisms to facilitate this, including the use of ON EXCEPTION and NOT ON EXCEPTION phrases.

Here is an example of incorporating error handling in a subroutine call:

```
IDENTIFICATION DIVISION.
PROGRAM-ID. MAINPROG.

DATA DIVISION.
WORKING-STORAGE SECTION.
01 WS-PARAM.
    05 WS-PARAM-VALUE PIC X(10).
01 WS-SUB-NAME PIC X(10) VALUE 'SUBROUTINE'.
01 WS-STATUS PIC S9(4) COMP.

PROCEDURE DIVISION.
0000-START.
    MOVE "Hello" TO WS-PARAM-VALUE.
    CALL WS-SUB-NAME USING WS-PARAM-VALUE
        ON EXCEPTION
            MOVE 1 TO WS-STATUS
            DISPLAY "Error in calling subroutine"
        NOT ON EXCEPTION
            MOVE 0 TO WS-STATUS.
     IF WS-STATUS NOT = 0 THEN
        DISPLAY "Handling Error."
     END-IF.
    STOP RUN.
```

This code illustrates the use of ON EXCEPTION to manage errors that occur during the call of the subroutine. If an exception is raised, WS-STATUS is set to 1, and a corresponding error message is displayed. Leveraging this technique ensures that the calling program can respond appropriately to any anomalies encountered when invoking subroutines, thereby enhancing the robustness and reliability of COBOL applications.

## 9.9 Error Handling in Subroutines

Error handling in subroutines is a critical aspect of developing robust and maintainable COBOL applications. Implementing effective error management strategies can prevent unexpected terminations and ensure that the program behaves predictably even under erroneous conditions. This section will discuss various techniques for handling errors within subroutines, focusing on best practices to enhance the reliability and maintainability of COBOL code.

Error handling mechanisms in COBOL can be implemented using several strategies, including the use of special error flags, the ON EXCEPTION clause, and custom error-handling routines. Each of these methods can be applied depending on the type of error being monitored and the desired response.

Consider an example where a subroutine is responsible for performing a division operation. A potential error condition is the division by zero. This can be managed using a combination of conditional checks and the ON SIZE ERROR clause. Here is a detailed illustration:

```
IDENTIFICATION DIVISION.
PROGRAM-ID. DivisionSub.

DATA DIVISION.
WORKING-STORAGE SECTION.
01 Num1 PIC 9(5) VALUE 0.
01 Num2 PIC 9(5) VALUE 0.
01 Result PIC 9(10)V9(5).
01 Error-Flag PIC X VALUE 'N'.

PROCEDURE DIVISION.
Main-Processing.
    MOVE 100 TO Num1
    MOVE 0 TO Num2
    PERFORM Division-Processing
    DISPLAY "Result: " Result
    DISPLAY "Error-Flag: " Error-Flag
    STOP RUN.

Division-Processing.
    IF Num2 = 0
       MOVE 'Y' TO Error-Flag
```

```
        DISPLAY "Error: Division by Zero"
    ELSE
        COMPUTE Result = Num1 / Num2
        ON SIZE ERROR
            MOVE 'Y' TO Error-Flag
            DISPLAY "Error: Size Error in Division"
        NOT ON SIZE ERROR
            MOVE 'N' TO Error-Flag
    END-IF.
```

In this example, the division operation is protected by a conditional check to ensure that the divisor Num2 is not zero. Additionally, the ON SIZE ERROR clause is used to handle any arithmetic errors that may occur during the computation. The Error-Flag variable is used to indicate whether an error has occurred, allowing the main processing logic to respond appropriately.

Another approach to error handling involves the use of DISPLAY statements to notify the user of an error. While this is a simple and straightforward method, it is often beneficial to implement more sophisticated error logging mechanisms for production systems. For example, errors can be written to a file or a database table for later analysis.

Consider an example where errors are logged to a file:

```
IDENTIFICATION DIVISION.
PROGRAM-ID. ErrorLogSub.

ENVIRONMENT DIVISION.
INPUT-OUTPUT SECTION.
FILE-CONTROL.
    SELECT ErrorLogFile ASSIGN TO 'errorlog.txt'
    ORGANIZATION IS LINE SEQUENTIAL.

DATA DIVISION.
FILE SECTION.
FD ErrorLogFile.
01 ErrorLogRecord.
    05 ErrorCode PIC X(3).
    05 ErrorMsg PIC X(50).

WORKING-STORAGE SECTION.
01 Division-Error PIC X VALUE 'N'.
```

```
PROCEDURE DIVISION.
Perform-Division.
    OPEN OUTPUT ErrorLogFile
    PERFORM Division-Processing
    CLOSE ErrorLogFile
    STOP RUN.

Division-Processing.
    COMPUTE Result = Num1 / Num2
    ON SIZE ERROR
        MOVE 'ERR' TO ErrorCode
        MOVE 'Division by zero or overflow' TO ErrorMsg
        PERFORM Write-ErrorLog.
    NOT ON SIZE ERROR
        MOVE 'NOE' TO ErrorCode
        MOVE 'No errors' TO ErrorMsg
        PERFORM Write-ErrorLog.
    END-COMPUTE.

Write-Error Log.
    WRITE ErrorLogRecord.
```

In this more robust example, errors are logged to an external file called errorlog.txt. The file is defined and controlled in the FILE-CONTROL paragraph in the ENVIRONMENT DIVISION. Upon detecting an error condition, the relevant error code and message are written to the log file using the WRITE statement. This approach facilitates post-mortem debugging and error tracking in live systems.

Finally, custom error-handling routines can be defined and used across multiple subroutines to ensure consistent error management. Such routines can encapsulate common error-handling logic, making the code more modular and reducing redundancy. Error-handling routines can perform actions such as rolling back transactions, setting error flags, or invoking alternate processing paths.

By integrating these techniques into your COBOL subroutines, you can improve the robustness and maintainability of your applications. Understanding and implementing effective error-handling strategies in COBOL is crucial for building reliable and resilient software systems.

## 9.10 Best Practices for Modular Programming

Modular programming is essential in COBOL for creating maintainable, scalable, and reusable code. This section elaborates on the best practices that facilitate effective modular programming, ensuring the resulting code is both efficient and easy to manage.

**1. Adopting a Consistent Naming Convention**

Adhering to a consistent naming convention for subroutines and functions enhances code readability and maintainability. Naming should be descriptive and indicate the purpose of a subroutine or function.

For example:

```
001000-PROCESS-INVOICE.
002000-CALCULATE-DISCOUNT.
```

001000- and 002000- are prefixes that indicate the logical sequence in which these subroutines may be executed. The names PROCESS-INVOICE and CALCULATE-DISCOUNT clearly state their functionality.

**2. Encapsulating Code Within Subroutines**

Encapsulation involves organizing code into discrete subroutines, each responsible for a single task. This ensures that each subroutine operates independently and interacts with other parts through well-defined interfaces.

```
    PERFORM 001000-PROCESS-INVOICE.
    PERFORM 002000-CALCULATE-DISCOUNT.
```

Encapsulation improves readability and makes debugging simpler because you can isolate problems within specific subroutines.

**3. Using Parameter Passing**

Passing parameters to subroutines allows them to operate on different data without global variables, thus improving modularity and reusability. Use COBOL's USING clause to pass parameters effectively.

Example of a subroutine receiving parameters:

```
CALL 'CALCULATE-DISCOUNT' USING SALE-AMOUNT
    RETURNED-DISCOUNT.
```

Subroutine definition:

```
001000-CALCULATE-DISCOUNT SECTION.
    USING SALE-AMOUNT RETURNED-DISCOUNT.
    ...
```

Ensure that parameters are correctly defined and used within the subroutine to prevent unintended side-effects and maintain data integrity.

**4. Error Handling**

Integrate error handling within subroutines to detect and manage exceptions. This approach ensures that errors are localized, making the program more robust and easier to debug.

Example of error handling in a subroutine:

```
001000-PROCESS-INVOICE SECTION.
    IF INVOICE-NUMBER IS NUMERIC
        ...
    ELSE
        DISPLAY 'ERROR: INVALID INVOICE NUMBER'
        MOVE 'N' TO VALID-INVOICE.
    END-IF.
```

Always check input parameters and return suitable error codes or messages to the calling program.

**5. Minimizing Dependencies**

Subroutines should have minimal interdependencies to reduce the risk of cascading failures and simplify maintenance. Each subroutine should have a clear purpose and interface, independent of other subroutines' internals.

STUBS-RESET should not rely on resetting procedures in other subroutines:

```
000100-INITIALIZE VALUES.
        PERFORM 001000-RESET VALUES.
```

Instead, the calling program is responsible for making necessary PERFORM calls, reducing the coupling between different subroutines.

**6. Using COPY and INCLUDE Statements**

Employing COPY and INCLUDE statements helps in reusing common code blocks and data definitions across multiple programs or subroutines, which ensures consistency and reduces duplication.

Example of a COPY statement:

```
COPY 'COMMON-ROUTINES' IN ENVIRONMENT DIVISION.
```

This practice keeps the codebase DRY (Don't Repeat Yourself) and can significantly decrease maintenance overheads.

**7. Modular Code Testing**

Thoroughly test individual subroutines before integrating them into the main program. Unit testing can be used to verify that each subroutine performs as expected under various conditions.

Example:

```
CALL 'CALCULATE-DISCOUNT' USING TEST-AMOUNT RETURNED-DISCOUNT.
DISPLAY 'Returned Discount: ' RETURNED-DISCOUNT.
```

This helps identify and resolve issues early in development, leading to more reliable applications.

**8. Documentation**

Document each subroutine's purpose, parameter list, return values, and any side effects. Proper documentation aids in understanding the code and ensures that future developers can maintain and enhance the system efficiently.

Documentation Example:

```
*----------------------------------------------------------*
* 001000-CALCULATE-DISCOUNT
* Purpose: Calculate the discount for a given sale amount.
* Parameters:
*  Input: SALE-AMOUNT (numeric)
*  Output: RETURNED-DISCOUNT (numeric)
*----------------------------------------------------------*
```

Clear documentation fosters collaboration and decreases the learning curve for new team members.

By adhering to these best practices, COBOL developers can enhance code modularity, resulting in applications that are easier to read, debug, maintain, and scale.

# Chapter 10

# Debugging and Error Handling

**Debugging and error handling are vital skills for ensuring robust COBOL programs. This chapter introduces debugging techniques including using tools, setting breakpoints, and step-by-step execution. It covers viewing and modifying variable values, understanding COBOL error codes, and managing SYNCHRONIZED and alignment issues. Additionally, the chapter discusses using DISPLAY for debugging, writing fault-tolerant code, and effective logging and tracing techniques for efficient error handling.**

## 10.1 Introduction to Debugging

Debugging is a crucial aspect in developing robust COBOL programs. It involves discovering, analyzing, and correcting errors or bugs within the code to ensure the program operates as intended. Mastering debugging techniques not only improves program reliability but also enhances the efficiency of the development process. This section provides a foundational understanding of debugging practices, focusing on the methodologies and cognitive approaches essential for addressing issues in COBOL programs.

Debugging refers to the systematic process of identifying and resolving defects or problems (bugs) in a program. Bugs can arise from syntax errors, logical errors, runtime errors, and data inaccuracies, among others. Effective debugging requires a methodical approach to isolate the problem, understand its root cause, and implement a solution.

- **Syntax Errors:** Occur due to incorrect usage of the COBOL language constructs. These errors are typically detected at compile time. For example, missing a period at the end of a statement or incorrectly specifying a COBOL keyword.
- **Logical Errors:** Occur when the program syntax is correct, but the logic implemented does not produce the desired outcome. These are often the most challenging to detect as they require a deep understanding of the program's intended functionality.
- **Runtime Errors:** Occur when the program encounters an issue while executing. Examples include division by zero or accessing an out-of-bound index in an array.
- **Data Inaccuracies:** Occur when the data being processed is incorrect or not as expected. This can be due to wrong input, miscalculations, or incorrect data handling.

Debugging in COBOL can be approached using several techniques.

- **Code Reviews:** Examining the code with colleagues to identify potential issues. Code reviews often reveal logical errors and help ensure adherence to coding standards.
- **Desk Checking:** Walking through the code manually to understand its flow and potential issues. This technique is especially useful for discovering logical errors and verifying algorithm correctness.
- **Static Analysis Tools:** Using automated tools to analyze source code for known patterns of errors or deviations from best practices.
- **Interactive Debugging:** Utilizing debugging tools that allow setting breakpoints and stepping through the code line by line, examining variable states and program flow in real-time.

Code Reviews involve a systematic examination of the source code by one or more individuals other than the author. The primary objective is to find and fix errors that might have been overlooked. Code reviews help in maintaining a high level of code quality and consistency.

Desk Checking is a process where the programmer manually simulates the execution of the code to predict its behavior. This method is useful in understanding the program's flow and identifying logical errors early in the development process.

Static Analysis Tools are automated tools that analyze the source code without executing it. These tools check for common programming errors, adherence to coding standards, and potential security vulnerabilities. They provide a quick way to detect errors that might not be obvious through code reviews or desk checking.

Interactive Debugging is perhaps the most hands-on approach. Debugging tools, such as IDEs (Integrated Development Environments), provide capabilities to set breakpoints, watch variables, and step through the code. This interactivity is essential for tracing the execution flow and understanding how data changes at each step.

The primary COBOL debugging commands and functions include:

```
STOP RUN.
DISPLAY "Debugging Information: " VARIABLE-NAME.
```

The DISPLAY statement is particularly useful for printing variable values and executing messages to understand the program flow and data changes during execution. Effective use of DISPLAY statements can significantly simplify the debugging process by providing clear insights into the program's operation.

```
Debugging Information: 100
```

Strategies for effective debugging include isolating the section of code where the bug appears, reproducing the error consistently, and simplifying the problem to its core components. Practicing these strategies enables developers to pinpoint issues more effectively, reduce time spent on debugging, and enhance the overall quality of their programs.

A common approach in debugging is the divide and conquer method. This involves breaking down the program into smaller sections and testing each section individually. By narrowing down the scope, it becomes easier to identify the precise location of the bug.

Furthermore, understanding and utilizing COBOL compiler options for debugging purposes can provide additional insights. Certain compilers offer options to generate detailed compilation reports or to include debug information in the compiled code, which aids significantly during the debugging process.

Effective debugging is an iterative process of hypothesizing, testing, and refining. It demands a disciplined mindset and thorough knowledge of the programming language and development environment. Through systematic approaches, such as those described, developers can enhance their ability to produce reliable, error-free COBOL applications.

## 10.2 Identifying Common COBOL Errors

In COBOL programming, identifying common errors is crucial for efficient debugging and error handling. This section elucidates typical mistakes that programmers encounter and provides strategies to recognize and rectify these issues. Understanding these frequent errors enhances the robustness of COBOL applications and optimizes the debugging process.

Compile-time Errors: Compile-time errors occur during the compilation of the COBOL program. They prevent the program from being successfully compiled into an executable. Common compile-time errors include syntax errors, missing or misplaced keywords, and incorrect statements. Here's an example of a compile-time error due to a missing period:

```
IDENTIFICATION DIVISION.
PROGRAM-ID. SampleProgram
WORKING-STORAGE SECTION.
01 WS-VAR PIC 9(3).

PROCEDURE DIVISION.
MOVE 100 TO WS-VAR
DISPLAY 'Value of WS-VAR' WS-VAR.
STOP RUN.
```

The missing period after PROGRAM-ID. SampleProgram results in a compile-time error. Ensuring that all COBOL statements are correctly terminated with a period is critical to avoid such errors.

Runtime Errors: Runtime errors occur during program execution and can cause the program to terminate unexpectedly or produce incorrect results. Common runtime errors include division by zero, file access violations, and memory issues. An illustrative case of a runtime error due to division by zero is shown below:

```
IDENTIFICATION DIVISION.
PROGRAM-ID. DivisionExample.
DATA DIVISION.
WORKING-STORAGE SECTION.
01 WS-NUM1 PIC 9(2) VALUE 100.
01 WS-NUM2 PIC 9(2) VALUE 0.
01 WS-RESULT PIC 9(4).

PROCEDURE DIVISION.
COMPUTE WS-RESULT = WS-NUM1 / WS-NUM2.
DISPLAY 'Result is: ' WS-RESULT.
STOP RUN.
```

Executing this code without proper error handling causes a division by zero error, leading to a runtime exception.

Logical Errors: Logical errors occur when the program executes but produces incorrect results due to flawed logic. These errors are challenging to detect as the program does not fail; instead, it delivers erroneous outputs. The following code snippet demonstrates a logical error in computing the factorial of a number:

```
IDENTIFICATION DIVISION.
PROGRAM-ID. FactorialExample.
DATA DIVISION.
WORKING-STORAGE SECTION.
01 WS-NUMBER PIC 9(2) VALUE 5.
01 WS-FACTORIAL PIC 9(6) VALUE 1.

PROCEDURE DIVISION.
PERFORM VARYING WS-NUMBER FROM WS-NUMBER
    BY 1 UNTIL WS-NUMBER = 0
    COMPUTE WS-FACTORIAL = WS-FACTORIAL *
        WS-NUMBER
END-PERFORM.
DISPLAY 'Factorial is: ' WS-FACTORIAL.
STOP RUN.
```

The logical error in the PERFORM loop causes the factorial calculation to fail since the terminating condition $\text{WS-NUMBER} = 0$ is never met.

Data-related Errors: Data-related errors arise from incorrect data definitions or unexpected input values. These errors include data truncation, incorrect data types, and mismatched data formats. Below is an example where input data does not match the expected format, leading to truncation:

```
IDENTIFICATION DIVISION.
PROGRAM-ID. DataErrorExample.
DATA DIVISION.
WORKING-STORAGE SECTION.
01 WS-NAME PIC X(5).

PROCEDURE DIVISION.
MOVE 'JOHNSON' TO WS-NAME.
DISPLAY 'Name is: ' WS-NAME.
STOP RUN.
```

The variable WS-NAME is defined with a PIC clause of X(5), which truncates the input 'JOHNSON' to 'JOHNS'. Proper definition and handling of data variables prevent such errors.

File Handling Errors: File handling errors are common when accessing or manipulating files in COBOL. These include file not found, file not open, and record not found errors. The example below demonstrates an error due to attempting to read a record from an unopened file:

```
IDENTIFICATION DIVISION.
PROGRAM-ID. FileHandlingExample.
DATA DIVISION.
FILE SECTION.
FD INPUT-FILE
    LABEL RECORD STANDARD
    VALUE OF FILE-ID IS 'input.txt'.
01 INPUT-RECORD.
    05 INPUT-DATA PIC X(10).

WORKING-STORAGE SECTION.
01 WS-DISPLAY-DATA PIC X(10).

PROCEDURE DIVISION.
READ INPUT-FILE INTO WS-DISPLAY-DATA
AT END
    DISPLAY 'End of file or file not found.'
```

```
    END-READ.
    DISPLAY 'Data: ' WS-DISPLAY-DATA.
    STOP RUN.
```

An attempt to read from INPUT-FILE without opening it leads to a runtime file handling error.

To effectively identify and mitigate these common COBOL errors, it is essential to rigorously review code, utilize debugging tools, perform thorough testing, and incorporate robust error handling mechanisms. Recognizing and addressing these errors at an early stage significantly enhances the reliability and performance of COBOL programs.

## 10.3 Using Debugging Tools

Debugging tools are indispensable when striving for error-free COBOL programs. These tools provide the means to track down and rectify errors efficiently, enhancing both productivity and code reliability. Various debugging tools are specifically designed for COBOL, each offering unique features to simplify the debugging process.

COBOL debugging tools enable developers to set breakpoints, step through code, inspect and modify variable values, and analyze the state of a program at any given point during its execution. These utilities can be classified into command-line tools and integrated development environment (IDE)-based tools.

**Command-Line Debugging Tools**

Command-line debugging tools provide robust functionality accessible through a text-based interface. A widely used command-line debugging tool for COBOL is cobol_debug. Below is an example to illustrate its usage:

```
cobol_debug -d my_program.cbl
```

This command initiates debugging mode for the COBOL program my_program.cbl. Once in debugging mode, various commands can be used to control the execution of the program and inspect its state. Key commands include:

- break line_number - Sets a breakpoint at the specified line number.

- run - Executes the program until it hits a breakpoint or completes.
- step - Executes the next statement.
- print variable_name - Displays the current value of a variable.
- modify variable_name=new_value - Changes the value of a variable.

For instance, to set a breakpoint at line 50, run the program, step through the next statement, print the value of a variable counter, and modify it, the following commands would be used:

```
break 50
run
step
print counter
modify counter=10
```

### Outputs in verbatim Environment

```
Breakpoint set at line 50.
Program running...
Breakpoint hit at line 50.
Next statement executed.
counter: 5
counter modified to 10
```

These outputs provide insights into the program's current state, helping pinpoint the exact location of issues and their cause.

### IDE-Based Debugging Tools

Integrated Development Environments (IDEs) offer a more user-friendly interface for debugging. Tools like IBM's RDz (Rational Developer for Z Systems) and Micro Focus COBOL Developer provide advanced debugging capabilities. These IDEs are equipped with graphical interfaces that facilitate setting breakpoints, stepping through code, viewing call stacks, and inspecting variable values.

Consider Micro Focus COBOL Developer. To debug a program within this IDE:

- Open the program source file.
- Set breakpoints by clicking on the left margin near line numbers.

- Use the debugging toolbar to control execution (e.g., run, step, stop).
- Inspect variable values through the variables panel.
- Modify variable values directly in the variables panel.

**Algorithm for Debugging Using IDE**

```
Data: COBOL source file in the IDE
Result: Identified and corrected error
Open the source file in the IDE;
Set breakpoints at suspected locations by clicking on the margin;
Initiate the debug session by clicking the Run button on the toolbar;
while program execution does not reach end do
    if breakpoint hit then
        Check variable values in the variables panel;
        if values are incorrect then
            Modify the values directly in the variables panel;
            Step through the next few statements using the Step button;
        else
            Continue execution by clicking the Continue button;
```

These detailed steps ensure that any discrepancies in variable values or logic are identified and corrected promptly.

Efficient use of debugging tools significantly enhances the accuracy and robustness of COBOL programs. They allow developers to explore the inner workings of their code, ensuring that all variables hold correct values and all logic paths are valid.

## 10.4 Setting Up Breakpoints

One of the fundamental techniques in debugging COBOL programs is setting up breakpoints. Breakpoints allow the programmer to temporarily halt the execution of a program at a specified location, enabling the inspection of variable values and program state at that point. This is essential for tracing logic flow and identifying errors.

To set breakpoints effectively, follow these steps:

- Identify the location in the program where a breakpoint is needed.
- Use the appropriate debugging tool commands to set the breakpoint.
- Run the program within the debugging environment to pause execution at the breakpoint.
- Inspect the program state and variable values at the breakpoint.

In a COBOL development environment, breakpoints can typically be set using an interactive debugger. Commonly used COBOL debuggers include IBM's Debug Tool for z/OS, Micro Focus Visual COBOL Debugger, and tools integrated within the Eclipse IDE.

```
IDENTIFICATION DIVISION.
PROGRAM-ID. BREAKPOINT-DEMO.
DATA DIVISION.
WORKING-STORAGE SECTION.
01 WS-VAR1 PIC 9(03) VALUE 000.
01 WS-VAR2 PIC 9(03) VALUE 123.
PROCEDURE DIVISION.
BEGIN-PARA.
    MOVE 500 TO WS-VAR1
    DISPLAY 'Value of WS-VAR1: ' WS-VAR1
    IF WS-VAR1 > 100
        CALL 'DEBUGGER-COMMAND' USING 'SET
            BREAKPOINT AT BEGIN-PARA'
    END-IF
    MOVE WS-VAR1 TO WS-VAR2
    DISPLAY 'Value of WS-VAR2: ' WS-VAR2
    STOP RUN.
```

In this example, a breakpoint is set at the statement where WS-VAR1 is moved to WS-VAR2. This allows the developer to pause execution before the variable WS-VAR2 is modified, thereby enabling the inspection of WS-VAR1's value after the conditional check.

Execution of the above COBOL program with breakpoints set can provide outputs similar to:

```
Value of WS-VAR1: 500
<Breakpoint reached at BEGIN-PARA>
```

Interactive debuggers also allow for setting conditional breakpoints based on specific criteria, enhancing the precision of debugging sessions:

```
IDENTIFICATION DIVISION.
PROGRAM-ID. CONDITIONAL-BREAKPOINT.
DATA DIVISION.
WORKING-STORAGE SECTION.
01 WS-COUNTER PIC 9(03) VALUE 000.
PROCEDURE DIVISION.
BEGIN.
    PERFORM UNTIL WS-COUNTER = 200
        ADD 1 TO WS-COUNTER
        IF WS-COUNTER = 100
            CALL 'DEBUGGER-COMMAND' USING 'SET
                COND BREAK IF WS-COUNTER = 100'
        END-IF
    END-PERFORM
    DISPLAY 'Final value of WS-COUNTER: ' WS-COUNTER
    STOP RUN.
```

In this script, a conditional breakpoint is set to trigger when WS-COUNTER equals 100. This targeted breakpoint approach allows for selective inspection, skipping iterations until the specified condition is met.

When the program is executed in a debugging environment, the expected output might be:

```
<Breakpoint reached at WS-COUNTER = 100>
Final value of WS-COUNTER: 200
```

Understanding the appropriate context and conditions for setting breakpoints is crucial for efficient debugging. Tools like Micro Focus Visual COBOL and IBM Debug Tool provide graphical interfaces where developers can set, enable, disable, and remove breakpoints interactively. These interfaces often provide features such as:

- Enabling/disabling breakpoints without deleting them.
- Viewing the list of active breakpoints.
- Navigation to the code associated with each breakpoint.

- Setting breakpoints based on line number, function name, or variable state changes.

To manage breakpoints programmatically, debugging tools expose specific commands. For instance, the command for setting a breakpoint at a particular line number in IBM Debug Tool could look like:

```
DEBUG TOOL COMMAND: AT LINE 10 BREAK ;
```

Setting breakpoints effectively requires understanding not only the debugging tools at one's disposal but also the flow of the program. It demands strategic thinking to select places in the code where stopping execution will provide the most useful information about the program's behaviour. This strategic placement ensures that debugging is both insightful and efficient, aiding in the rapid identification and resolution of issues within COBOL applications.

## 10.5 Step-by-Step Execution

Step-by-step execution, also known as single-stepping, is a debugging technique that allows a programmer to execute a program one statement at a time. This granular level of control facilitates the identification of logical errors, variable value anomalies, and unintended control flow within a COBOL program.

To initiate step-by-step execution, a debugger tool must first be activated and the program loaded into it. Most COBOL compilers provide an integrated debugger or support third-party debugging tools. Here, we illustrate the general process using a hypothetical COBOL debugging environment.

After loading the program into the debugger, various commands are used to step through the code:

```
PROCEDURE DIVISION.
...
0000-MAIN.
PERFORM 1000-INITIALIZE.
PERFORM 2000-PROCESS.
PERFORM 3000-TERMINATE.
STOP RUN.
```

Assuming we have the following segment of a COBOL program, the debugger is set up and ready to execute the program step-by-step.

To begin, place a breakpoint at the start of the 0000-MAIN paragraph:

```
(break) 0000-MAIN
```

Execution begins, and the debugger halts at the start of 0000-MAIN. At this point, the following options are typically available to the programmer:

- next (n): Execute the next statement but do not dive into any performed or called paragraphs.
- step (s): Execute the next statement and dive into performed or called paragraphs.
- continue (c): Resume program execution until the next breakpoint or the end of the program.

By executing the next command, the debugger will proceed to the PERFORM 1000-INITIALIZE statement:

```
(n) 0000-MAIN.
    PERFORM 1000-INITIALIZE.
```

To observe what happens within the 1000-INITIALIZE paragraph, use the step command:

```
(s) 1000-INITIALIZE.
    MOVE 0 TO COUNTER.
    MOVE SPACES TO INPUT-RECORD.
```

The debugger now steps into 1000-INITIALIZE and executes the MOVE 0 TO COUNTER and MOVE SPACES TO INPUT-RECORD statements. At each step, the programmer can inspect the values of variables.

For example, to check the value of COUNTER after its assignment:

```
(display) COUNTER
0
```

This confirms that COUNTER has been correctly initialized to 0. Stepping further allows the programmer to examine every operation within the $1000 - INITIALIZE$ paragraph.

If the programmer wants to skip detailed inspection of a performed paragraph and move to the next mainline statement, the next command can be employed:

```
(n) 1000-INITIALIZE EXIT.
    PERFORM 2000-PROCESS.
```

This is useful for focusing on particular sections of the code which are suspected of causing issues.

Furthermore, the debugger facilitates modifying variable values during step-by-step execution. This can help test various scenarios without modifying the actual source code.

Assuming an error might be due to an unexpected value of COUNTER during the 2000-PROCESS paragraph, one could set COUNTER to 5 before stepping into the PERFORM 2000-PROCESS:

```
(set) COUNTER = 5
```

Now, while stepping into the 2000-PROCESS paragraph, one can observe the effects of COUNTER being 5.

Lastly, step-by-step execution is significantly potent when dealing with conditional statements and loops. It helps evaluate the truthfulness of conditions and the number of loop iterations explicitly, reducing the guesswork involved in debugging.

Consider the loop in 2000-PROCESS:

```
03. 2000-PROCESS.
04. PERFORM UNTIL COUNTER > 10
05. ADD 1 TO COUNTER
06. DISPLAY "Counter: " COUNTER
07. END-PERFORM.
```

Stepping through this loop helps ensure that COUNTER increments correctly and that the loop terminates as expected. Each iteration can be visually confirmed in the debugger output:

```
(s) ADD 1 TO COUNTER.
(display) COUNTER
1
(s) DISPLAY "Counter: " COUNTER
Counter: 1
...
```

By continuing with the next command until the loop concludes, the execution count can be validated precisely.

The concept of step-by-step execution, supported by relevant debugger commands and practical illustrations, is instrumental in isolating and resolving logical errors within COBOL programs. This debugging approach cultivates a deeper understanding of program behavior at a microscopic level.

## 10.6 Viewing and Modifying Variable Values

In the debugging process, effective strategies for viewing and modifying variable values can significantly streamline finding and fixing bugs. Being able to inspect the contents of variables at various execution points aids in understanding the program's behavior and ensures that the variables hold expected values. This section explores different methods and tools available for viewing and modifying variable values in COBOL programs.

### Viewing Variable Values

One common approach to inspect variable values in COBOL is to use the DISPLAY statement. It outputs the value of variables to the console, allowing the programmer to check values at different execution stages. Here's an example:

```
IDENTIFICATION DIVISION.
PROGRAM-ID. SampleProgram.
DATA DIVISION.
WORKING-STORAGE SECTION.
01 WS-VAR1 PIC 9(3) VALUE 100.
01 WS-VAR2 PIC X(10) VALUE 'HELLO'.
PROCEDURE DIVISION.
DISPLAY 'The value of WS-VAR1 is: ' WS-VAR1.
DISPLAY 'The value of WS-VAR2 is: ' WS-VAR2.
STOP RUN.
```

Executing the above code will produce the following output:

```
The value of WS-VAR1 is: 100
The value of WS-VAR2 is: HELLO
```

While the DISPLAY statement is straightforward and easy to use, it does have limitations. It adds lines to your source code that need to be removed after debugging, and it might not be suitable for large-scale variable inspection.

### Using Debugging Tools to View Variables

Most COBOL development environments provide debugging tools that allow for on-the-fly viewing of variable values. These tools enable the programmer to inspect variables without modifying the source code. Two examples of such debugging environments are IBM's Integrated Debugger and Micro Focus' Visual COBOL.

**Example with IBM Integrated Debugger:**

To view variable values using the IBM Integrated Debugger, perform the following steps:

- Run your COBOL program in debug mode.
- When execution pauses at a breakpoint, enter the command Var = * to display all variables in the current scope.
- Or, use Var = var-name to display a specific variable's value.

**Example of Viewing Variables in Visual COBOL:**

- Start the program in debug mode.
- Insert a breakpoint where you want to inspect the variable.
- When execution pauses, hover over the variable in the code editor to view its value.
- Alternatively, use the Watch window to add and monitor specific variables.

### Modifying Variable Values

Another critical aspect of debugging is the ability to modify variable values during execution. This can be particularly beneficial to test how the program reacts to different data without altering the original source code permanently.

### Using DISPLAY for Modification

Directly modifying a variable value in the source code using the MOVE statement allows you to check the program's behavior with new data. Here's an example:

```
MOVE 200 TO WS-VAR1.
DISPLAY 'New value of WS-VAR1 is: ' WS-VAR1.
```

This will produce:

```
New value of WS-VAR1 is: 200
```

### Using Debugging Tools for Modification

Most debugging tools support modifying variable values in real-time, which streamlines the testing process. Here are steps to modify values using common debugging environments:

**With IBM Integrated Debugger:**

- Pause the program at a breakpoint.
- Enter $\text{Var} = \text{var-name, new-value}$ to assign a new value to the variable.

**With Visual COBOL:**

- Pause execution at the breakpoint.
- In the $\text{Watch}$ window, double-click the value column next to the variable name.
- Enter the new value and press Enter.

Here is an algorithm demonstrating value inspection and modification using debugging tools:

**Algorithm 1:** Algorithm for Viewing and Modifying Variable Values in Debuggers

```
Data: Program paused at breakpoint
Result: Inspect and modify variable values
Viewing Variable Value:
Inspect variables using debugger commands/tools ;
if using IBM Integrated Debugger then
    Use command Var = var-name to view the variable value;
else if using Visual COBOL then
    Hover over variable or use Watch window to view;
Modifying Variable Value:
Enter new value using debugger commands/tools ;
if using IBM Integrated Debugger then
    Use command Var = var-name, new-value to modify the
     value;
else if using Visual COBOL then
    Double-click in the Watch window and modify the value;
```

Proficiency in viewing and modifying variable values is indispensable for effective debugging. Utilizing the $\text{DISPLAY}$ statement provides quick insights, while debugging tools offer more sophisticated capabilities for real-time inspection and modification. Fine-tuning these skills can lead to more efficient identification and rectification of issues within COBOL programs.

## 10.7 Understanding COBOL Error Codes

Understanding and efficiently handling error codes are crucial for maintaining the robustness and reliability of COBOL programs. COBOL's error handling capabilities can be categorized into compile-time, run-time, and logic errors, each with distinct characteristics and methods for detection and resolution.

Compile-time errors are identified during the compilation of the program. These errors often include syntax errors, data declaration issues, and incorrect usage of COBOL reserved words. The COBOL compiler generates error messages that provide specific line numbers and descriptions of the issues encountered. Understanding these messages requires familiarity with common error codes and the context in which they occur.

```
000100 IDENTIFICATION DIVISION.
000200 PROGRAM-ID. SampleProgram.
000300 ENVIRONMENT DIVISION.
000400 DATA DIVISION.
000500 WORKING-STORAGE SECTION.
000600 77 SAMPLE-VAR PIC 9(5).
000700 PROCEDURE DIVISION.
000800 MOVE 12345X TO SAMPLE-VAR.
000900 DISPLAY 'SAMPLE-VAR: ' SAMPLE-VAR.
001000 STOP RUN.

Output during compilation:
Error: Line 800: Invalid character 'X'
```

In this example, a compile-time error arises from an invalid character in line 800. The error message's clarity enables quick identification and resolution by correcting the syntax.

Run-time errors manifest during the program's execution, often due to data-related issues such as division by zero, file not found, or out-of-range array access. These errors are captured using COBOL's USE statements and special registers like FILE-STATUS. Each run-time error is associated with a specific code, providing insights into the nature of the error.

```
000800 PERFORM DIVIDE-ACTION.
000900 DIVIDE-ACTION SECTION.
001000 DIVIDE 10 BY 0 GIVING RESULT.

Output during execution:
Error: Attempt to divide by zero.
```

To handle run-time errors effectively, the FILE STATUS clause is frequently used to capture error codes associated with file operations. A FILE STATUS clause is associated with a file and specifies a data item where the file's status code is stored.

```
000100 IDENTIFICATION DIVISION.
000200 PROGRAM-ID. FileStatusExample.
000300 ENVIRONMENT DIVISION.
000400 INPUT-OUTPUT SECTION.
000500 FILE-CONTROL.
000600 SELECT MYFILE ASSIGN TO 'mydata.txt'
000700 ORGANIZATION IS SEQUENTIAL
000800 FILE STATUS IS WS-FILE-STATUS.
000900 DATA DIVISION.
001000 FILE SECTION.
001100 FD MYFILE.
001200 01 MYFILE-RECORD.
001300 05 FIELD-1 PIC X(10).
001400 WORKING-STORAGE SECTION.
001500 77 WS-FILE-STATUS PIC XX.
001600 PROCEDURE DIVISION.
001700 OPEN INPUT MYFILE.
001800 IF WS-FILE-STATUS NOT EQUAL TO '00'
001900 DISPLAY 'ERROR: ' WS-FILE-STATUS.
002000 CLOSE MYFILE.
002100 STOP RUN.

Output during execution:
ERROR: 35
```

In this example, the WS-FILE-STATUS variable captures the file status code after attempting to open a file. Code '35' indicates a file not found error.

Logic errors represent the most complex type of errors, as they do not generate error codes directly. These errors occur due to flawed program logic, leading to incorrect outputs or unintended behaviors. Identifying logic errors involves thorough testing and reviewing program flow and data manipulation.

Common COBOL error codes include:

- $00$: Successful completion.
- $02$: Duplicate key in $\mathrm{ISAM}$.
- $22$: Data not in correct $\mathrm{MODIFIED\ SEQUENCE}$.
- $23$: Record not found.
- $34$: Permanent error condition.
- $35$: File not found.
- $37$: Permanent error on open.
- $39$: Record is too large.

Errors such as $02$ (Duplicate key) and $23$ (Record not found) are specific to indexed files and often require thorough validation and error handling mechanisms within the application logic.

Understanding these error codes necessitates not only recognizing their numerical values but also implementing appropriate error handling constructs within the COBOL program. This ensures that the program can gracefully manage errors, provide meaningful error messages, and maintain data integrity through proper error handling practices.

To systematically handle errors, it is essential to use structured error reporting mechanisms, keep detailed logs, and implement checks at critical points in the program. Robust error handling and logging facilitate proactive error detection and resolution, thereby enhancing program reliability and maintainability.

## 10.8 Handling SYNCHRONIZED and ALIGNMENT

Proper handling of the SYNCHRONIZED clause and data alignment are critical for ensuring the accuracy and efficiency of COBOL programs. Misalignment or improper synchronization can lead to unexpected behavior, performance degradation, and errors that are difficult to trace. This section explains the significance of these concepts and provides detailed instructions on how to manage them effectively in a COBOL environment.

The SYNCHRONIZED clause specifies that a data item should be aligned on a storage boundary corresponding to its length, which can enhance performance on certain hardware architectures. This clause is particularly useful for binary data types, which often benefit from being stored in positions that align with the hardware's word boundaries.

```
01 DATA-ITEM PIC S9(4) COMP SYNC.
```

In the example above, DATA-ITEM is a binary field that will be aligned according to the machine's word boundaries because of the SYNC clause.

Understanding the concept of 'ALIGNMENT' is pivotal in managing the allocation of data items in memory. COBOL allows for the declaration of data items with varying lengths and data types within a record, and improper alignment can lead to inefficient memory access or, in some cases, invalid data interpretations, especially on systems with strict alignment requirements.

To illustrate the importance of alignment, consider the following example where different data items are declared without the SYNC clause:

```
01 RECORD.
    05 ITEM-1 PIC X(1).
    05 ITEM-2 PIC S9(4) COMP.
```

Here, ITEM-2 may not be aligned on a word boundary, potentially affecting access efficiency. To rectify this and ensure proper alignment, the SYNC clause can be applied:

```
01 RECORD.
    05 ITEM-1 PIC X(1).
    05 ITEM-2 PIC S9(4) COMP SYNC.
```

The SYNC clause ensures that ITEM-2 is aligned appropriately, which can enhance performance on systems where alignment impacts memory access speed.

The detailed rules for alignment are dependent on the specific COBOL implementation and the underlying hardware. For instance, on systems where a 4-byte integer must be aligned on a 4-byte boundary, failing to use the SYNC clause could result in misalignment. The following guidelines are generally helpful:

- Use SYNCHRONIZED for binary, packed-decimal, and floating-point data types.
- Consider alignment requirements for REDEFINES clauses to ensure that all possible redefined items are correctly aligned.
- Be aware of default padding applied by the compiler when SYNCHRONIZED is used.

Another example demonstrates a more complex structure where multiple data items must be correctly aligned:

```
01 COMPLEX-RECORD.
    05 ALPHA-ITEM PIC X(5).
    05 BINARY-ITEM PIC S9(4) COMP SYNC.
    05 ANOTHER-ALPHA PIC X(1).
    05 FLOAT-ITEM COMP-1 SYNC.
```

In this structure: - BINARY-ITEM is a 4-byte binary field. The SYNC clause ensures that it starts at a word boundary. - FLOAT-ITEM, a binary floating-point number, is also aligned according to the system's requirements for floating-point fields.

Managing alignment and synchronization closely ties into the use of the REDEFINES clause, which allows multiple data items to share the same storage area. Ensuring that all redefined items adhere to alignment requirements is essential for program correctness:

```
01 REDEFINED-RECORD.
    05 FIRST-FIELD PIC 9(4) COMP SYNC.
    05 FILLER PIC X(1).

01 REDEFINED-RECORD REDEFINES FIRST-FIELD.
```

```
05 SECOND-FIELD PIC 9(2) COMP-3.
```

In the redefined record example, FIRST-FIELD and SECOND-FIELD must be carefully aligned to ensure correct interpretation and efficient memory access.

By attentively leveraging the SYNCHRONIZED clause and understanding the principles of data alignment, COBOL programmers can enhance both the reliability and performance of their applications. Detailed attention to these aspects ensures that data is stored and accessed efficiently, reducing the likelihood of runtime errors and enhancing overall program stability.

## 10.9 Using DISPLAY for Debugging

The DISPLAY statement in COBOL is a fundamental tool for debugging and inspecting the flow and state of program execution. By leveraging DISPLAY, programmers can output the values of variables and literals to the console or any specified output device, which facilitates the examination of the program logic and variable changes in real-time.

The basic syntax for the DISPLAY statement is as follows:

```
DISPLAY identifier-1 [identifier-2 ...] [LITERAL]
```

Each identifier can represent either a variable or a group data item, and the LITERAL can be a string constant enclosed in quotation marks.

**Examples:**

The following example demonstrates how to use DISPLAY to output the value of a single variable:

```
WORKING-STORAGE SECTION.
01 WS-NUMBER PIC 9(3) VALUE 123.

PROCEDURE DIVISION.
    DISPLAY "The value of WS-NUMBER is: " WS-NUMBER.
```

In the execution of this COBOL code, the output will be:

```
The value of WS-NUMBER is: 123
```

Multiple variables can be displayed in a single DISPLAY statement, from both the WORKING-STORAGE and LINKAGE sections, as shown in this example:

```
WORKING-STORAGE SECTION.
01 WS-NUM1 PIC 9(3) VALUE 456.
01 WS-NUM2 PIC 9(3) VALUE 789.

PROCEDURE DIVISION.
    DISPLAY "Values: " WS-NUM1 " and " WS-NUM2.
```

The corresponding output will be:

```
Values: 456 and 789
```

The alterability highlights pragmatic use when debugging logical flow:

```
PROCEDURE DIVISION.
...
PERFORM VARYING WS-INDEX FROM 1 BY 1 UNTIL
    WS-INDEX > 5
    DISPLAY "Current index value: " WS-INDEX
END-PERFORM.
...
```

As the loop executes, it will produce:

```
Current index value: 1
Current index value: 2
Current index value: 3
Current index value: 4
Current index value: 5
```

**Complex Structures:**

The debugging capability extends to complex data structures, where group items can consolidate multiple elementary items. Here is an example illustrating DISPLAY output for group data items:

```
WORKING-STORAGE SECTION.
01 WS-DATE.
    05 WS-YEAR PIC 9(4) VALUE 2023.
    05 WS-MONTH PIC 99 VALUE 12.
    05 WS-DAY PIC 99 VALUE 25.

PROCEDURE DIVISION.
    DISPLAY "Full date: " WS-DATE.
```

The expected output would be:

```
Full date: 20231225
```

For improved readability, individual components of the group item can be displayed separately:

```
PROCEDURE DIVISION.
    DISPLAY "Year: " WS-YEAR " Month: " WS-MONTH "
        Day: " WS-DAY.
```

This will result in:

```
Year: 2023 Month: 12 Day: 25
```

**Debugging Numeric Computations:**

When diagnosing arithmetic errors, the DISPLAY statement is indispensable. The following example demonstrates how to track variable values before and after arithmetic operations:

```
WORKING-STORAGE SECTION.
01 WS-NUM1 PIC 9(3) VALUE 10.
01 WS-NUM2 PIC 9(3) VALUE 20.
01 WS-SUM PIC 9(3).

PROCEDURE DIVISION.
    DISPLAY "Before addition: " WS-NUM1 " + " WS-NUM2.
    ADD WS-NUM1 TO WS-NUM2 GIVING WS-SUM.
    DISPLAY "After addition - Sum: " WS-SUM.
```

The resulting debugging output:

```
Before addition: 10 + 20
After addition - Sum: 30
```

This clarity assists in verifying calculations and detecting overflow, truncation, or unexpected values.

**Best Practices:**

When incorporating DISPLAY statements for debugging, it's important to employ meaningful messages that indicate the specific section or operation being debugged. Consistently using labels with variable names enhances traceability:

```
DISPLAY "DEBUG: Entering Compute Section"
DISPLAY "DEBUG: WS-NUM1 = " WS-NUM1 " WS-NUM2 =
    " WS-NUM2
```

Additionally, removing or commenting out DISPLAY statements after debugging ensures cleaner production code. Managing these through compilation flags or conditional compilation is advisable for larger projects.

```
*> DISPLAY "DEBUG: WS-INDEX = " WS-INDEX
```

By systematically utilizing the DISPLAY statement, debugging becomes an integrated part of the development process, promoting thorough analysis and precise identification of logical flaws and unexpected behavior in COBOL programs.

## 10.10 Writing Fault-Tolerant Code

Fault-tolerant code is essential for increasing the reliability and robustness of COBOL programs, ensuring they can handle unexpected conditions gracefully without failing. This section outlines various strategies and practices for writing fault-tolerant code in COBOL, focusing on validation, exception handling, and redundancy to achieve a resilient application.

In COBOL, fault-tolerant code can be achieved by integrating thorough error handling, validating input and output, and preparing for unexpected scenarios. Let's examine these techniques in detail.

**Validation: Input and Output**

Input validation is the process of ensuring that any input to a COBOL program is accurate and conforms to expected formats and conditions. Output validation ensures that the results produced by the program are within the expected ranges. Proper validation can prevent many runtime errors and reduce the likelihood of unexpected behavior.

To perform validation in COBOL, the IF statement is commonly used. Below is an example of input validation:

```
DATA DIVISION.
WORKING-STORAGE SECTION.
01 WS-USER-INPUT PIC X(10).

PROCEDURE DIVISION.
    PERFORM GET-USER-INPUT.

    IF WS-USER-INPUT IS NUMERIC AND
```

```
        WS-USER-INPUT > 0
        MOVE "VALID INPUT" TO WS-MESSAGE
    ELSE
        MOVE "INVALID INPUT" TO WS-MESSAGE.

GET-USER-INPUT.
    DISPLAY "Enter a number: ".
    ACCEPT WS-USER-INPUT.
```

In this example, WS-USER-INPUT is validated to ensure it is numeric and greater than zero. This kind of validation ensures that the program only processes valid data, preventing potential failures or unexpected results.

### Exception Handling

Exception handling in COBOL involves detecting and managing errors during program execution. COBOL provides specific keywords and sections to handle different types of exceptions, including file handling errors and computational exceptions.

FILE STATUS and USE AFTER EXCEPTION are commonly used to manage exceptions in file handling:

```
FILE SECTION.
FD INPUT-FILE
    LABEL RECORDS ARE STANDARD
    BLOCK CONTAINS 0 RECORDS
    RECORD CONTAINS 80 CHARACTERS
    DATA RECORD IS INP-REC.

01 INP-REC PIC X(80).

DATA DIVISION.
WORKING-STORAGE SECTION.
01 WS-FILE-STATUS PIC XX.

PROCEDURE DIVISION.
    OPEN INPUT INPUT-FILE
    IF WS-FILE-STATUS NOT = "00"
        DISPLAY "File open error: " WS-FILE-STATUS
        PERFORM ERROR-ROUTINE.

READ-FILE.
```

```
    READ INPUT-FILE INTO INP-REC
    AT END
        MOVE "10" TO WS-FILE-STATUS
    NOT AT END
        PERFORM PROCESS-RECORD
    END-READ
    IF WS-FILE-STATUS NOT = "00"
        PERFORM ERROR-ROUTINE.

CLOSE-FILE.
    CLOSE INPUT-FILE
    IF WS-FILE-STATUS NOT = "00"
        DISPLAY "File close error: " WS-FILE-STATUS
        PERFORM ERROR-ROUTINE.

ERROR-ROUTINE.
    DISPLAY "An error occurred. File status: " WS-FILE-STATUS.
```

WS-FILE-STATUS is used to check the status of file operations. If an error occurs (i.e., the file status is not "00"), the error routine is invoked, reporting the error and handling it gracefully.

### Redundancy

In fault-tolerant systems, redundancy involves duplicating critical components or data to ensure system reliability and availability. Implementing redundancy can range from simple data backups to more complex algorithms for data integrity checks.

Consider a COBOL program that makes a backup of a critical data file before processing to ensure data integrity. Below is an example that demonstrates this redundancy:

```
FILE SECTION.
FD BACKUP-FILE
    LABEL RECORDS ARE STANDARD
    BLOCK CONTAINS 0 RECORDS
    RECORD CONTAINS 80 CHARACTERS
    DATA RECORD IS BKP-REC.

FD ORIGINAL-FILE
    LABEL RECORDS ARE STANDARD
    BLOCK CONTAINS 0 RECORDS
    RECORD CONTAINS 80 CHARACTERS
```

```
    DATA RECORD IS ORG-REC.

01 BKP-REC PIC X(80).
01 ORG-REC PIC X(80).

PROCEDURE DIVISION.
    OPEN OUTPUT BACKUP-FILE
    OPEN INPUT ORIGINAL-FILE

    PERFORM BACKUP-DATA
    CLOSE BACKUP-FILE
    CLOSE ORIGINAL-FILE.

BACKUP-DATA.
    READ ORIGINAL-FILE INTO ORG-REC
    AT END
        DISPLAY "End of file reached."
    NOT AT END
        WRITE BKP-REC FROM ORG-REC
        PERFORM BACKUP-DATA
    END-READ.
```

In this example, the BACKUP-DATA routine reads records from the original file and writes them to the backup file. This redundancy ensures that a copy of critical data is available even if the primary file gets corrupted during processing.

#### Graceful Degradation

Graceful degradation ensures that when a failure occurs, the system continues to operate at a reduced level rather than completely failing. This concept is imperative in fault-tolerant systems to maintain a minimum required functionality.

Below is an example in COBOL that demonstrates the use of graceful degradation:

```
DATA DIVISION.
WORKING-STORAGE SECTION.
01 WS-PRIMARY-RESOURCE PIC X(1) VALUE "N".
01 WS-SECONDARY-RESOURCE PIC X(1) VALUE "N".

PROCEDURE DIVISION.
    PERFORM USE-PRIMARY
```

```
    IF WS-PRIMARY-RESOURCE = "N"
        PERFORM USE-SECONDARY.

USE-PRIMARY.
    IF FUNCTION-TRY-PRIMARY > 0
        MOVE "Y" TO WS-PRIMARY-RESOURCE
    ELSE
        DISPLAY "Primary resource failed."

USE-SECONDARY.
    IF FUNCTION-TRY-SECONDARY > 0
        MOVE "Y" TO WS-SECONDARY-RESOURCE
    ELSE
        DISPLAY "Secondary resource failed."
```

In this example, the program attempts to use a primary resource first (USE-PRIMARY). If the primary resource fails, indicated by WS-PRIMARY-RESOURCE remaining "N", it proceeds to use a secondary resource (USE-SECONDARY). This ensures that the program does not cease functioning entirely if the primary resource is unavailable.

Fault-tolerant code in COBOL ensures reliability and robustness by incorporating effective validation, exception handling, redundancy, and graceful degradation. These strategies collectively allow COBOL programs to handle unexpected situations gracefully and continue to provide essential functionality without failing.

## 10.11 Logging and Tracing Techniques

Accurate logging and effective tracing are indispensable techniques for diagnosing and rectifying issues in COBOL programs. This section elucidates methodologies to implement logging and tracing mechanisms, ensuring detailed insight into the program execution flow and promptly identifying errors.

Logging involves recording information about the execution state of the program, while tracing entails tracking the sequence of executed operations. Both methods serve to provide context for debugging, understand program behavior, and document runtime conditions.

- Ensure that sufficient detail is captured to allow identification of not only errors but also their causes.

- Maintain readability and manageability of log files, balancing the granularity of logged information with performance impacts.
- Implement logging in a modular manner, encapsulating related logging logic.

### Implementing Logging in COBOL

In COBOL, logging can be implemented using the DISPLAY statement to write log messages to the standard output or to a specified file.

```
IDENTIFICATION DIVISION.
PROGRAM-ID. SampleLogging.

ENVIRONMENT DIVISION.
INPUT-OUTPUT SECTION.
FILE-CONTROL.
    SELECT LOG-FILE ASSIGN TO 'logfile.txt'.

DATA DIVISION.
FILE SECTION.
FD LOG-FILE.
01 LOG-RECORD PIC X(80).

WORKING-STORAGE SECTION.
01 WS-LOG-MESSAGE PIC X(80).

PROCEDURE DIVISION.
    OPEN OUTPUT LOG-FILE.

    MOVE 'Start of Program Execution' TO WS-LOG-MESSAGE.
    WRITE LOG-RECORD FROM WS-LOG-MESSAGE.

    * Program execution continues here *

    MOVE 'End of Program Execution' TO WS-LOG-MESSAGE.
    WRITE LOG-RECORD FROM WS-LOG-MESSAGE.

    CLOSE LOG-FILE.
    STOP RUN.
```

This example demonstrates basic logging to an output file. It opens a file, writes messages to it, and then closes it. Each log message conveys critical execution points.

### Tracing Execution Flow

Tracing involves tracking specific points within the program to observe sequence and timing of executed operations. This helps in understanding program workflow and identifying stages where issues arise.

```
IDENTIFICATION DIVISION.
PROGRAM-ID. SampleTracing.

ENVIRONMENT DIVISION.
INPUT-OUTPUT SECTION.
FILE-CONTROL.
    SELECT LOG-FILE ASSIGN TO 'tracefile.txt'.

DATA DIVISION.
FILE SECTION.
FD LOG-FILE.
01 LOG-RECORD PIC X(80).

WORKING-STORAGE SECTION.
01 WS-TRACE-MESSAGE PIC X(80).

PROCEDURE DIVISION.
    OPEN OUTPUT LOG-FILE.

    MOVE 'Entering Section A' TO WS-TRACE-MESSAGE.
    WRITE LOG-RECORD FROM WS-TRACE-MESSAGE.

    * Execute Section A operations *

    MOVE 'Exiting Section A' TO WS-TRACE-MESSAGE.
    WRITE LOG-RECORD FROM WS-TRACE-MESSAGE.

    MOVE 'Entering Section B' TO WS-TRACE-MESSAGE.
    WRITE LOG-RECORD FROM WS-TRACE-MESSAGE.

    * Execute Section B operations *

    MOVE 'Exiting Section B' TO WS-TRACE-MESSAGE.
    WRITE LOG-RECORD FROM WS-TRACE-MESSAGE.
```

```
    CLOSE LOG-FILE.
    STOP RUN.
```

Here, the program records entry and exit points of critical sections. This level of detailed tracing enables pinpointing unsuccessful operations or performance bottlenecks.

**Enhanced Logging and Tracing with Timestamps**

Including timestamps in logs and traces greatly enhances the information's utility. This enables tracking the temporal sequence of events and understanding timing-related issues.

```
IDENTIFICATION DIVISION.
PROGRAM-ID. TimestampsLogging.

ENVIRONMENT DIVISION.
INPUT-OUTPUT SECTION.
FILE-CONTROL.
    SELECT LOG-FILE ASSIGN TO 'timelog.txt'.

DATA DIVISION.
FILE SECTION.
FD LOG-FILE.
01 LOG-RECORD PIC X(100).

WORKING-STORAGE SECTION.
01 WS-LOG-TIMESTAMP PIC X(20).
01 WS-LOG-MESSAGE PIC X(80).

PROCEDURE DIVISION.
    OPEN OUTPUT LOG-FILE.

    CALL 'CURRENT-DATE' USING WS-LOG-TIMESTAMP.
    STRING WS-LOG-TIMESTAMP DELIMITED BY SPACE
           ' - Start of Program Execution' DELIMITED BY SIZE
           INTO WS-LOG-MESSAGE.
    WRITE LOG-RECORD FROM WS-LOG-MESSAGE.

    * Program execution continues *

    CALL 'CURRENT-DATE' USING WS-LOG-TIMESTAMP.
```

```
STRING WS-LOG-TIMESTAMP DELIMITED BY SPACE
       ' - End of Program Execution' DELIMITED BY SIZE
       INTO WS-LOG-MESSAGE.
WRITE LOG-RECORD FROM WS-LOG-MESSAGE.

CLOSE LOG-FILE.
STOP RUN.
```

This example embeds current timestamps into log messages, offering precise information on when log entries are recorded. The CURRENT-DATE COBOL intrinsic function is used to obtain the current timestamp.

**Best Practices for Logging and Tracing**

- Regularly review and maintain log files to prevent unnecessary accumulation of data.
- Ensure sensitive data is appropriately obfuscated or anonymized to maintain data security.
- Modularize log and trace capabilities to enable selective detailing, adjustable per development or production needs.
- Incorporate log rotation mechanisms to manage file sizes and archive older logs.
- Develop conventions for log message formats to ensure consistency and readability.

Logging and tracing are fundamental practices for maintaining high reliability in COBOL programs, aiding in the detection and diagnosis of issues, ultimately enhancing program robustness and stability.

## 10.12 Best Practices for Error Handling

Effective error handling is crucial in ensuring the robustness and reliability of COBOL programs. The strategies discussed herein are designed to help developers anticipate, detect, and resolve errors efficiently, thereby safeguarding the integrity of the entire system.

**1. Leveraging COBOL Built-in Functions and Verbs:** COBOL provides various built-in functions and error-handling verbs that can be strategically utilized to manage exceptions and errors. For instance,

ON SIZE ERROR and INVALID KEY clauses can be added to critical arithmetic operations and I/O statements, respectively. These clauses will trigger specific error handling procedures when uncommon conditions occur.

```
IF NUMB-1 > 0 AND NUMB-2 > 0 THEN
  DIVIDE NUMB-1 BY NUMB-2 GIVING RESULT
    ON SIZE ERROR
      PERFORM SIZE-ERROR-HANDLING
END-IF.
```

INVALID KEY flag on READ statements ensures that attempts to read a non-existent record are properly managed:

```
READ FILE-NAME INTO REC-AREA
  INVALID KEY PERFORM INVALID-KEY-HANDLING.
```

**2. Structured Error Handling with Declaratives:** Declaratives are a powerful feature in COBOL for handling exceptions. They allow programmers to define specific sections of code that are executed when certain conditions arise. A declarative block typically comprises USE statements, housing the error-handling logic.

```
DECLARATIVES.
INPUT-ERROR SECTION.
USE AFTER EXCEPTION ON INPUT FILE-NAME.
    DISPLAY "Error reading file: " FILE-STATUS.
    PERFORM EXIT-APPLICATION.
END DECLARATIVES.
```

**3. Consistent Data Validation:** Perform data validation checks consistently throughout the application. These checks should verify the format, type, and range of input data before processing it. Such defensive coding practices prevent corrupt data from propagating through the system and causing more severe issues.

```
IF INPUT-DATE IS NUMERIC AND
   FUNCTION NUMVAL(INPUT-DATE) <= 31129999
   CONTINUE
ELSE
   PERFORM INVALID-DATE-HANDLING.
```

**4. Utilizing DISPLAY Statements for Debugging:** DISPLAY statements are invaluable during the development and debugging phases. They help in logging the program flow and variable states. However, these should be appropriately documented and eventually streamlined to avoid performance overheads in production environments.

```
DISPLAY "Start of Routine-X".
DISPLAY "Variable VAR-A Value: " VAR-A.
DISPLAY "End of Routine-X".
```

**5. Log Messages for Error Reporting:** Implement a comprehensive logging mechanism that records error messages and statuses to an external file. This practice enables post-mortem analysis and helps in diagnosing application issues that may arise in the production environment.

```
OPEN EXTEND LOG-FILE.
WRITE LOG-RECORD FROM ERROR-MESSAGE.
CLOSE LOG-FILE.
```

**6. Defining Exit Handlers:** Ensure that the program exits gracefully by defining specific exit handling routines. These routines should perform necessary cleanup operations, such as closing files and flushing buffers, to maintain data consistency and system stability.

```
EXIT-HANDLING.
    CLOSE FILE-NAME.
    RELEASE FILE-RESOURCES.
    STOP RUN.
```

**7. Modularizing Error Handling Code:** Organize error-handling code into separate, reusable modules. This modular approach simplifies maintenance and enhances the clarity of the main program logic by isolating error management routines.

```
CALL 'ERROR-MODULE' USING ERROR-CODE.
PERFORM HANDLE-ERROR-MODULE.
```

**8. Handling SYNCHRONIZED and ALIGNMENT Issues:** SYNCHRONIZED and alignment issues are common pitfalls in COBOL programming, often leading to subtle and hard-to-diagnose errors. Utilize the appropriate SYNCHRONIZED clause to ensure proper alignment of data structures.

```
01 RECORD-DATA.
```

```
    03 VAR-1 PIC X(10).
    03 VAR-2 PIC 9(5) SYNCHRONIZED RIGHT.
```

**9. Providing Detailed Error Messages:** When errors occur, detailed messages should be provided to explain the nature of the problem and possible resolutions. These messages facilitate rapid troubleshooting and enhance the usability of the program for end-users and support personnel alike.

```
DISPLAY "Error: Invalid account number. Please check the input and
    try again.".
```

**10. Continuous Monitoring and Proactive Error Management:** Implement continuous monitoring techniques to routinely check for atypical patterns and preempt potential errors. This proactive approach includes setting up alerts for unusual system behavior, thereby addressing issues before they escalate.

```
PERFORM MONITOR-SYSTEM AT INTERVAL.
```

These error handling best practices ensure that COBOL programs are resilient against potential issues, thereby enhancing their reliability and maintainability.

Made in the USA
Monee, IL
13 September 2026

62980073R00164